DATE DUE			

Bitter Choices

Women in Culture and Society
A series edited by Catharine R. Stimpson

Bitter Choices

*Blue-Collar Women
in and out of Work*

Ellen Israel Rosen

The University of Chicago Press
Chicago and London

Ellen Israel Rosen is associate professor of sociology at Nichols College.

331.4125
R726
146467
May / 1989

The research for this book was conducted under a grant from the Employment and Training Administration, U.S. Department of Labor, research and development grant no. 21–25–79–19.

The University of Chicago Press, Chicago 60637
The University of Chicago Press, Ltd., London

96 95 94 93 92 91 90 89 88 87   5 4 3 2 1

Library of Congress Cataloging-in-Publication Data

Rosen, Ellen Israel.
    Bitter choices.

    (Women in culture and society)
    Bibliography.
    Includes index.
    1. Women—Employment—United States.   2. Labor and
laboring classes—United States.   I. Title.   II. Series.
HD6095.R74   1987   331.4'125'0973   87–5867
ISBN 0–226–72644–4

Contents

Series Editor's Foreword

Between 1979 and 1983 in the United States, 35 percent of all "displaced workers" were women. In New England, 40 percent of all "displaced workers" were women. Since the mid-1960s, the textile industry has lost 800,000 jobs. Many of them belonged to women.

Out of callowness, callousness, or cruel ignorance, many people pass such facts by. Ellen I. Rosen asks us to confront them and their significance. "Displaced worker" is a euphemism for the victims of the structural transformation occurring in the United States economy since the middle of the twentieth century. Industrial and manufacturing jobs have disappeared, and "service" jobs with lower pay and less unionization have replaced them. The hard hat has given way to the paper cap of the counterman or cashier in a fast food franchise. The United States buys and sells, gets and spends, within a global economy that puts men in one kind of job, women in another, and uses them all.

Bitter Choices illuminates the lives of a group of victims largely invisible to the academy and the media: married, working-class women who carry the burden of the "double day." They have responsibilities both at home and in the semiskilled or unskilled public labor force. They have assembled light bulbs, inspected golf balls, stitched garments in factories where employers have demanded that they move smartly, at a faster and faster pace. A bullying piecework system has often dictated the wages for this labor.

Bitter Choices looks most closely at the married women of "Milltown," a New England industrial city. They differ amongst themselves. Some, born in America, are middle-aged or older. Others, also born in America, belong to a younger generation. Still others are Portuguese immigrants who find the patriarchal values from an older culture bearing down on them. By explicitly comparing these three groups, Rosen shows the inseparability of the accurate study of gender from that of class, ethnicity, and age.

Bitter Choices then measures the pain in "Milltown" that comes with job insecurity, unemployment, and new jobs that pay less in poorer working conditions than the jobs that have vanished. Psychologically and economically, women and their families must adjust to having less than they once did, and their hopes of mobility, of gaining more within the system, must contract. Rosen also shows the social costs of deindustrialization. Because good economic opportunities for working-class women are diminishing, even though more women need those opportunities, the chances for gender equity in employment must decrease as well.

Although the women of *Bitter Choices* are victims, they are neither passive nor pathetic. Sympathetically, Rosen listens to their stories, traces their life cycles, and watches them manage circumstance. She documents the women's strategies, such as good relations among co-workers, for coping with the stresses of the factory floor and the tensions that class and gender breed. The women of Milltown are aware of their motives for devising such strategies and for seeking work in the first place, especially if the work pays well. They want to help maintain, sustain, and improve family life. Moreover, women's earnings can gratifyingly stimulate greater authority and esteem for women within the family; thus, women's wages strengthen, rather than corrode, family life.

That binding sense of family often leads to a distrust of feminism when working-class women believe that feminism is challenging the nuclear family and the dignity of husbands, brothers, and fathers. Feminists then seem to resemble the forewomen of a destructive change that will leave members of the working-class vulnerable to capitalism's power.

Bitter Choices is a careful monograph. Rosen scrupulously describes her place, methods, and findings. Careful, however, has a second meaning as well: to be full of care, concern. Rosen is rightly suspicious of social and economic processes that milk the diligent women of Milltown of their toil, discard them, and then go on to exploit female labor in a developing country thousands of miles away. *Bitter Choices* suggests what the United States might do to help the women whom the system has not yet laid off and thrown aside. We might manage our trade policy more effectively; we might creatively restructure the industries, like the textile industry, that employ many women; we might have more retraining programs, especially for younger women. Yet, these remedies will be only blueprints or scenes of social engineering unless a passionately voiced question animates them: "When will we have work, in families and factories, as if workers mattered?"

Catharine R. Stimpson

Acknowledgments

I used to wonder why so many people were mentioned in book acknowledgments. Now I know. Producing a book is in large part a solitary endeavor. However, after doing the research and getting some answers to the puzzling questions that plagued one at the outset, the impetus to maintain the discipline that writing requires is impossible without the help and encouragement of so many others. So let me begin offering my thanks to all the people who kept me at my word processor day after day.

First I would like to thank those who made it possible to do the research in the first place. I want to thank all those who helped fund and administer a large grant from what used to be the Employment and Training Administration of the Department of Labor. They are responsible for the large grant that enabled me to take two years out of my teaching career to do the research for this book. I am also indebted to the union educators and officials who live daily with the problems described in this book and therefore recognized the importance of the research. Frank Lyons of the University of Massachusetts; Nick Roussos and Carl Proper of the ILGWU; Pete DeCicco, Al Cummings, and Robert Pierce of the IUE; Bill Kennedy, Theresa Asselin, and Claire Belleville of the USWA; Ron Carver of the UE; Arthur Osborn and Kay Beecher of the IBEW; Bronwen Zwirner of the ACTWU; David Murray of the Bakery, Confectionary, and Tobacco Workers Union; and Betsy Munzer of the Massachusetts Department of Employment Security. I would also like to thank Gerry D'Amico, former Democratic State Senator from Worcester, for recognizing the political importance of this research. The more than four hundred women who told us about their lives are, of course, too numerous to mention here.

Then there is the staff of the Social Welfare Research Institute at Boston College. These individuals provided me with a home for two years and helped me deal with the mass of data we collected. Thanks to Barry Bluestone, Michele Garvin, Françoise Carré, Paul Schervish, Lynn Ware, Alan Matthews, and Virginia Richardson.

I want to thank my friends and colleagues, who read the proposal and the manuscript at various earlier stages, whose comments, criticism, and encouragement kept me aware that I had embarked on a truly worthwhile endeavor—Naomi Kline, Rosalyn Feldberg, Nona Glazer, Carol Brown, Susan Ostrander, JoAnn Miller, Sara Bershtel, Barbara Ehrenreich, Myra Ferree, Elizabeth Useem, Elizabeth Markson, Mary Stevenson, Elsa Dixler, Robert Fitch, John Van Maanen, Paula Kline, Kay Snyder, Tom Nowak, Amy Ansara, Paul Osterman, and John Williamson.

I would like to thank some of the people at Nichols College, particularly Ed Warren and Lowell Smith. They had confidence in the importance of what I wanted to do and were responsible for making sure I had the time I needed to write the book. Without the generosity of Reed Holden, who helped make computer time available, the book would not have been completed.

I want to thank my parents, Ruth and Benjamin Israel, for bringing me up with the sensitivity to understand what the women factory workers, whose story this is, had to say about their work and their lives. Lastly, and certainly not least, I want to thank my family, Richard and Jeremy Rosen, who really wanted to see this book written. Not only did they provide the emotional support and encouragement that allowed me to persevere, they also contributed essential technical assistance.

1   Blue-Collar Women:
An Introduction

$\mathbf{M}$ARIA SANTOS[1] IS THIRTY-EIGHT YEARS OLD. She is a pocket setter in a garment factory and married to a man who works in a metal foundry. The Santos' have been married for sixteen years and own their own home in a working-class suburb near a large industrial city in New England. They have two sons, aged twelve and fourteen. Maria has always been a garment worker. Since she left high school at seventeen, she has stopped working and left her job only twice—for several months each time one of her sons was born. Maria has to work. "If I didn't work," she says candidly, "we couldn't pay for this house."

Maria is a pieceworker; on a good day she can earn between $5 and $6 an hour, or about $40 a day for a seven-hour shift.[2] Maria says, "The piece rate system is a lot of pressure. You gotta push all the time." Time is important to Maria, whether she is at work or at home, and Maria feels that she doesn't have enough of it for her family. "You have to rush when you get home. I come home, do some chores, do the dinner. I have no time to spend with them [her children]. During the weekend I have the shopping, the laundry, the house to clean." Despite the hectic pace of her life at home and at work she told us, "I like working—and that relieves some of the pressure."

What does she find to like about her job? First she mentions her boss, who often lets her leave early if she has an errand to run. This was particularly important to Maria when her children were small. Maria also likes the people she works with. "You get very close to the people who are sitting right near you. You become good friends." But most importantly, Maria feels that she earns "good money."

Sylvia DeNiso was an assembler in a firm which made electrical cords and cables. Six months before she was interviewed, she lost her job. She is forty-three years old, married, and like Maria Santos, also a homeowner. The DeNisos have three teenage children. Sylvia was laid off with about three hundred other workers, 80 percent of whom were women, when the parent company of the firm she worked for, a multinational conglomerate, made a decision to move the plant to Mexico.

In her eighteen years of working at Cerulean Electric, Sylvia felt she had always done a good job. She felt she gave the company "everything I've got." She was making $8.25 an hour and was to be promoted to a supervisory position when the news of the plant closing came. Like Maria Santos, Sylvia also liked her job. "I've heard people talk about factories as sweatshops," she said, "but I was lucky. I had a good job and good friends." She adds, "When you work the second shift [2:00 P.M. to 10:00 P.M.], you spend more time with these girls than you do with your family." Sylvia echoes the views of many social critics, when she speaks of being laid off from her job.

> What really gets me is that this company is moving out of the country. They are putting a lot of people out of work. They do not get taxed for moving out of the country. They do not charge extra for imports. They are runaway shops. The government does nothing to keep companies from leaving. And any legislature that has tried to put through laws has been knocked down. . . . This country does nothing to stop it.

Sylvia's husband is a factory worker who has had his job for twenty-one years, and the company appears to have a good future. She is still collecting unemployment insurance and is not desperately worried about how her family will eat or pay its bills—in the short run. But last year, Sylvia earned about 40 percent of her family's total income. Unless she finds work soon, the DeNisos will be in serious economic trouble. But what kind of work can she get which will pay as well, or even nearly as well, as what she was earning at Cerulean? Perhaps even more importantly, what kind of work can she find that will reproduce a workplace she has known for almost twenty years?

A younger co-worker is going back to college to study "computers." But Sylvia's children are almost ready for college. "My husband can't afford to send me back to school, so where am I going to get the money?" Sylvia sees her choices as having to "scrimp and save and try to work your way through . . . or just get some stupid job to try to tide you over . . ."—not a promising future.

This book is about the lives of women like Maria Santos and Sylvia DeNiso. It is exclusively about married women and mothers, who work in New England's mills and factories and whose work lives are now being seriously threatened. Most of these "blue-collar" women work year round and full time as they raise their families and maintain homes and marriages. Members of today's dual-earner families, they work on assembly lines for much the same reason women have always done so—to earn a living for themselves and their families.

Working-class women work in factories because they must; their families need the money they earn. Yet, in New England, the older, unionized, mill-based industries, despite their decline in the past twenty-five years or so, have continued to provide many "good" jobs. Demanding as the work is, a good number of these factory jobs permit many of the married women who hold them to fashion lives sustained by a modicum of financial security and a real sense of efficacy, purpose, and accomplishment. Indeed, the women who work on assembly lines often feel that factory jobs are decidedly more attractive than other work they have the skill and experience to do. Many feel their jobs provide them with important resources they can use to meet their needs and the needs of their families. Within the constraints of class and gender, blue-collar women have, through their work, found ways to achieve the goals they set for themselves. If the lives of these women are not always a bed of roses, neither are they always a "world of pain." The major issue for them is not whether or not to work but the availability of more and better jobs.

However, women like Sylvia DeNiso and Maria Santos are now witnessing firsthand, the deterioration of their work environments, the destruction of their unions, and the loss of their jobs. How do these women cope with their vulnerability as they see their already limited control at work diminish, as they see how difficult it may be in the future to earn the money they need to keep their families from poverty? If the balance so many of these women maintain between their work and family lives is already so demanding, how will they fare in leaner times as they face more pressure at work, lower wages, and new uncertainties about continued employment? The purpose of this book is to begin to answer such questions.

But why, one might ask, in the context of the decline of manufacturing in America, should we concern ourselves with the lives of women factory workers? In 1980 women employed in "blue-collar" jobs like the ones we will be looking at—traditional female production jobs defined as "unskilled and semiskilled"—made up only 12 percent of the female labor force.[3] Many believe blue-collar women are disappearing from the American employment landscape. The focus of today's research on working women suggests that if we are concerned with the problems of today's working women, we should concern ourselves primarily with the difficulties experienced by the evergrowing numbers of women who work as secretaries, clerks, cashiers, waitresses, and saleswomen.[4] Is it merely nostalgia then, a wistful and academic concern to mark the passing of an older way of life that motivates an interest in the lives and problems of women who still work in our nation's mills and factories?

There is surely something powerful and compelling about the image of the traditional New England mill town. A whole generation of social and labor historians have recently begun to rescue from obscurity the lives of men and women who lived and worked in America's factory towns and industrial communities in the nineteenth and early twentieth century. They have given us access to generations of working-class men and women whose efforts, struggles, and hopes for their children built the communities we know today. The work of these scholars[5] has shown us how family and community life, culture and religion, provided comfort and identity to new groups of immigrants, generating a basis for resistance to industrial exploitation. Many of these historians have described the mix of exploitation and opportunity that factory work provided for women as they came to participate in paid industrial labor. Indeed, if contemporary "blue-collar" women do represent the last chapter in an older way of industrial life, that in itself would warrant the telling.

Yet, the changes that are occurring in New England's mill towns and industrial cities reflect more than the passing of an older, simpler, and more parochial way of life. What is happening to the blue-collar women in these communities is the result of vast industrial transformations which are changing the entire shape of the American labor force—and indeed, the global economy. These transformations are best known for the ways in which they have affected the jobs of millions of male industrial workers and the lives of Third World women. What is less well known are the ways in which they have begun to undermine a century of progress in wages and employment conditions for America's women factory workers.

While it is not well known, during the years following World War II unionized women factory workers achieved a considerable wage advantage over women employed in the fast growing sales, service, and clerical sectors. However, as a result of the new global trends this advantage is eroding. What is perhaps most ironic and most saddening is that the wage declines and the demise of women's manufacturing jobs have occurred just at the point when large numbers of married women with children need and want well-paid employment more than ever before. Indeed there are still many women, some of whom are the subjects of this book, who hold relatively high-wage, unionized production jobs. Yet the changes which are now taking place are having fearful consequences for the lives of these working-class women—and for their working-class families as well.

Women's Labor Market Equality and the Working-Class Family

In recent years there have been broad-ranging debates about the ways to achieve women's labor market equality. Underlying this overall concern has been a growing awareness that there are class issues which divide women as well as men. Certainly more women than ever before are going to law school, medical school, and business school. However, as these women begin to take their places in the professions and the executive suites, the growing number of jobs available to the 80 percent of "ordinary" working women[6] continue to reproduce the existing sexual division of labor, and with it, the large pay inequities between men and women.

Despite our stated national commitment to women's equality, the industrial changes we are seeing today are working at cross-purposes with the goals of our equal employment opportunity policies. These changes result, some argue, from management's control over the workplace, from employers' ability to create workplace hierarchies, and from its power to develop and employ selected technologies and maintain hiring and wage policies which channel women into low-wage, sex-typed jobs. New studies of secretaries and clerical workers, saleswomen, computer programmers, and telephone company personnel testify to the rapid growth of "women's work," work which continues to be "unskilled" and poorly paid.[7]

Some of the same problems exist for women in production jobs. Capital shifts and technological changes have made possible worldwide industrial transformations which threaten to undermine a century of social progress for today's blue-collar women. International and domestic industrial shifts, added to regional growth and decline, have created new forms of labor market segmentation in production work. As we will see, new female job ghettoes are emerging in new industries, while women employed in older industries face deunionization, wage declines, and unemployment.

These changes in the structure of women's employment, the growing divorce rate, and the continuing wage gap between men and women have made us increasingly aware of women's poverty—particularly the poverty of women who support children often on salaries that average about 60 percent of what men earn.[8] Though this impoverization is concentrated among women who head families, it is not without consequence for married women. Today, the wives and mothers of working-class families find themselves working in jobs such as these in order to complement the earnings of male breadwinners.

Some analysts argue that the advent of the new, two-paycheck, working-class family (as opposed to the "dual-career," middle-class or professional couple and their children) is a clear sign of the declining fortunes of the working class and is, therefore to be resisted.[9] Feminists have of course criticized the notion that paid employment for working-class women is simply another, newer form of "oppression." They point, with skepticism, to the vision of a period in industrial history when working men actually "supported" their families. But what is even more compelling is the fact that if women did stay home in the early postwar years, when they went back to work in the late 1960s and 1970s large numbers apparently seemed to enjoy working. We must now come to grips with more than a decade of historical and social research on working-class women which shows how women in working-class families have benefited in a variety of ways from holding paid jobs—even those jobs at the lowest occupational levels.

It has been almost a decade since Patricia Sexton, in response to the dearth of studies at that time, pointed to the need to know more about the lives of women in working-class jobs. [10] As she put it, "Statistical reports on wages, employment and related matters, useful as they are, tell us very little about who these working-class women are, how they fare and what they want from their working lives." Despite the studies that have followed her call for more research, we still know relatively little about working-class women and the dynamics of their "dual-earner families."[11]

What follows then, must be seen as an attempt to answer some of the remaining questions, to contribute to the debate about contemporary working-class families as they face these trying economic times; to see whose interests are served when women work outside the home. This book is also an attempt to change the parameters of the debate by beginning to focus on the quality of work that is available to working-class women. If "good" jobs are important to them, in many ways, as we shall see, many of New England's unionized factory jobs are "good" jobs. They often permit women with little education and few job skills to earn more money than they could in other kinds of employment available to them.

By bringing to light the experience of women who work in today's unionized factory jobs we begin to discover what working-class women get from "good jobs." By exploring the tradeoffs such work both requires and justifies in terms of women managing the "double day," we will highlight the sacrifices blue-collar women and their families make in order to improve their families' standard of living. At the same time, the resources and benefits available from these blue-collar jobs offer the women and their families some real advantages compared to many of the alternatives available for working-class women in today's labor market. By comparing the lives of women who have managed to get and keep unionized factory jobs with those who have lost such jobs, we will be able to see quite clearly what women are getting from full-time, blue-collar work—and, inevitably, what so many now stand to lose.

There is certainly nothing sacrosanct about working in a factory as opposed to an office, hospital, store, or restaurant. There is no intrinsic advantage involved in producing goods rather than services. Yet what is happening in New England's mill towns offers us a window on the transition that is taking place in the lives of millions of other working-class women who confront the need to work and the decreasing availability of jobs which meet their needs. The job crisis that is occurring for blue-collar women allows us to witness what happens to married women and their families when they are forced to make the transition to more marginal work at lower wages. It suggests how women and families suffer when mothers and wives find themselves without access to needed earnings.

The lives of blue-collar women also allow us to see how a woman's job affects her family. It is generally assumed that a married woman's paid work is essentially contingent on the needs of her husband and children, that her domestic responsibilities inform her view of the appropriate job market and her concerns about paid work. Often it is assumed that her preference is to stay home. Family is primary and work is secondary. Women are "pushed" and "pulled" in and out of the labor market largely in response to family concerns. Rosalyn Feldberg has called this approach the "ragdoll theory of women's labor force participation." Yet, as we will see, it is not only family concerns which influence women's work behavior. The quality of her job may also influence the nature of a woman's labor force participation as well as her relationships with the members of her family.

In many ways then, this book can make a new contribution to feminist theory by providing a detailed empirical study which explores the relationship between women's work and family life. By turning our attention to the internal dynamics of families with two paychecks among the working class, we can begin to more fully understand the relationship between class and gender and the impact of capitalism and patriarchy on working-class women in dual-earner families.

Since 1977 when Patricia Sexton asked what working-class women wanted from their jobs, new theoretical approaches to this question have been developed. The approaches of Benenson, Rapp, and Ferree[12] taken together, can provide a paradigm for understanding the experiences of the women described in this volume. The approaches of these three challenge the class biases inherent in so much of the literature on dual-earner families.

Benenson demonstrates that middle-class dual-career families, families where women pursue "careers" and egalitarian marriages, represent only a tiny minority of dual-earner families in America. Yet the research literature reifies their experience as the norm of the new feminist consciousness. In comparison to this model, working-class women in dual-earner families, who share neither the opportunities nor the experience of professionally trained or managerial women, are seen as "traditional" or "familistic."

The purpose of this work is not primarily to compare the middle-class and working-class experience of married working women, but to demonstrate how working-class women's class situation structures their opportunities, choices, and attitudes. As Rapp argues, a modicum of financial resources enables working-class families to participate in the economic mainstream of American life. She emphasizes how the availability of these resources is essential to the stability of the working-class family. Today the legitimacy of married women's participation in paid work enables working-class families to obtain these resources for their families. As compared to twenty years ago, today more and more working-class wives experience both the necessity and the opportunity to contribute resources through paid work. "Liberation" is in no way seen as freedom to be a homemaker. Married, working-class women want more access to good jobs and better pay.

Ferree shows, through her exposition of the work of German feminist sociologists, that women's attempts to combine work and family life is more than just a double burden. Access to both paid work and family life fulfills both psychological and economic needs, needs which, as I will show, are inextricably bound together. Wanting to work and having to work are not seen as polar opposites. Balancing work and family life is certainly a burden for these women. But because neither paid work nor housework alone is fully satisfactory, it is a burden they choose to carry, leading to what Ferree calls a "divided life."

While this "family centered instrumental orientation" is not so different from the lives of working-class men, according to Ferree, wives have an alternative way to acquire resources—through marriage. The poverty of their labor market options makes the exchange of domestic work for financial support something that is highly valued. Thus, married, working-class women do not seek an egalitarian division of labor in the family. Moreover, while domestic work is burdensome it also is seen as providing rewards in terms of intimacy, pride and autonomy, things not available in the commodity-oriented, exploitive marketplace. Ultimately then, paid work and unpaid domestic work are both valued. Each holds a part of what the other cannot offer. Domestic work is seen as a partial escape from the nonhuman demands of paid work while paid work is seen as a partial escape from the demands of patriarchal relations within the family.

If "good" jobs for married, working-class women hold a key to the women's sense of efficacy and control over their lives and the stability of their working-class families, this book will allow us to see how capital's changing requirements for women's cheap labor bends women's aspirations for better employment to its own requirements for continued profit. As we witness a new chapter in the history of America's women factory workers, we will see how changes in production work continue to dehumanize women's work experience, which inevitably, destabilizes their family lives. As a "new international division of labor" transforms the industries in which they work, the pressures of factory work grow more intense, and the conflicts women experience become more difficult to resolve. Hidden in the mill towns and small industrial cities of New England, the story of these changes remains to be told and will be told in what follows.

Most of what follows describes the blue-collar world of women factory workers. It provides a portrait of the social milieu in which women grow up, marry, and typically become lifelong factory workers. It chronicles the daily experience of blue-collar women—on the job and at home. We will look closely at the pressures of the workplace as they affect women's family lives at different stages of the life cycle and as they influence women who come from different cultural backgrounds. The book will probe the women's feelings about the role of work in their lives and explore the impact of factory life on their identities as women. Finally, we will explore the growing anxieties of blue-collar women as they cope with the economic and family issues raised by a deteriorating work situation, growing job insecurity, and the fearful experience of actually losing their jobs. In sharing their experiences with us, women who work in traditional female factory jobs begin to provide us with a glimpse of their hopes, dreams, and aspirations as well as the problems they now confront.

Blue-Collar Women and the Changing Employment Structure

The story that will emerge is, for the most part, a result of a two-year study I conducted to explore the impact of job loss on women factory workers. The context of this research was New England's changing economy; the transformation of the region from a manufacturing employment base to one centered on high technology, service, and trade. I was primarily concerned with understanding the economic, social, and emotional consequences of layoffs and unemployment for blue-collar women and their families. For four decades since the Great Depression, researchers have concerned themselves with the way families respond to the job loss of male breadwinners. The purpose of this research was to discover what transpired in a contemporary working-class family when a wife and mother, not a male breadwinner, was laid off from a factory job.

Today plant closings and contractions in the "smokestack" industries challenge the long-term economic well-being of millions of industrial workers and their families. These events threaten the stability of whole communities as contemporary American manufacturing firms find themselves unable to compete with European and Japanese efforts to make steel and build automobiles. Numerous books and articles have appeared in the past five years about the industrial decline of cities like Youngstown, Ohio, Pittsburgh, and Detroit.[13] Some of this work is quite graphic in describing the pain experienced by blue-collar families when the men lose their jobs. Through his music, even Billy Joel has enhanced the national awareness of the crisis that is taking place in America's "Allentowns."

Yet, we have heard little about the small mill towns and industrial cities where women industrial workers have, for the past forty years, been losing "good" jobs and facing unemployment. Today we know little about what the future holds for such women. In the past twenty years 800,000 jobs have been lost in the clothing, apparel, and textile industries, a group of industries which even today employs one out of eight production workers, most of whom are women. Despite large employment declines then, these industries still employ more workers than basic steel, auto assembly, and chemical refining combined.[14]

A recent study by the Bureau of Labor Statistics of the Department of Labor shows that 35 percent of "displaced workers" counted between 1979 and 1983 were women. In most regions women represented between 30 and 40 percent of the displaced workers. New England, however, had the highest percentage of displaced women, 40 percent of all the displaced workers.[15] Yet there is only beginning to be a body of research which explores the impact of job displacement on women and their families.[16]

As I began this research and began to explore the issue of women's unemployment, the "data" eventually took me well beyond my original question. It became clear that job loss and unemployment was only part of a larger story that needed to be told. The loss of these jobs and the effects on the women and their families could not be understood outside a framework which explained the causes of this unemployment, particularly the new role women have come to play in the industrial transformations that are now taking place throughout the world.

In what follows I will say more about the ways in which a growing global economy affects women's employment domestically and throughout the world. The changes wrought by the new international division of labor now threaten a century of social progress for many of today's women production workers. These changes are leading to the growth of new and cheaper forms of domestic production work. They have begun to undermine the protections and wage gains won by generations of working women during almost a century of struggle and are causing many women to lose their jobs. These events are occurring at a time when women need well-paid work perhaps more than ever before.

The Research

The research which will be described here was made possible by a generous grant from the Department of Labor's Employment and Training Administration. This support made it possible to interview more than four hundred women who were employed full time (thirty-five hours a week or more) in blue-collar occupations in the manufacturing industries which were disappearing from the New England region. The women we talked with were garment workers; they were assemblers of electrical cords, cables, and light bulbs; they processed leather goods; they wrapped and packaged a wide variety of consumer products, from toys to food items—fish, candy, bread. About two-thirds of our sample, 273 women, were workers who had lost their jobs in the previous six months. The remainder, 141 women, were currently employed in comparable occupations and industries. Almost all the women we talked to, 92 percent, worked in unionized firms.[17]

The women we interviewed were employed in occupations which have traditionally been reserved for women. As stitchers, packers and wrappers, assemblers, and operators of small machines, these women had jobs which were classified by the Department of Labor as "unskilled and semiskilled."[18]

The vast majority of blue-collar women work in manufacturing jobs like these, despite more than a decade of efforts at affirmative action designed to get more blue-collar women into more highly paid "skilled" craft jobs. In the past ten years we have, no doubt, seen more TV commercials and magazine ads where women are wearing hard hats and breaking up pavement on construction crews. Yet despite the changing image, in 1980, after about a decade of affirmative action, 94 percent of all skilled, blue-collar workers were still men.[19] Indeed, most blue-collar women are not climbing telephone poles but, like the women we spoke to, are working in factories on assembly lines.

This book is not about the lives of all 414 women interviewed. It is only about the 233 married women, most of whom had children as well as husbands. Most of us are well aware of the economic problems faced by women who head their own families. The feminization of poverty and the pauperization of women have been treated extensively in both the scholarly literature[20] and the popular press.

I decided to focus on married women, in part because the impact of low wages on women with spouses has not been treated extensively. Moreover, the major purpose of this book is to contribute to a better understanding of women's experience in working-class dual-earner families. Finally, an essential purpose of this work is to explore the impact of job displacement on married women. Although there is no doubt that the financial consequences of job loss are likely to be greater for women who head families, this book attempts to refute the notion that job loss is of little import for married women. Finally, my goal here is to compare the effects of job loss on married men and married women. In doing so I hope to show how married women's employment maintains the stability of working-class families. In this context it will become possible to develop a new framework for understanding the impact of the loss of jobs on both husbands and wives.

Unlike many other studies of working-class family life, the married women in this book are not all from ethnically homogeneous families with young children at home. Instead we will look at the way women in three different types of working-class families deal with factory work, family life, job loss, and unemployment. First we will take a look at "prototypical" families, the families of women between the ages of twenty-five and forty-five who have dependent children and were born in this country. Then we will look at the older generation of women factory workers, women who continue to make up a large part of the labor force in traditional female production work. These women were also born in America and are between the ages of forty-six and sixty-five. Most of these women have husbands who are still working, but some have spouses who are retired. About a third of these women have teenage children at home. The others mostly have grown children who are on their own. The third group of women, whose lives we will compare with their native-born counterparts, are Portuguese immigrants. These women are married, between the ages of twenty-five and forty-five, and have dependent children. Today, large numbers of Portuguese immigrant women live in eastern Massachusetts and Rhode Island and work in the same shops and factories as their American-born sisters.

This book then, is based on the reports of home interviews with 233 women, or 56 percent of the original sample. The interviews lasted approximately an hour and a half and were designed to elicit information about a wide range of subjects. The women answered questions about their family backgrounds (mothers' and fathers' work experiences). They were asked about their own education, work histories, current work tasks, work satisfaction, and what they valued most in a job. We collected data on current wages and benefits, home ownership, savings and childcare methods. We asked the women about their attitudes toward employment and elicited responses to questions about work satisfaction, sharing of domestic chores between spouses, feelings about the stresses involved in balancing work and family life and the feminist movement. We collected data on husbands' earnings and other sources of income available to families. Data was also collected on the women's marital satisfaction as well as their perceptions of their husbands' attitudes toward their employment.

We also asked detailed questions about the women's experiences after the loss of their jobs. Open-ended and structured questions were designed to elicit the women's personal responses to displacement and to assess the financial impacts on their families. We also asked the women how they felt their husbands responded to the loss of their jobs. We inquired about public and private income supports available to them (i.e., unemployment insurance, severance pay, continuation of health insurance benefits). We asked about the length of the women's unemployment, their job search behavior (including help received with retraining and job search). We inquired about their reemployment outcomes, such as whether or not they found jobs, what kind of jobs they found, and whether they lost or gained wages. We elicited information about public and private help with job search. We sought information on the actual financial losses incurred by the women and their families. We inquired about cutbacks, family problems, and health problems that ensued after job loss. Using projective tests we tried to assess the impact on the women's mental health as well.

The breakdown of employed women and job losers was as follows:

	Employed	Job Losers		Totals
		reemployed	not working	
American-born Women				
Younger	29	21	23	73
Older	34	36	22	92
Portuguese Women	28	30	10	68
			Total	233

Women and Their Work

One advantage of selecting a sample of working-class women on the basis of the work they do rather than on the neighborhoods they live in or the men they are married to is that their employment becomes a constant. In this research it allowed us to explore the changing role of work over the course of the women's life cycle. It hardly needs mentioning that children in working-class families grow up and leave home. When they depart, their mothers face new balances between work and family life. Today, as women's life expectancy expands, these changes need to be explored more than ever before. By focusing on women and their work rather than on families at a particular stage of the life cycle, we can see how work and family life change as women reach the crucial forks in their lives and face "empty nests," widowhood, and retirement.

A second advantage of the selection of women by their work is the cross-cultural comparison it makes possible. These comparisons proved just as important as those we made between generations. Initially we chose to include Portuguese women in the research because they were heavily represented in the industries and occupations we were studying. Their experience is important, and necessitates recording.

It was not the importance of the Portuguese as new players in the American immigrant drama which motivated the decision to include them in our study. The Portuguese are not extensively represented among new immigrant groups across the country. They are largely concentrated in eastern Massachusetts and Rhode Island. As new immigrants, however, the Portuguese play an important role in the new international division of labor, a role we were able to explore further.

But perhaps even more importantly, the old-world, patriarchal attitudes of the Portuguese family gave us the opportunity to raise some important theoretical questions about the influence of "patriarchy" and "capitalism" on working-class women. Comparisons between the lives of

Portuguese women factory workers and those of American blue-collar women were especially useful in pinpointing more precisely, the sources of "oppression" for these women in their experience of class and of gender, in their families and their workplaces.

Working-Class Women: Pain and Pleasure

Sometimes academics tend to either pity or romanticize the quality of working-class life, seeing in the people they study either their own worst fears or their greatest hopes. Those who pity their subjects see either limited aspirations or limited opportunities. They see people without the inner resources to enrich the quality of what, to middle-class observers, appear to be rather dreary lives. Or, they see workers and their families as too overwhelmed with life's troubles to do much about private "worlds of pain." On the other hand, there are those who see the working class, men and women, as agents of social change. These analysts look for courage and resistance in the face of exploitation. Hopefully, this book will show the fruitlessness of simple dichotomies which mask the complexities of people's lives. Instead we will show that it is often the personal circumstances of women and their changing fortunes which explain a variety of responses to the demands of work and family and a disparity of attitudes about what life has to offer.

The research, as the following pages and chapters will reveal, certainly sharpened some of our theoretical understandings about the lives of working-class women. Yet at the same time, we could find no modal "working-class" female personality that could be deduced from theoretical considerations of class and gender. There was no lesson we could learn about some inevitable political response that could be expected to emerge among working-class married women with children. Class and gender do, of course, create the options and limits in which blue-collar women formulate a broad set of values and goals. But the goals and principles which guide them do not determine a fixed set of attitudes or behaviors.

Women work in factories to assure the harmony and integrity of their families. Therefore, blue-collar women cannot afford to become passive victims; they must find ways to resist the degrading aspects of their jobs—to find the strength to remain vigilant—in order to maintain their involvement in the labor force. Sometimes this is a heavy burden, but one women often bear with equanimity and integrity. In our interviews we heard strains of traditionalism and also of feisty courage. We saw passivity as well as activism, acquiescence and anger. The work which follows demonstrates how eloquently the women spoke of the constant pressure of factory work, of their exhaustion at the end of the day, of the problems involved in balancing the demands of jobs and families, of their worries about money. There was fear, diffidence, and occasionally a sense of hopelessness. Yet we also heard expressions of pride in one's "trade." We heard about strong friendships, accomplishments at work, and gratifying family lives.

What will emerge here is a look at the day-to-day experience of contemporary blue-collar women, women with no public voice and no public image. In part it is written to give a voice and an image to people who have not found a way to speak for themselves. In introducing these women we must first understand the historic and contemporary employment context which today forms their best hopes and their worst fears. The next chapter will introduce this context, describing some of the larger events which are shaping the employment situation of America's and New England's blue-collar women.

Following that, in chapter 3, I will introduce some of New England's unionized blue-collar women. We will learn who these women are and how they have come to work in factories. Here I will explain how and why women make the choice to become blue-collar workers. No one shoulders the "double burden" of full-time factory jobs and family responsibilities with equanimity. Yet, for many of the unionized, blue-collar women, factory work is a choice, despite the fact that it is often made within the constraints of personal histories and financial need. If the necessity is a lash that drives the women to the factory gates, blue-collar women have decided to take on this struggle on the shop floor and at home. The combined enterprise often permits them a sense of control and accomplishment.

In the next two chapters, chapters 4 and 5, we turn to the shop floor. We see how blue-collar women use the resources in their workplace to resist management's attempts to hold them hostage to their own economic need. Their efforts reflect more than an attempt to preserve their sanity in an "alienating" work environment, as some have argued.[21] Women learn to manage the "action" on the shop floor in order to meet their individual and collective needs. They devise strategies to secure their welfare, negotiate conflict, cope with the piece-rate system, and master the technology designed to thwart their control.

In chapter 6 we turn to the women's families. We follow the three groups of women as they leave the factories and go home. We explore how husbands and wives negotiate their rights and obligations in marriages where a woman's blue-collar job requires an extensive commitment of her time and effort; the demands of a woman's job and the money she earns gives her leverage in a wide range of family decisions. Women balance their need for self-assertion against the needs of their husbands and children in view of the values they share with their men about the proper place of men and women in the family.

In this chapter we look at the working-class family economy, at the issue of women as "supplementary earners," or "breadwinners." Are they

working for "pin money" or, like their husbands, to "support the family."
As we will see, the limiting factor for blue-collar women, in terms of the
contribution they make to the family economy, is in the options available to
them in the labor market. Inevitably then, while women and their families
depend on women's blue-collar jobs, the women also see the value of maintaining legitimate access to the resources of spouses in exchange for domestic work.

Even as "secondary earners," women who work full time and year-
round in factories do not consider their jobs marginal. It does not take a
back burner to the women's concerns with their homes and families. Indeed,
the more we talked with the women and analyzed the data, the more we
came to understand how central "good" jobs were. In fact, it would not be
overstating the case to say that the limitations of class and gender women
face are frequently created by limited work options rather than "authoritarian" husbands or "patriarchal" families.

If today's women factory workers fare well at home when they fare
well at work, how must they fare in response to the deterioration of their
work and the loss of their jobs? Chapters 7 and 8 describe the experience of
job loss for blue-collar women and their families—the labor market consequences they face and the impacts on their families. These chapters explore
how job displacement and women's weakening employment situations
shake the foundations on which their sense of control and personal efficacy
are largely based.

As we will see, women do not experience the loss of their jobs in the
same way that men do. That does not mean, however, that the "male model
of unemployment" can be used as a benchmark for measuring the suffering
of unemployed women. Women see their work differently than men, both
in relation to their identities, and in terms of their family obligations; there
are aspects of a woman's unemployment experience that are different from
those of men. Nevertheless, as we will see, the experience of job loss and
displacement can lead to the impoverishment of the women's families as
well as the impoverishment of women's spirits, just as they do for men.

In the concluding chapter, chapter 9, I will try to summarize what we
have learned about the lives of New England's blue-collar women, about
their work, their families, and the way these blue-collar families respond to
the impact of women's job displacement. I will show how their class experience shapes their attitudes about questions of equality and inequality between men and women. Faced with deteriorating work conditions, declining wages, and the insecurity that comes with the increasing threat of
job loss, factory women often see the gains of the contemporary women's
movement as irrelevant, or worse still, as a cruel reminder that other wom-
en, better placed in the social hierarchy, have been able to improve the

quality of their lives. In that sense, they often see the women's movement as a consequence of class privilege.

At the same time, the value many blue-collar women find in traditional roles has not led to their seduction by the Moral Majority. Few of these women have ever had the option of being fully supported bv a man. They recognize their need for access to the labor force and they support women's struggles for well-paid work.

Learning about the lives of blue-collar women and the crises they now face cannot be divorced from the question of what must be done about solving these problems, issues which will also be discussed in the concluding chapter. Is it feasible to save the mill towns and small industrial cities, in New England and throughout the country, which have for more than a century offered employment and a way of life to millions of blue-collar women and their families? What are some of the solutions which are being discussed to improve the crisis these women now face?

What will become of the jobs of these married, unionized, female production workers—and what will happen to the women who do them? Today one of the major contradictions of our society lies in the fact that we have become a nation which officially champions the goal of women's labor market equality while at the same time we support an economy which is based on the employment of women as a source of cheap labor. Whether or not America or America's women can live with this contradiction remains to be seen.

Today the fate of America's women production workers is bound up with the past history and the current transformations that continue to change the international division of labor. These transformations continue to influence both the quality and the availability of paid work for American women. In many parts of the country, not only New England, unionized production jobs have enabled women to fashion meaningful lives, lives sustained by a fair degree of material comfort for their families and a personal sense of efficacy and purpose. It is now time to get to know some of these women. But before we can know them, we need to find out what is happening to their jobs. To do this we must know something about their past as well as about the new developments in the global economy, a subject to which we now turn.

2   Women Factory Workers and the Transformation of American Manufacturing

B EFORE WE BEGIN TO EXPLORE the dilemmas faced by women who now work in New England's factories, we need to understand the historic experience of American women who have worked in manufacturing jobs. Further, we need to see how the work lives of almost five million women who now work in our nation's mills and factories are being changed by the transformation of American manufacturing generated by what some have described as a new international division of labor. This chapter will set the stage for an exploration of what C. Wright Mills once called the "intersection of history and biography." It will provide a framework and a context for viewing the lives of the blue-collar women whose stories will appear in the pages of this book.

The Historical Context

Women have always worked in factories. Indeed it was women's labor that was initially responsible for the very beginnings of the industrial revolution. In the late eighteenth and early nineteenth centuries, the young, unmarried daughters of farmers and tradesmen left the farms and villages of rural New England to work in the burgeoning textile mills of towns like Lawrence and Lowell, Massachusetts. Like today, they worked in jobs designed specifically for female labor.

As the growth of modern industry claimed the labor of men, it transformed the nature of work discipline and undermined the independence of craftsmen; but with the advent of the modern factory system, traditional views of men's and women's roles continued to prevail. A sharp line continued to be drawn between the jobs that were considered appropriate for males and females, and women were relegated to some of the worst paid, least "skilled" jobs. Later, male-dominated unions collaborated with management to keep females out of the better paying, more highly skilled, industrial work.[1]

Historically then, men and women employed in manufacturing have worked in different industries and occupations. Men have typically worked as craftsmen or skilled workers in "heavy," capital intensive industries, such as the steel and auto industries and machine tools manufacturing. Women, however, have more frequently done unskilled or semiskilled work in labor intensive, nondurable goods manufacturing, like the apparel-textile complex, the shoe and leather industries, and more recently in cosmetics, food processing, and electronic assembly.

Even though women factory workers have always been confronted with sex segregation and lower earnings than their male counterparts, they have often responded positively to opportunities for factory employment. Such jobs, despite the low status, hard work, and presumed unsuitability for "ladies," has frequently offered better earnings than the other alternatives that were available to working-class women—jobs like domestic service, sales work, and, of course, agricultural labor.[2]

Women have traditionally accepted job segregation and lower wages in part because they had little choice and in part because earning well has never been an activity that provided much social esteem for women who have usually been brought up to believe that their primary obligations, and their greatest happiness, were to be found in commitments to home and family. By restricting the kind of work women could be asked to do, even protective labor legislation functioned to keep women in women's jobs and, of course, to keep women at home.[3]

Such solutions had more appeal in earlier days when factory conditions were abhorrent, when women spent much of their adult lives in childbearing, and when housekeeping remained a full-time activity. Many working-class wives and mothers could also find alternative ways to be economically productive outside the paid labor force by keeping gardens, doing laundry, and taking in boarders. Moreover, a century ago, children could more easily be sent to work at an early age to help support the family.

Yet if women accommodated to low wages and sex segregation in industry half a century ago, today this solution is increasingly less tenable. By the 1960s wives and mothers could no longer send their teenagers out to work. Instead they themselves took paid jobs in order to earn money to send their children to college. Today working-class women need jobs most of their adult lives. Like women in other occupations, blue-collar women, women who work in sex-segregated factory jobs, are now part of what Ralph Smith has called the "subtle revolution."[4] Blue-collar women have participated in the changes which have affected family employment patterns in the post–World War II period. They have become "working mothers" and members of "two-paycheck families."

In discussing the postwar changes in women's labor force participation, however, social scientists have given scant attention to contemporary women factory workers.[5] Perhaps this relative neglect results in part from the illusion that the prosperity of the postwar years made it possible for most working-class men to support their families on one paycheck. After ten years of depression and four more of war, it may have been comforting to believe that America's male workers had achieved the "family wage," and that Rosie the Riveter simply packed up her tools to retire to Levittown to raise her 2.3 children.

The truth is considerably less benign. Indeed, recent historical work suggests that one might well argue that while most women did leave their factory jobs when the men came home from overseas, countless others resisted being displaced from the high-wage jobs in heavy industry that labor shortages caused by the war had made available to them.[6]

Many women in the postwar period did, of course, find other jobs. They worked in the sales, service, and clerical sectors as corporate America built high-rise office buildings and shopping malls. Yet large numbers of women continued to work in factories throughout the 1950s and 1960s in order to contribute to the material comfort of their families. A substantial number of these women continue to do so. Compared to other working-class women, many unionized women workers have earned relatively high wages and received good fringe benefits, paid vacations, and pensions. These are gains which were achieved by over a century of union and political struggles and which are now being threatened by the transformation of the global economy and the new international division of labor.

As we will see, what is happening to New England's contemporary blue-collar women is a direct result of previous patterns of sex segregation in American manufacturing. The problems they are experiencing are also a consequence of recent postwar changes in the global economy, changes which have transformed all of American manufacturing in the past twenty years or so. Because women have been employed in different industries and occupations, they have experienced the impact of the new international division of labor in different ways than men have. How then, in the light of past developments, have recent transformations in the international division of labor affected today's American women who work in domestic production jobs? What are the implications of these changes for the women who live and work in unionized factory jobs in the mill towns and small industrial cities of New England? We must look first to the recent growth of a worldwide economic system.

The New International Division of Labor

What many now call "the global economy" or "the new international division of labor" has been discussed extensively in a large, and still growing, body of research which explores the growth of multinational corporations in the past forty years or so.[7] Much of this work theoretically and empirically examines not only the structure and patterns of the new global industrial shifts, but the consequences of these patterns for employment—both domestically and abroad.

In brief, it is argued that the past forty years have witnessed the growth of vast, often American-dominated, multinational corporations which have achieved new levels of centralization and control over a worldwide network of productive enterprises. The growth of multinational corporations since World War II has generated a massive restructuring of worldwide industrial production. The existence of American industrial hegemony after World War II initiated this growth, which was also made possible by the development of technological breakthroughs in transport and communication and by supportive federal tax and trade policies which favored capital integration. The reemergence of European and Japanese capital, with a greater investment in new, labor-saving technologies, has, however, begun to challenge American hegemony as the leader of international capitalism.

At the forefront of new technological breakthroughs in steel, automaking, and microelectronics, European and Japanese firms have become, in the past twenty years or so, serious rivals to America's industrial hegemony in world markets. One of the most serious consequences of these changes has been the loss of high-wage, unionized, manufacturing jobs. These losses have fallen mostly on male workers who are employed in the steel, auto, machine tool, and other "heavy" industries. The inability of American manufacturing to continue to compete with the higher productivity and typically lower wages of foreign manufacturing has mobilized public attention and has generated serious policy discussions about a new industrial policy for America.

Cities like Youngstown, Ohio, Pittsburgh, and Detroit continue to provide graphic examples of the toll in human suffering wrought by "deindustrialization." Barry Bluestone and Bennett Harrison estimate that there has been a loss of fifteen million jobs in this country between 1968 and 1976 as a result of industrial contractions and plant closures. In addition to large-scale unemployment, these changes have created severe problems for a labor movement weakened by the waning number of jobs. The past fifteen years or so has witnessed new onslaughts of union busting and intensified demands for concessions.

Another important thrust of research concerned with the effects of the new international division of labor has focused on the changed economic relations between developed and Third World countries.[8] These scholars point out that until recently many Third World countries were primarily sources of cheap raw materials which were transported to industrialized countries to be used in domestic manufacturing. Today, instead of exporting raw materials, these underdeveloped countries are exporting their labor.

Multinational corporations, in search of cheaper labor, have set up new, deskilled manufacturing operations abroad. Or, indigenous manufacturing operations have "run away" to "export processing zones" where they benefit from low taxes and most importantly, low wages. June Nash and Patricia Fernandez-Kelly write,

> According to the United Nations Industrial Development Organization, there are at present almost 120 export-processing zones in areas as far distant from one another as the Orient, Latin America, Africa, Western Europe, and the United States. Almost two million people are currently employed in EPZs throughout the world and many more are directly or indirectly affected by their existence.

Wages in these zones are far below what comparable workers in the United States would be paid. The average wage in Hong Kong in $1.18 per hour, Taiwan offers $.57, South Korea $.63. In the Peoples Republic of China wages are $.16 an hour.

Grossman and Ehrenreich have documented some of the effects of what they call "the global assembly line."[9] They point out that most of the manufacturing to be found in the new export processing zones provides few jobs for skilled workers. Instead, recent technological changes have made it possible to deskill production processes, enabling the multinationals to hire large numbers of young, peasant women who are "first generation immigrants" to industrial society. Grossman estimates that there are more than two million, mostly young, unmarried women, employed in places like Malaysia, Taiwan, and in Mexican border towns, making garments, textiles, toys, footwear, pharmaceuticals, appliances, and computer components.

Many anthropologists[10] who have studied the effects of this development have concluded that it is not only destructive to the texture and fabric of traditional ways of life, but it is extremely exploitative of young women. Unfettered by protective labor legislation or regulation of any kind, these enterprises have recreated industrial conditions similar to, perhaps worse, than those found in the workshops of Europe and America more than a hundred years ago. The women work long hours, often in dangerous settings, where many are exposed to a variety of health hazards. Ehrenreich describes "wages on a par with what an 11-year-old boy could earn on a paper route, and living conditions resembling what Engels found in Manchester." Further, management has found ways of manipulating the subservience of traditional women in order to keep the "factory girls" in line and avoid protest or rebellion.

The employment dislocations wrought by the new international division of labor, however, are not limited to Third World women and American men. Though few observers have noticed their plight, women in domestic manufacturing have also suffered from the effects of these international economic transformations. Unable to compete with women in South Korea who earn $.63 an hour, they have been losing their jobs in record numbers for the past twenty years. As I have already pointed out, in the past twenty years 800,000 jobs have been lost in the clothing, apparel, and textile industries, industries which employ women extensively.

Both the *New York Times* and *The Wall Street Journal* ran a series of front-page stories describing the personal and family effects of mass unemployment during the 1981–82 shakeout in the steel and auto industries. The men who lost their jobs were some of the most highly paid workers in the country, backed by powerful labor unions. Most were heads of families who had wives, children, and mortgages to support. Yet the quiet desperation of countless numbers of displaced women workers in garment shops and light manufacturing plants all over the country has been publicly ignored.

As Sol Chaikin, President of the International Ladies' Garment Workers' Union, has pointed out in testimony before the Subcommittee on Economic Stabilization of the House Committee on Banking, Finance and Urban Affairs,

> In the process of assessing the growing decline of capital intensive industries, the equally, and in a sense, more severe problems confronting labor intensive manufacture are being overlooked. Perhaps this occurs because labor intensive manufacture is, by and large, conducted on a small scale with the average firm employing fewer than fifty workers. For example, when an apparel factory, employing an average of fifty workers, mainly women, closes, it attracts little media attention. Even if 200 such shops around the nation close at one time—as is the case—the same lack of attention prevails. When a steel or auto plant closes down, on the other hand, the unhappy event usually results in front-page stories and extensive television coverage.[11]

Perhaps there is no TV coverage when garment shops close because the displaced workers are "only women."

The failure to notice the impact of unemployment on women results from erroneously accepting the conventional wisdom. First, many believe that women don't need jobs to support themselves and their children. Second, it is assumed that losing a "woman's" blue-collar job does not represent much of a problem. Presumably, if garment workers are unable to compete with women in South Korea who earn $.63 an hour they can simply get other low-wage jobs which are in plentiful supply; they can become secretaries and waitresses. As we will show in this volume, both of these assumptions are frequently belied by the evidence.

But the problems of today's women factory workers are not limited to job displacement and unemployment. The new international division of labor has also contributed to the reversal of a historical trend in which women had begun to considerably improve their situation in manufacturing employment. In the 1960s changes began to occur in women's production jobs just at the point that paid employment became increasingly important to millions of working women, married women with children. The effects of a deteriorating work situation are felt unevenly across industries and between regions. However, many blue-collar women who continue to work in manufacturing are experiencing significant wage declines and an overall deterioration in their working conditions.

There are new case studies of women employed in a variety of domestic manufacturing jobs which give us a glimpse of the exploitation that is currently being experienced by women in production jobs. [12] Researchers and journalists have recently documented the existence of small shops in which recent immigrants, both legal and illegal, work in sweatshops for less than the minimum wage. [13] New forms of industrial homework are emerging in the assembly of electronic equipment. [14]

Competition with women employed on Third World global assembly lines is not only creating unemployment for domestic women production workers. It is also creating downward pressure on the wages of women who continue to be employed in our nation's mills and factories. In 1971 women who worked full-time and year-round as "operatives" in manufacturing [15] earned 107 percent of the wages of comparably employed saleswomen. By 1981, their earnings had dropped to 91 percent of the earnings of full-time women salesworkers. In 1971 women operatives earned 115 percent of the wages of women in service jobs. Ten years later they earned only 103 percent of what women service workers made. Their earnings compared to women in craft jobs had dropped as well. In 1971 they earned 88 percent of craft workers salaries. By 1981 the proportion had dropped to 78 percent. [16]

The wage declines experienced by America's blue-collar women have been exacerbated by massive regional shifts of employment from the Frost Belt to the Sun Belt. Inevitably, these changes have meant the deunionization of America's women factory workers. For ultimately it was unionization which created the wage advantage experienced by blue-collar women in the postwar period. A comparison of statewide employment data from the 1970 and 1980 census shows that the greatest increases in women's blue-collar jobs were in Texas, Florida, and California, while the greatest declines were in New York, New Jersey, and Pennsylvania. [17]

As firms in the older, mill-based industries have closed their doors in the heavily unionized industrial areas, blue-collar women have inevitably left the union rolls. While it is difficult to get complete data on union membership we do know that between 1956 and 1976 blue-collar unions lost roughly 100,000 women members. The apparel and textile unions lost the greatest number of women members; but the Bakery Workers, the Electrical Workers (IUE), the Meatcutters and the Auto Workers also lost women union members during this period.[18]

The deunionization of America's women production workers, and indeed, all workers, has been exacerbated by the new forms of union busting we have begun to see during the past decade. In a brilliant article in the *University of California Law Review*, Jules Bernstein has described some of the more sophisticated strategies management consultants have begun to use against union organizing efforts.[19]

Union busting efforts are certainly not limited to women or to workers in manufacturing jobs. But blue-collar women may become increasingly vulnerable to the efforts of employers to prevent them from organizing, primarily because management can now more easily threaten to relocate jobs overseas.[20] Firms can threaten to move production sites not only from region to region domestically, but to the new export processing zones outside the country in order to head off union drives. A variety of untenable working conditions may become more acceptable if the alternative is to be without any work at all.

Women employed in other types of work have not yet become as vulnerable to deunionization as their blue-collar counterparts. During the same period that blue-collar unions lost 100,000 women members, a total of 1.1 million working women joined labor unions. They accounted for about half the growth in total union membership in the twenty-year period. While union membership rose only 13 percent during this period, the numbers of women in unions rose by 34 percent. The greatest increases in women's union membership between 1956 and 1976 were among teachers, government workers, and not surprisingly, among service employees and retail clerks.[21] Growing numbers of blue-collar women then will probably continue to be susceptible to both lower wages and the risk of displacement in coming years. It is hardly surprising that black women, immigrants, and other minorities are increasing their numbers in these jobs as they become less desirable to hold.[22]

Blue-Collar Women in New England and the Global Assembly Line

We are moving toward a world in which there is an increasing concentration of capital and a growing integration of the processes of production. As women employed in particular kinds of manufacturing jobs, New England's unionized blue-collar women are a central link on a chain that ties the parts of the "global assembly line" together.

The women whose world we will enter in the following chapters share some important experiences with their counterparts who work as assemblers in Silicon Valley's electronics plants and with women who work for $.63 an

hour in Korean garment shops. What they share is the experience of working at industrial jobs which have been designed with women's lives in
mind.

However, the woman who earns upwards of $5.00 an hour in a union-
ized factory job in Milltown, New England enjoys a way of life that is vastly
different—both materially and culturally—than her counterpart who works
in a garment shop in Korea for $.63 an hour. It is her way of life, built on
the progress of a hundred years of workers' struggles, which is now being
called into question. The value of these relatively well-paid jobs to the
women and their families, then the loss of these jobs, and finally the aftermath of unemployment and reemployment in new, lower paid work, is the
drama that will be played out in the pages of this book.

Some have argued that the totality of economic changes we are witnessing now threaten to polarize the nation into a group of haves and have
nots; that the middle class is now in the process of "disappearing." New
England's unionized blue-collar women are part of that "disappearing middle." Indeed, what many who concentrate on male blue-collar workers forget is that when the "middle disappears" women will be among the first
groups to suffer. Finally, then, the lives of the women factory workers we
will meet in the following chapter allow us to witness the importance and
the value of good jobs that are now being threatened by the international
division of labor. We will begin to see the value of what so many blue-collar
women are now in the process of losing.

3   A Profile of America's Forgotten Working Women

Driving down the interstate highway in New England, as you approach "Milltown" the first thing you see are the smokestacks of the old textile factories and paper mills. As you get closer you approach the old gray stone or red brick buildings that stick out against the sky. Most are three or four stories high with neat rows of darkened windows. The boldness of their symmetry expresses the power and optimism of the entrepreneurs who started the industries they were built to house. At first the mills appear to be empty—some are. But the gray smoke pouring out of chimneys tells you that many are still in use.

The industries most of these factories were put up to house are gone now. Either the goods made are obsolete, or the mills have been relocated elsewhere—like the Sun Belt or overseas, in places where employers can offer lower wages than they would have to pay in New England. Today, small garment shops occupy the lofts which remain. Some space is also filled with other manufacturing firms which produce a variety of products—from electrical equipment and hardware to toys and golf balls. Near the old gray and red structures stand modern, one-story, aluminum-sided buildings with new neon signs to mark the continuing presence of manufacturing in late twentieth-century New England.

Beyond the factory buildings is the central business district—Main Street—in various states of prosperity and repair. Some of these old "downtowns" are decaying while others are in varying stages of urban renewal. The insides of turn of the century buildings have been gutted and restored; new and tasteful signs hang outside. The people who work in the nearby factories come here to do their shopping, meeting and greeting one another and inquiring about each other's health.

A few blocks beyond the center of town one is likely to find a Catholic church. Usually it is surrounded by a small lawn beyond which are rows of residential streets. Sometimes these streets are lined with trees, but more typically there are only wood frame and triple-decker houses. Some have chipping paint and sagging porches which suggest the same state of affairs within. Yet with real estate prices what they are, most are in good repair—freshly painted with new aluminum storm windows and screen doors. At the corners of the streets are grocery stores where various ethnic foods are sold—Polish, Italian, French Canadian, or Portuguese—depending on the neighborhood. Some of the older, larger homes have been turned into funeral parlors.

If you stay in your car and drive down these streets, the triple-deckers give way to a more suburban setting, where modest two- and three-bedroom ranch houses predominate. These neighborhoods, built during the last twenty-five years or so, are flanked by newer shopping centers and malls with department stores, movie theaters, supermarkets and fast-food restaurants. Then this "suburb" gives way to the countryside and the route to the interstate which connects you, after a drive of an hour or two, to Boston, Worcester, Providence, or Hartford.

Sometimes "Milltown" is more than a town. It is a small industrial city. Or Milltown used to be a city but has become annexed to a larger metropolitan area as expanding populations and urban growth have made it into an industrial suburb. Whatever its actual size, it is a community, or a series of adjacent communities, of working people. It is a place where men and women spend their days shuttling between the gates of a factory and modest triple-decker apartments and ranch houses, working hard, saving, and hoping for a better future for their children.

In the century or so that it has been a factory town, Milltown has changed. But in many ways it has remained the same kind of place it has always been—a blue-collar, working-class community. Industries have come and gone, leaving in their wake extended periods of unemployment, poverty, and human suffering. Several times in the past hundred years the city has confronted the prospect of becoming a ghost town. Yet, periods of industrial revitalization have followed the declines, putting those who remained, their children, and a sizable contingent of newcomers to work once again.

The community retains its tradition of class consciousness and labor militancy. If the red flags and socialist picnics of earlier days have been replaced by TV, the Knights of Columbus, and Sunday football games, the union hall is still located in the center of town. While many of the children and grandchildren of older ethnic groups have gone to college, new streams of immigrants have come here from various parts of the world to find work and build new lives. Today they continue to come. Homes, entire neighborhoods, have changed hands in the past twenty-five years. In certain parts of town the restaurants and grocery stores of one group have been replaced by those of another.

Yet it is not restaurants and grocery stores but manufacturing which has created this continuity. Moreover, the mills and factories of New England, unlike those of Pittsburgh, Youngstown, and Detroit, have traditionally employed large numbers of women. Indeed, despite the thousands of factory jobs which women have lost in the past two decades, in 1980, women production workers in Massachusetts still comprised almost 25 percent of the female labor force in the state. Who are these women and why do they work in factories? With the increase in employment opportunities for women in offices, restaurants, and shopping malls, what does a factory job offer a woman today? How does it provide a way for women as wives, mothers, even as grandmothers to earn a living and make a home for themselves and their families?

The Women Who Work in Factories

The women who work in New England's mills and factories, the women who live in the neat triple-deckers on Main Street and the modest ranch houses have no public image and no public voice. Although they are indeed "working women," you are not likely to read about them in newspapers or magazines. These blue-collar women do not appear in the columns of *Ms. Magazine* or *Cosmopolitan*. Nor will you see them in feature stories about welfare mothers or female family heads. They are frequently older, and more often than not, married. With little education, few have either the experience, the language, or the confidence to break the silence about their lives in the midst of discussions about "working women."

There are common threads that run through the lives of all blue-collar women which emerge from the experience they share as factory workers. What they share, however, as working-class women and as factory workers is limited by their stage in the life cycle, the history of the times through which they have lived, as well as by their ethnic culture and background. In this chapter I will introduce the women and examine some of the great divides between older women whose families are, or soon will be, behind them, and younger women with children who still need their care and their financial support; between women who were born and raised in America and those who are new arrivals. In many ways the young, the old, and the foreign-born women have different reasons for working in a factory.

Moreover, while factory jobs like these may seem the same to the uninitiated observer, women who actually spend their days at benches assembling the components of light bulbs or sewing together slacks and pajamas often feel there is a world of difference between a "good" job and a poor one. The needs of the women and the real options available to them sometimes allow a "fit" then between what the women seek from their work and what they get. Blue-collar women do work which is dirty, difficult, and sometimes dangerous, but they don't always see their jobs as a "last resort."

Older, American-born Women

What is perhaps most striking about the women employed in New England's production jobs today is their advanced age. The women who work in today's factories tend to be older than women who do most other types of work. The average age of the 414 women in our sample was forty-three; a full 47 percent, almost half, were forty-five or older. Despite the recent influx of new groups of younger immigrant women,[1] most (75 percent) of the older women factory workers, those between forty-six and sixty-five, were born in America. By and large they are the daughters and granddaughters of earlier immigrants who worked in the region's manufacturing jobs when they migrated to New England fifty to one hundred years ago.

The ninety-two American-born women in our study who are now forty-five years or more grew up and came to maturity during the Great Depression. The children of immigrants and factory workers, few could afford to finish high school.[2] Like their parents before them, most of the women started working early in life, about sixteen or seventeen. This was for them just before, or a few years after, the second World War.

Women in this cohort may be the first generation of American-born women industrial workers to spend most of their adult lives working in factories.[3] Before it was fashionable they were members of "dual-earner" families. Certainly most dropped out of the work force in the 1950s and 1960s to marry and to bear and raise their children. But unlike their predecessors, when their sons and daughters finished grade school or reached adolescence, these women returned to jobs in factories much like the ones they had left ten and fifteen years before. They returned to work when their children's growing needs, inflation, and later, the changing attitudes about married women's employment, made a national trend of their experience.

The length and continuity of the women's work histories are at odds with the prevailing image of wives and mothers dropping in and out of the work force throughout their adult lives. With a mean age of fifty-five, our subjects have spent an average of twenty-five years doing paid work—most of this time after their children were in school. Virtually all of the women who were forty-five years of age or older had started their careers doing production work. Like the generations of women before them, when they left to get married, few expected to return. Nevertheless, when the growing financial needs of expanding families in the 1950s and early 1960s made it clear they could not remain housewives, a factory job was something they knew how to do.

Some of the oldest women, women preparing to retire, reported working twenty-five to thirty years in one firm. Yet a good deal of movement from firm to firm has characterized the work histories of the women in this cohort. The job changes, in some cases, were the result of opportunities for higher wages or better hours. Sometimes changing jobs followed an absence from the labor force, to get married or have another baby. Women reported gaps in employment lasting six months to several years, or job changes, which have also resulted from labor market forces beyond the women's control—particularly the contraction of employment in the industries which have employed them. The desire and financial wherewithal to take some time off has sometimes meant that layoffs which occurred at the "right" time (when children were small or husbands earning well) were sometimes extended. Yet sooner or later the women went back to work; most often they went back to factory jobs. Indeed, these women are lifelong factory workers. We calculated that 92 percent of the women's working lives had been spent at blue-collar jobs.

A few of these blue-collar women had worked as secretaries, waitresses, saleswomen, clerks, or chambermaids. Others had tried being hairdressers. Yet for women who started their work lives on the assembly line, work in these expanding "pink-collar" ghettoes frequently seems unstable, marginal, and temporary. It may be necessary to take such a job as an interim measure; sometimes it is a way of making do for a while after a layoff or a way to reenter the labor force. But, having a full-time, unionized production job with a seniority system and fringe benefits is having a "trade." The lives of Celia Triano and Marcia Penvert illustrate the attractions that blue-collar jobs can have for older women.

When we spoke with her, Celia Triano was sixty years old. She was currently employed full-time as an assembler in a small firm that made electrical wires and cables. Her husband, Bud, was a metal worker in a local plant that manufactured machine tools. As our interviewer walked through the door, she was welcomed, offered a seat, and almost instantly regaled with photographs of the Trianos' two grown sons. Both had graduated from college and Celia proudly showed the pictures of her sons' graduations—and then the photographs of their weddings.

Celia began working in 1939 when she was eighteen in a rubber factory where, for thirteen years, she made golf balls. Unlike most of her contemporaries, she married late, at the age of thirty-two, the year Eisenhower was first elected president. She stopped working for a full eighteen years while she bore and reared her two sons. In 1970, at the age of fifty, Celia went back to work to put her two sons through college.

Celia's children are somewhat unusual. Most of her friends at work have grown sons who are blue-collar workers and daughters who are secretaries. Yet there is a sizable minority of women who have children who are currently enrolled at the state university. Others have sons and daughters who have already become nurses, engineers, and accountants. One woman on our study, a stitcher in a garment shop, has a son who is a student at

Yale. Clearly he is somewhat atypical. Yet, Tina Bologna, his mother, expressed the feelings and aspirations many women have for their children when she told us, "I would stitch any time to send him to school."

When Celia decided to go back to work ten years ago the only job she could find was as a part-time file clerk in a real estate office in her town. She worked there for about nine months and quit when the production job she now holds became available. Working in the cable plant paid more money—money she felt she needed at that point. She has worked there, full-time, for the past nine years.

Celia admits that her husband does not believe that women should work. Yet, he apparently acknowledges that they couldn't have sent their two boys to school without her salary. He would like her to quit now that their children are out of school and on their own, but Celia continues to work. She says she likes having the extra money. She doesn't have anything special to do now that her children are gone and enjoys being with her friends at work. She said she would like to retire at sixty-two when she becomes eligible for a small pension.

Marcia Penvert was forty-six when we interviewed her, almost fifteen years younger than Celia Triano. She was a garment worker, married to a man who made his living as a postal clerk. The daughter of immigrant parents who worked in the textile mills, she quit school at sixteen to work in a garment shop. At twenty she married but continued to work until her children were born—a son when she was twenty-four and a daughter two years later.

Marcia stopped working when her children were born. But unlike many of the women in Celia Triano's age group who did not work until their children were adolescents, when Marcia's daughter entered kindergarten she started thinking seriously about going back to work. Because she felt she could "do better" than work in a garment shop for the rest of her life, she went back to school and got her high school equivalency degree. Taking typing and shorthand she prepared for a step up in the world—a job in an office.

When her daughter entered first grade and both of her children were in school all day, Marcia got work as a secretary, "a little typing, a little filing and answering the telephone." Marcia was pleased with the status; she liked "getting all dressed up every day." Yet after about six months she quit her job and went back to work in a garment shop, the same firm where she has continued to work for the past fourteen years.

One of the problems she had with her office job was the work itself. She described it as "boring" and felt there was not enough to do to keep busy all day. Another problem was childcare. She left the office at 5:00 P.M. but her kids got home from school at 3:00 P.M. Her mother-in-law was taking care of her son and daughter after school but Marcia could not be there to get them until 5:30. In the garment industry, work starts at 7:00 A.M. but it ends at 3:00 P.M. When she worked as a stitcher she could get her children at 3:30 and be home with them all afternoon. As she put it, "I was the mother. I had to be home for the children." But the bottom line was the money! She was earning considerably less than the women she knew who were still working in a garment shop.

Unlike Marcia, many of the older women had never thought of doing alternative kinds of work. When we asked them if they had ever considered taking another kind of job, most of the women simply responded by saying that they lacked education, and consequently, had never had the opportunity to do anything else. Such a response is an accurate enough representation of their situation. Few women with their backgrounds, growing up in the Depression, managed to finish high school. Indeed, without a high school diploma, a woman's employment options are very limited.

Yet there is more to be said about why these older women continue working in factories. Like Celia Triano and Marcia Penvert, most older blue-collar women started their work lives in factory settings. As their children got older and they recognized the need to shore up the family wage package, they went back to factory jobs because it was something they knew how to do. Some women, mostly those who finished high school, thought about or, like Marcia Penvert, actually tried office work. Others, without a high school degree, may have worked as waitresses or become saleswomen or hairdressers for a time. But ultimately, despite the low status and hard work, the women decided in midlife that a factory job was the better option for them.

Graying hair and thickening waistlines keep some older women in factories where youth and sex appeal are not required. Maura Ellis actually went back to school to become a bookkeeper when she lost her job as a stitcher in a garment plant and qualified for federally funded subsidized retraining. She appeared at the local community college, registered for a course in accounting, and went to school for a full semester. As she put it, "I've always enjoyed school. I love reading! So I thought TRA is going to pay for it. They were going to pay me to go. I'd be a fool not to try it."

Maura liked going to school, but felt her long-term options were better in her stitching job, despite the fact that the garment industry is in serious decline. She felt there was no future for her in trying to start a new career as a bookkeeper. Maura told our interviewer,

> I thought, this isn't for me. I knew it would be hard to get work. I'm not some 22-year-old. I had a couple of pounds I didn't want. So even if I did come out with straight A's, there wouldn't be any security, no union. So maybe somebody would hire you because they were under pressure and they

really needed somebody desperately. So he hires you. You work for three or four weeks and then he goes out for a few martini lunch. Some waitress adds up the slip and he says, 'Hey, she is good at figures.' Well, there isn't anybody there to protect your job. It is up to his discretion. And I just didn't think that was the spot for me.

Maura was lucky; she had the choice to make and went back to her job as a stitcher when the firm reopened.

For other women it was primarily the earnings which kept them employed on the shop floor, despite the fact that they would have preferred doing something else. Many of the older women told us they would really like to work with people, in a helping capacity. Some said they wanted to work in a nursing home while others expressed a preference for working with children. Eliza Mather was a 55-year-old garment worker who never finished high school. In our conversation with her, she said nostalgically, "About fourteen years ago I worked as a saleslady for about two years. But the wages were too small. I loved everything else about it."

Whatever their reasons for continuing their employment in production work, older women seemed to accept their situation as factory workers, seeing their situation, their lack of "opportunity," as simply part of the experience of women of their class and generation. The women felt that they had started out as factory workers and it was too late for them to change. Yet, at the same time, others developed a sense of vocation, a feeling that over the years they had mastered a "trade."

Helen Safa[4] has pointed out that older women are so heavily represented in these light manufacturing jobs because younger women have willingly left them the field. She argues that today, the daughters of these workers finish high school or go to college, moving into higher-paying, cleaner work as secretaries and other white-collar workers.

However, the allocation of these factory jobs to older women does not necessarily mean that they have been left with the most exploitative work. Indeed, the choice many have made to remain in factories attests to the value their jobs have for them as women of a particular class, historical period, and stage in the life cycle. It is important to remember that many of these older women went back to work in the 1960s, a period when factory work paid well compared to the existing alternatives. Even though the wage advantage the average blue-collar woman held has eroded over the years, and the wages they earn would barely keep a family of four above the poverty level, as unionized women, many feel they still make good money and have more job security than they would in other jobs. Despite their age and lack of education and skills, it is important to remember that these women do have some choices. Work for women in the sales and service sectors has expanded enormously in the past twenty years. Today there are many older women who are waitresses and saleswomen. Many older women without skills do things like office cleaning. Yet, as we have seen, work like this often seems decidedly less attractive to them than factory jobs.

Perhaps what is most important, however, in motivating the women to stay in factory work is the desire to collect their pensions. In most unions, the longer women work (until the age of sixty-two or sixty-five) the greater their pension checks will be when they do retire. Indeed, Agassi[5] has pointed out that jobs like these with pension programs tend to keep older women, who might otherwise withdraw from the work force, on the job until retirement age. Blue-collar jobs then, provide a cushion for older women who, because they work, can manage to live in modest comfort.

Among the ninety-two older women we surveyed, few lived in poverty; 83 percent reported they had savings and the majority, 59 percent, owned their own homes. In looking toward retirement, few of these women expected to live on their pensions. Nevertheless, with Social Security, homes that are largely paid for and a little savings, their pensions are expected to help mitigate the increasing vulnerability older women expect to confront as the years bring impending widowhood and the potential for chronic and costly illness.

Immigrant Women in New England's Factory Jobs—The Portuguese

If the daughters and granddaughters of these older blue-collar women will not replace their forebears on the assembly lines of Milltown, there are younger women, new groups of immigrant women, who will. Just as earlier groups of immigrant daughters and wives replaced the native farmgirls in the nineteenth-century textile and shoe factories of Lowell, Lynn, and Fall River, new groups of immigrant women continue to find production jobs in Milltown, as native-born women in their fifties and sixties make plans for retirement. The new immigrants are from different places. They now come from Haiti, Cuba, Puerto Rico, Indochina, and the Portuguese Azores. They are taking the place of Jews, Italians, Poles, Irish, Greeks, and French Canadians.

As researchers we wanted to capture some of the dynamics of ethnic change in the factories and neighborhoods of contemporary New England. Even more importantly we felt it was essential to explore how women from different cultural backgrounds responded to the demands of factory work in America. Because we couldn't study them all we made a decision to select one ethnic group and focus our attention on the women from that group. Because they were so prevalent in the industries we were studying, we chose the Portuguese, those who have recently come here from the mainland and from the Portuguese Azores.

While there has been a new influx of Portuguese immigrants to New England during the past twenty years or so, the Portuguese have been represented in the U.S. since the seventeenth century. They began coming to this country in large numbers, however, only in the last hundred years—largely to work in the cotton mills of southeastern Massachusetts. While the size of their community has fluctuated for years, the past two decades have witnessed a sizable increase in the number of new arrivals. These newcomers are largely from the Azores, a group of Portuguese islands located off the mainland of Portugal.

The Azores have been described as "agrarian, semifeudal and dependent." The economy is based on the production and export of agricultural products. In the past twenty years or so, these islands have experienced the centralization of land ownership and the mechanization of agricultural production. The land is dominated by large landowners while most of the people who till the soil are small holders, renters, or day laborers. It is also estimated that 73 percent of the privately owned holdings are too small to support the families that work them. At the same time there is an underdeveloped industrial sector which employs only 17 percent of the labor force. High birth rates contribute to the growth of a rural poverty, while the pace of urbanization and industrial development at home has not been sufficient to absorb the numbers of people who need work.

These are some of the classic conditions which have traditionally generated emigration. It is hardly surprising then, that during the 1960s 75,000 Azoreans left their homeland, and more than half of these came to the United States. In this ten-year period the number of immigrants from the Portuguese mainland and the Azores increased almost 400 percent over the previous decade. The liberalization of immigration policies in the 1960s facilitated this migration. By eliminating quotas and giving preference to those with relatives already living here, the new wave of immigrants have been able to join other family members who have already settled in New England.[6]

The women we interviewed came from backgrounds such as these. Over half, 54 percent, of the Portuguese and Azorean women we spoke with had fathers who were tenant farmers or fishermen. Only 25 percent reported fathers who had worked in factories. The remaining 21 percent said their fathers had been self-employed—they owned small parcels of land or tiny businesses.[7] Three-quarters of the women had mothers who were "housewives." But as Portuguese housewives in agrarian settings, these women not only cared for their homes and children, many grew food in the family garden, washed clothes by hand, tended animals, and helped with the harvest.[8]

Most of the immigrant women in our study came to America as adults, as adolescents, or as married women. Having grown up in traditional families in an agrarian society, their arrival in southeastern Massachusetts marked an abrupt transition. Like so many immigrants before them, only a few days "off the boat" most women found themselves living in an urban environment and working in factories. However, the transformation from agricultural labor to industrial wage work has meant far more than just coming to terms with an urban, industrial environment. With immigration these Portuguese women have experienced some profound changes in the way their work and family lives are integrated. As we will see in the chapters which follow, Portuguese women in America continue to be subordinated to the demands and values of a very traditional and patriarchal family life at the same time they must confront new forms of exploitative work relationships outside the home.

Portuguese families, like most families from traditional, patriarchal societies, support values which uphold the domination and the authority of husbands and fathers over their wives and daughters. Before marriage, daughters are closely chaperoned. In the Azores courtship is supervised by the family and sometimes marriages are arranged. The husband is clearly the head of the household. His authority in the family is heavily sanctioned by the Church. Within the family he receives deference and makes the decisions. Moreover, there is no place for women outside the protection of the family.

The continuity of this patriarchal traditionalism in America is reflected in the extremely high proportion of immigrant women who are married and living with their husbands and children. Almost 90 percent, sixty-eight out of the seventy-eight Portuguese women we interviewed who were between the ages of twenty-five and forty-five were married.[9] Among the remaining ten that were not married, six were young women who lived at home with their parents. Three of these ten women had been widowed. One woman we interviewed initially avoided questions about her marital situation. After some probing, the interviewer realized her husband had left her, a fact that was embarrassing to her and that she was trying to hide.[10]

In part, so many women are married because of U.S. immigration policies which give preference to families or relatives joining families in America. But at the same time, the virtual absence of divorced or separated women in the Portuguese immigrant community suggests the shame that falls on women who do not have husbands. It is extremely unusual for a young, single woman in the Portuguese immigrant community to take an apartment alone or live with a roommate. Until she marries, a woman lives under her parents' roof and gives her paycheck to her father at the end of the week.

The patriarchal traditionalism of the Portuguese family in America, however, has adapted to the need for daughters, wives, and mothers to work outside the home. Women's employment has been part of the immigrant strategy for survival and upward mobility in America. Even when it was considered unseemly for married women and mothers to have paid jobs, immigrant women, many of whom were married and had small children, worked in factories. In today's Portuguese immigrant community the wife's earning capacity is also put to the service of her family. At the same time her virtue is protected by the network of kin and neighbors who live in the ethnic community and work with her in Milltown's unskilled production jobs.

Today as always, kin and neighbors in ethnic communities are still enlisted in helping newcomers find work when they arrive. Women are taken in hand by their sisters and cousins and helped to apply for production jobs in a variety of low-wage industries. This method of recruitment means that Portuguese women tend to be concentrated and segregated in particular firms or particular departments within firms. On the shop floor they find themselves working with sisters, cousins, and other relatives and going home with them at night to the same neighborhoods. Because they are living and working with other Portuguese women there is often little incentive even to learn English. Indeed, almost two-thirds of the women we interviewed, 62 percent, spoke only Portuguese, despite the fact that most of them had been in this country more than a few years.

The work and family patterns of the Portuguese immigrants in New England today parallels some of the experiences of other European immigrant women who came to the United States in the late nineteenth and early twentieth century. Jews, Italians, Poles, and other groups came from impoverished, often rural communities seeking economic mobility through employment in some of most exploitative industrial jobs available, jobs American-born workers were often unwilling to take. The traditional values and strong family bonds these groups brought with them helped to mitigate the stresses involved in the adjustment to industrial life in America. At the same time, there is ample literature which demonstrates how the traditionalism of the older generation and the patriarchal nature of the family has often thwarted the desires of women, wives, and daughters to experience the freedom and opportunity promised by the American experience.[11]

As we will see in the following chapters, the lives of blue-collar women are characterized by a variety of struggles and tensions. Yet, for those who are immigrants, the struggles that confront working-class women, because they work in factories, are intensified. Immigrant women have fewer choices—both at home and at work. In the factories of Milltown, whether they are stitching sportsclothes or assembling electrical equipment, they work for some of the lowest wages. In the evening, as they move beyond the factory gates, going home to modest apartments in neat wood-frame triple deckers, they exchange one form of male authority for another. They go from work which is paid, albeit poorly, to work which is not—washing floors, making dinner, and caring for their children in a family system where men have considerable rights and relatively few obligations to help wives with their "double burden."

Lucia Costa is typical of the many Portuguese women who live in New England's ethnic communities and work in its factories. She is thirty-five years old and came to the United States with her husband twelve years ago as a bride. The Costas are both from the island of St. Michael in the Azores. Her father was a farmer. Unlike the majority of those who tilled the soil in St. Michael, Lucia's father was not a tenant but owned his own land. Lucia describes her mother as a "housewife." Like her parents before her, Lucia had only four years of schooling, which completed her education in the Azores. [12] When she came to America, she could read and write Portuguese, but even after twelve years of living and working here she still only speaks a few words of English.

The week after the newlyweds arrived in Milltown, Lucia's cousin took the Costas to the employment office of the garment shop where she worked. They were very lucky; there were jobs for them both. Lucia's husband, Paulo, was offered a job as a presser and Lucia got work as a stitcher. After twelve years in America the Costas feel their lives have gone well. Both are still working at the same jobs. They have managed to buy a house and they have three children, two daughters, now ten and five, and an infant son who is two.

Lucia feels fortunate that the company where both she and her husband are employed has done well. There have been only a few, short, temporary layoffs since they began working there. Some of her friends have lost job after job, as firms have closed and contracted. Because she has had a steady job, yearly pay increases have brought her wages to $6.00 an hour. But despite the fact that she is earning more than many of her friends, Lucia is tired of working so hard. She did take some time off when her three children were born, but each time she was only home with her newborn for three months. The strain and fatigue she felt when each of her children was born and having to go back to a physically demanding, full-time job with an infant made her deeply resentful of not having more time to be home with her babies.

Lucia's older sister, Maria, the children's godmother, has always taken care of the Costas' children when she works. Since the two girls have been in school they spend only an hour or so in the afternoon at their godmother's house until their mother comes to get them and their baby brother. Maria cares for Eduardo, the Costas' baby son, all day. Lucia pays her sister $40 a week for this and says she is very happy with this arrangement. "Maria loves the children and takes good care of them. She is my sister. I have confidence in her."

Lucia thinks her husband, Paulo, would like it better if she didn't have to work and could be home with the children. But the Costas both realize that is simply out of the question. In America women need to work; as most women put it, "You need two pays."

Lucia earns 45 percent of her family's income. She also does the shopping, makes dinner, washes the dishes, does the laundry, and cleans the house. Every Friday she gives her paycheck to her husband. Paolo pays the bills and puts whatever is left in their joint savings account.

While Lucia is tired of working so hard and wishes she might have more time off, she sees no way to make her hopes a reality. Before the Costas bought their house, she felt she was working to save enough for the downpayment. But now she realizes she needs to keep working. Without her salary there would be no way to pay the mortgage. Hard work has become a way of life and Lucia has no intention of retiring. Besides as her two daughters get older they help her more with the housework.

Researchers have recently documented the working conditions of contemporary immigrants, often illegal immigrants, employed in some of the newer nonunion sweatshops in the garment and electronics industries in New York and California. [13] In these firms, which often employ illegal aliens, compliance with minimum wage laws or with standards of safety and cleanliness appear to be unknown. These researchers recognize that the new international division of labor is responsible for the reemergence of these sweatshops.

The employment of low-wage, Portuguese immigrant women in New England's manufacturing firms is certainly part of this very same pattern. Portuguese immigrants have been well received by employers in New England's garment shops, jewelry firms, and many of the region's insulated wire and metal processing plants. Indeed, many of the firms that employ immigrants have remained in New England and have not relocated in the Sun Belt or abroad because manufacturers have continued to enjoy the benefits of the immigrants' willingness to work at low wages. Lucia Costa's experience in America, and the experience of women like her, show that Portuguese immigrant women who come here to work in New England's garment shops and wire plants work hard for some of the lowest wages. As we will see, the Portuguese do earn less than their American-born counterparts.

Yet the sample of Portuguese women we interviewed who have come to America with a commitment to hard and unrewarding work live in families which have made some impressive gains. Few of the families we studied lived in poverty; virtually no one we spoke with was on welfare. Indeed, in the years they have been here, 65 percent of the women we interviewed told us their families had managed to buy a house and 65 percent reported savings. As it has in the past, America has given many of these immigrant women and their families, not an easy life, but an opportunity to fare better than they could have had they remained in their native countries. [14] Indeed, as I will show, many of the problems Portuguese women face are tied, not only to exploitative jobs but to the very same families that give them comfort and sustenance in a strange and sometimes frightening country. As we will see, traditional, patriarchal families are an important source of the "oppression" felt by many Portuguese women.

While immigrant wives and mothers like Lucia Costa typically accept the basic contours of their work and family obligations, there is evidence that the patriarchal values are changing as the Portuguese rub elbows with life in contemporary America. Portuguese women's conflict with the traditionalism of family life usually takes place in the second generation, between fathers and daughters rather than between husbands and wives. Daughters are expected to marry early, about sixteen or seventeen, or to quit school as soon as they are legally able in order to work (often in a factory) and contribute to the family's income. The goals of the family as a unit are expected to supersede those of the individual. Economic success in Portuguese families is measured by the economic mobility of the family rather than the individual mobility of the children. Therefore, dutiful children, sons and daughters alike, are expected to earn money as soon as they are able. This means leaving school as soon as the law permits and earning money for the family.

This pattern has apparently functioned well in the Azores. Where young people grow up to be fishermen and farmers, extended education is neither available or important for most people. Four years of schooling is sufficient and is all that is required. But the immigrant women who came here as children and those who were born here of immigrant parents must attend school, usually until the age of sixteen, because it is mandated by law.

Sometimes there is generational continuity. Sonia Soares is twenty-one years old and lives with her parents. Her mother, father, and oldest brother are all employed in local factories where they have been working since the family came to America from the Azores three years ago. Sonia has also worked in a garment shop since she came with her family to America. Sonia was upset when she was laid off several months ago because she was saving her money for a trip to the Azores. Her fiancé is still there. When they are married, in St. Michael, the couple will return to the United States to live. Recently Sonia found another job. A new wedding date has been set, and she is "glad that things are returning to normal."

Sometimes there is generational conflict. Maria Mendes is nineteen and complains bitterly about her life. She works in a firm where she packs electrical cords and earns $4.25 an hour. Maria came to America with her parents as a child of ten and attended school until three years ago. Her father claims the family needs her to work in order to be able to pay the mortgage on the house the family bought three years ago. Yet she has two older brothers who live at home and contribute their earnings. After some bitter fights, Maria finally compromised with her father. She works during the day but is permitted to leave the house at night to go to school to get her high school equivalency degree. When she graduates she would like to try going to college. She wants to be a nurse.

Immigrants and the children of immigrants to America have always dropped out of school early and gone to work to help support their families, to pay the mortgages, and to allow their parents some comfort and security in their old age.[15] At the same time, American literature is also full of stories about intergenerational conflicts, of tensions between immigrant parents who want their children to retain both the old culture and their ties to the family and children who want to fulfill their own dreams. Both of these dramas are, once again, being played out in homes of new Portuguese immigrant families of Milltown, New England. The intensity of the passions they raise are an index of the economic opportunities in this country which may or may not allow immigrants to see a better life for their children.

Midlife American Women—The Attraction of High-wage Work

It may not seem surprising that older women or immigrant women, women who are marginal to the labor force, are employed in blue-collar manufacturing jobs. Such workers have little education and few job skills. Yet, the factories of New England also provide work for a third group of women. These women were younger; between the ages of twenty-five and forty-five. They were born in this country and typically have been educated through high school. Why, one might ask, with the wider options available to women with a high school degree, do these women continue to work in blue-collar jobs? The reason is simply that even with a high school education, many of the women in our study found that the sales, service, or clerical work available to them, unlike the factory jobs they finally found, did not allow them to earn a living for themselves and their families.

As we will see, production jobs are not all alike. There are "good" jobs and "bad" ones, jobs which pay well and those which pay poorly. The younger women in our sample, those who were born in New England and typically finished high school, had more of the "good" jobs. They earned wages which were, on average, about 10 percent higher than the older women and about 20 percent higher than women who were Portuguese immigrants.

It is difficult to fully understand the reasons for these wage differentials. One way to explain them, however, is by reference to "human capital" theory. This theory holds that workers who are more productive earn higher wages. Those more able-bodied, more educated, more experienced, and more "skilled" workers should earn more money. Yet there is no simple relationship between experience and education. Older women, both native- and foreign-born, tend to have more experience on these jobs. Nevertheless they earn less than younger women with less experience. At the same time, Portuguese women, with the lowest level of education, earn the lowest wages. Therefore it is not at all clear what effect the differences in these workers' "human capital" have on their productivity. Ultimately the relationship between experience and education works at cross-purposes in these assembly jobs and cannot account for wage differences for the three different groups of women.

Certainly younger women born in this country have the most education. They are more likely to have finished high school than their older, native-born cohorts. Moreover, virtually all American-born women, regardless of their age, attended school longer than immigrant women. However, it is also difficult to see how the "skills" they received from this schooling could influence their productivity on an assembly line, as human capital theorists would argue.

A more plausible explanation is that labor market forces maintain wage differentials between women in different age and ethnic groups, creating labor market segmentation. First of all, wage levels seem to be a function of employment in high-wage or low-wage firms. Portuguese women tended to be absent from high-wage firms and concentrated in low-wage firms, while younger, American women were concentrated in high-wage firms. For example, we interviewed women in two different firms in the same city, which produced the same products (electrical cords and cables) and in which women were employed in identical jobs. In one firm, the women were American-born and most had completed high school. The other firm employed mostly Portuguese women. In the first company, the American women earned wages that were 40 percent higher than those of the Portuguese women in the other company—despite the fact that both firms were also unionized.

It is difficult to explain the reasons for these seemingly arbitrary wage differentials. In part, they are the result of each firm's unique history of being incorporated into a different trade union organization. The high-wage firm which employed American-born workers was part of a multinational conglomerate and had, thirty years before, been incorporated into a powerful trade union. The other firm, which employed mostly Portuguese workers, many of them women, had only recently been unionized. The wage differentials between American-born and immigrant workers were initially due to this historical difference and had been reinforced by recruitment practices in which hiring is typically done through informal networks based on word of mouth. New employees are generally brought in by neighbors and kin. Evidently, new immigrants can be excluded from high-wage firms if the initial labor force of a particular firm was comprised of earlier immigrant groups and their children.

Exclusionary as these processes are, the historical patterns of industrialization and unionization in the northeast have created a stratum of high-wage, native-born women in manufacturing jobs. Even women with high school degrees are anxious to get such jobs because they often pay so well. Today, more and more of these high-wage women's jobs are disappearing from New England. Nevertheless, many of the women who have found a way to get these jobs, and who are willing to make the trade-offs factory work requires, have found the choice they made both lucrative and satisfying.

But what is it in a woman's life which motivates her decision to work in a factory? What creates the impetus for a woman with small children and a home to care for to spend thirty-five to forty hours on an assembly line instead of taking any number of other, perhaps easier jobs available to today's high school graduates in offices, stores, or hospitals? The midlife women factory workers we spoke to described the dynamics of work and family needs that shaped their choice.

Like other women of their class and generation, most of the women who were between the ages of twenty-five and forty-five started working in the late 1950s and early 1960s. Those that finished high school, about 50 percent of the cohort, got jobs right after graduation. Others entered the labor force at sixteen or seventeen. Some of the women we spoke to started their careers in factories. Yet unlike their older predecessors, the women who started their factory careers twenty years before, many women in this younger generation began their work lives as clerks, waitresses, secretaries, or cashiers, inevitably in response to the growth of the new sales and service sector jobs that became available to women during this period.

However, regardless of whether they began their careers in blue-collar, white-collar, or pink-collar jobs, most of the women's first years out of school were usually characterized by considerable movement between jobs. As young, single women they moved in and out of the labor force in response to boyfriends, families, bosses who bugged them, or low wages. For those who started working in factories, low seniority sometimes meant frequent layoffs. As young women entering the work force in a period of economic prosperity, many had parents to fall back on. With few financial responsibilities, most expected to marry and simply put a moratorium on decisions about work.

Most of the women did marry within a few years of leaving school[16] and soon started having children. If at eighteen or twenty women gave little thought to their future in the labor force, often floating from job to job, once they were married, with growing children, perhaps wanting to buy a house in a period of inflation and high interest rates, the need to have a well-paying, steady job began to take on new meaning. As they approached their thirties and found their growing families unable to live comfortably on their husbands' earnings, these women began to view the importance of paid work with increasing seriousness.

Many of these women who started their work lives in sales, service, or clerical jobs switched to assembly lines specifically because of the higher wages and good benefits. Elaine Barnes, a married woman with two children, ages eleven and eight, heard about her factory job from a friend in her neighborhood. She told us, "I worked at [Town Hospital]. I was a dietary aide. The money was lousy and they couldn't give me full-time. So I quit . . . I had to wait a year to get in there [Condo Electric, where she now works]. I finally did and the money is terrific." When our interviewer asked Elaine what her primary attraction was to her job at Condo Electric, she replied without hesitation, "Money, definitely the money."

Sylvia Brentano, a friend and co-worker of Elaine's, told us how she had come to work at her job. She said, "I had done various other kinds of work. I did office work and I worked in stores." When our interviewer asked Sylvia what attracted her to Condo Electric, she gave the same answer, "Money!"

Some women took a factory job because it was high-wage, full-time work that could be done at night when husbands could be home to care for young children. Work on the second shift usually begins at 3:00 or 5:00 P.M. and ends at 10:00 P.M. or midnight. Although these hours make it possible for women to manage their work and family obligations, working such hours does not always make life easy. Sarah Bellows described her job at Cerulean Electric, saying, "I work 3:30 to midnight. By the time you get to bed it's 1:20. Then I get up early to get the kids to school. Then back to bed and sleep all morning until I get up to do my housework. Then its time to go to work. I have absolutely no time to myself." After this the interviewer asked, "What do you enjoy most?" She gave the same answer as Sylvia Brentano and Elaine Barnes, "Money. Definitely the money . . . I wouldn't be there if it weren't for the money . . . that's for sure."

In several cases women reported taking a factory job when their husbands became unemployed or disabled—like Linda Staller. When we spoke with her she was twenty-seven, married to a truckdriver and had two children, ages six and seven. Linda had quit high school at seventeen to get married. For three years after that she worked in a discount store as a cashier. When her second child was born, Linda took a part-time job selling newspaper subscriptions. This worked out well until her husband was laid off.

Fortunately, soon after her husband lost his job, Linda ran into an old friend whose husband told her about an opening for production workers in the firm where he worked. Linda applied and got a job as an assembler. The firm makes hydraulic tools. When her husband was called back to his job Linda continued to work forty hours a week and now makes $5.90 an hour. The Stallers' two little girls are in school all day now. After school they spend the afternoon with Linda's sister-in-law, where they play with their cousins until she picks them up. Linda says she feels the children are in good hands and willingly pays her sister-in-law $30 a week.

Certainly the inflation of the 1970s has pushed more working-class women with growing families into the labor force. While Linda Staller took a factory job because her husband was out of work, other women, like Sylvia Brentano and Elaine Barnes, simply responded to inflation, expanding families, and the needs of growing children—all of which were putting a greater burden on their family's income. Yet few of the blue-collar women we spoke with had gone from being full-time housewives to working in factories. Their move into a factory job usually came with the realization that the marginal work they were already doing would no longer suffice. Already working, they looked for better jobs. Unlike other women of their class and in their situation, these women were lucky to find their high-paying, blue-collar jobs.

While most of the women in the cohort of older women had waited at least until their children were in school to return to work, these younger women worked when their children were small. They managed work and childrearing in a variety of ways. Some left the labor force for a few years after their children were born. But most struggled with a variety of babysitting arrangements and continued to work. The lives of Sally DeNardo and Mary Howe represent some of the alternative ways women chose to deal with the dilemmas of work and family obligations during the years when the needs of dependent children were greatest.

When we first met her, Sally DeNardo was thirty-five years old. She had been married to Tom DeNardo, a shipping clerk, for fourteen years. The DeNardos had four children, ranging in age from thirteen to two. Sally finished high school when she was seventeen and then went to work as a stitcher in a garment shop. During the next seven years she held jobs in several firms, as she put it, "on and off." During this time she got married and had her first child. She was laid off twice but she also quit two jobs because she felt they didn't pay enough. After her baby was born, when she was twenty-two, she left the job she had because, with the cost of a babysitter, she felt it didn't pay enough, but a year later, she got a job that did. For the past eleven years she has worked steadily as an overlocker, taking only a few months off when each of her other children was born.

Sally feels fortunate to have a steady job where she can earn $5.50 an hour. With four children, including a two-year-old, she works full-time and except for a few "slow" weeks during the summer, year-round. She has friends in other shops, though, who have had very little work; Sally worries about layoffs. She plans to work until she retires, at age sixty-two if she and her husband can afford it, but at sixty-five if not.

Mary Howe has managed her job and family somewhat differently. She is forty-two years old and for eight years has been working as an assembler of light bulbs at Condo Electric. She started working as a saleswoman after she finished high school at the age of eighteen. She worked in a series of different department stores until she married at twenty-five. Then she quit her job and stopped working for five years while she had her two children, now fourteen and sixteen. Then she went back to work again. For a few months she worked nights as a waitress at a local restaurant until she found the job she has now as an assembler. She has been working at Condo Electric for the past eight years and was earning $6.50 an hour. Mary has no plans to leave.

The work histories of these blue-collar women suggest we need to modify the conventional belief that suggests women enter and exit from the labor force primarily in response to their family obligations, or as a way of coping with periodic fluctuations in the earnings of their husbands.[17] When children are young, the choice between low-wage jobs and the relatively high cost of childcare can minimize the women's motivation to work. But it appears that the higher wages sometimes provided by factory jobs may serve to bind women to the labor force, especially when, as mothers, they begin to envision their children entering school. As the women, and their children, get older, the work patterns of these blue-collar women became increasingly more stable. "Liberation" is not seen as the freedom to make a career out of homemaking. Instead, these women want to work and they are willing to work harder for a higher wage.

Indeed, blue-collar jobs may bind working-class women even more tightly to the labor force, creating a work commitment which persists despite the presence of small children and despite changes in their husbands' earnings. Indeed once they are past the first years of their children's lives, the work histories of the women we interviewed suggest employment patterns not much different from those of blue-collar men.[18] Being married and having small children can become an impetus for women to find a way to earn more money to meet the needs of their growing families. Just like men, families may make women increasingly attached to highly paid work. As we will see, New England's high-wage, unionized, blue-collar jobs often permit women to be the providers their families need them to be.

Many of the women we spoke to were keenly aware of the status deprivation they suffered by working in factories. They view white-collar work as more suitably feminine and as more desirable—but only if one can afford the luxury of getting paid less for the pleasure and ease of working in more attractive surroundings. Yet, in many cases their own experience of sales, service, or clerical work reinforces the view they share with scholars that office and factory work are becoming increasingly similar. Caroline Benuto was thirty-eight; she had been working part-time as a typist when her growing family generated a need for more income. Four years ago, she went to work at Condo Electric, packing light bulbs. She told our interviewer, "I think that in clerical or sales work, you think that because you are not getting dirty that everything is all right—and it really isn't. The women who work in those jobs are in just as much trouble as we in the factories are in terms of having demeaning jobs. The only thing is they can get dressed up so it's glossed over. And they get paid less."

Factory Work—Struggles and Challenges

If given the choice, most of us would not wish to spend our lives working in a factory in an unskilled job on an assembly line. As we will see, the work is tedious, stressful, and physically difficult. But if the women who do it have been shaped by its pressures, they have not been deformed. In many ways, the public image of factory workers, in no small measure aided by social scientists, has created a grotesque caricature of the factory worker, leading us to believe that they are downtrodden, sometimes as mindless and stupid as the jobs they do. But few of the women were mindless or stupid. When we listened to them and heard their stories, we came to understand how they had made their choices, each woman in her own way, meeting her own needs as she saw them.

Older women work in blue-collar jobs because they started their lives as factory workers in a different era. Many have worked to buy homes and put their children through school. Their ability to continue working gives them the chance to earn the money they need to retain their economic independence and to live with dignity when they retire.

Immigrant women made their choice in deciding to come to America. Portuguese women hold jobs which compare poorly with the ones held by their American-born counterparts. They are indeed, some of the most recent victims of the new international division of labor. Yet the jobs they do are the same kind of work that has enabled immigrants to achieve some upward mobility and help their children move into the mainstream of American life. Many of those who study the patterns of ethnic assimilation fear that such jobs are disappearing.

Perhaps most striking is the value of blue-collar jobs for midlife American women. Many of these women with growing families have chosen to do the hard physical work that is required in factory jobs rather than spend their days doing work that is physically less demanding but often pays less. They live with the heat and the noise of the production lines to be able to give more to their children.

All of these women must adjust to the possibilities that life and society have made available to them, to the limits created by their class and gender. But when we go beyond the images of victimization and "oppression" that are associated with those who work with their hands, we discover that the women shape the circumstances of their lives as well as being shaped by them. They do this each day as they enter the factories, punch the time clock, and take their places on the assembly lines.

4 Within the Factory Gates

WHAT IS IT LIKE TO WORK in a factory? What lies behind the facade of brick walls, behind the neat rows of windows that typify the factories of Milltown, New England? What happens within those factory gates where blue-collar women spend seven or eight hours a day, five days a week, fifty weeks a year? Most of us spend our working hours in offices of steel or glass, in shops, hospitals, schools, or restaurants, whether we clean floors or give orders. Working in a factory is not the same. When you leave your car in the parking lot and walk past the gate in the chain link fence, the difference becomes apparent.

You enter the building by a heavy steel door and find yourself at the bottom of a dimly lit staircase. The staircase has no windows and no light except for the metal fixture on the wall at the top of each landing. As you go up the staircase you come to a small glass-enclosed office on the third floor. Inside, two secretaries are at work at heavy wooden desks. The wall behind them is lined with green metal filing cabinets where piles of leather-bound ledgers are stacked. A large calendar hangs on the wall, reminding one, by the steepled white church, the rolling hills, and the gold-red leaves, that it is September in New England. To the right side of the office is a door with an opaque glass window. It leads down a corridor which, in turn, empties into the locker rooms. Beyond the locker rooms, on a far wall is the time clock, nestled between rows of paper cards which sit neatly in a metal rack.

Beyond the time clock is the shop floor, a loft space that seems about half the size of a football field, with creaking, grease-stained, wooden floors. The ceiling is about twelve feet high and is held up by heavy circular beams. Windows on each side of the loft let in the morning and the evening light. The room is filled with machinery. Garment shops have row upon row of sewing machines. Some of these are recognizable as sewing machines. But the new often computerized equipment, with multiple needles and flashing lights comes in a variety of unexpected sizes and shapes. Much of the technology bears little resemblance to the sewing machines we have in our own houses or remember in our mothers' and grandmothers' parlors.

If the machines are not for sewing clothes, they are for making light bulbs, or electrical cords and cables, for mixing the ingredients to bake, wrap, and pack bread and candy. There are lathes, presses, and molding machines. Conveyor belts are everywhere. But whatever the product or technology, there are overhead pipes, there is peeling paint, dust, grease, and what seems to the uninitiated observer like an overwhelming amount of noise.

Factories clearly lack the charm and comfort of other contemporary workplaces where women are employed today, even if they are production sites which are housed in modern structures with good lighting and shiny new cafeterias. But it is not only the setting which determines the way factory jobs are experienced but the kind of work the women do.

Women are concentrated in some of the least desirable production jobs in manufacturing. The majority are still concentrated in low-wage, nondurable goods industries. Moreover, whether or not they work in low-wage industries, they are likely to be found in "low-skilled" occupations. Only about 10 percent of all women who do production work do "skilled" craft jobs; the remainder are employed as "unskilled" and "semiskilled" operatives and laborers. Finally, these unskilled and semiskilled operatives and laborers tend to be employed in female job ghettoes. The jobs they hold typically pay about 60 percent of what male operatives and laborers earn.

The blue-collar women we studied did "bench work"—typical women's work. They were assemblers, checkers and examiners, packers and wrappers, and sewers and stitchers. They did things like putting together the components of light bulbs and lighting fixtures. They cut and wound copper wire to make electrical cords and cables, they crated golf balls and auto parts, packed and wrapped bread and candy, or set pockets and zippers into men's suit jackets and children's play clothes.

According to the demographics of blue-collar employment, most of us will never work in a factory. We will never know the pressure or the stress involved in sitting at a sewing machine and making blouses—of packing light bulbs or wrapping loaves of bread and boxes of candy. We may imagine such jobs to be mindless and boring. Yet, despite a decade of research exploring the "alienation" of production work, this book will show that it is not tedium which characterizes the work that women do in factories. Instead, what appears to be the worst part of their jobs is the pressure involved in dealing with the fast pace and the low wages of the piece-rate system— particularly in declining industries.

What follows is an effort to explore the organization of women's factory work and the responses of the women who do it to what they feel are the worst pressures and the greatest rewards. Blue-collar women often find ways to cope with their demanding jobs, using whatever resources their work provides as weapons in what can be seen as a daily struggle. At the same time, many of the women also take pride in what they do, finding ways to control the work process and defend themselves against its worst abuses. As we will see, what they want from their jobs—and what they get—can vary depending on the work they do and the firm in which they work.

The daily experience on the shop floor is more than just a perennial conflict with battle lines sharply drawn between the women and their employers. There are informal rules of exchange and reciprocity which moderate the tensions of the factory floor and make the workplace livable. Moreover, women want different things from their work depending on their age, their family situations, and their stage in the life cycle. What a woman's job offers then is, in part, a result of the nature of her job. But it is also a function of the implicit requirements each woman brings with her to the factory floor.

The Piece-rate System

In many production processes, conveyor belts and assembly lines control the speed at which workers do simple repetitive tasks. However, where workers do bench work, putting together the component parts of a product, where they inspect, or package and wrap, the speed at which each task is performed may still, in part, be under the control of the workers. Inevitably, management has set production norms and quotas. But it is not only the quotas which create the focus for the struggle which occurs on the shop floor between women workers and management, but the wage incentive or piece-rate system.

The specific rules which govern the way piecework is organized vary widely between firms and industries. Nevertheless, despite the myriad of differences between them, all piece-rate systems are based on a common set of principles. Workers get paid a minimum hourly wage rate for producing a certain quota of "pieces." They must set a minimum number of pockets, or pack a particular number of light bulbs in an hour, but, for each piece of work produced over and above the minimum amount, the worker earns a specified increment in hourly earnings.

Within this system there is presumably an "incentive" for workers to produce as fast as humanly possible. The system, however, benefits management more than workers, because it maximizes productivity. In most firms management brings in its own engineers who time each operation and set the rates. Surely both men and women who work in unskilled and semiskilled factory jobs suffer from the pressure of fast-paced jobs. Nevertheless, the sexual division of labor we witnessed in one firm illustrates the ways in which piece-rate systems may be used to intensify the pressures on women who do bench work and other kinds of simple assembly operations.

The firm—we will call it Cerulean Electric—was a small plant which employed about three-hundred-fifty workers on two shifts and produced electrical cords and cables. On the first floor, thin copper wires on spools were mounted on winding machines which transformed them into cords and cables of varying lengths and thicknesses to be used for different industrial and nonindustrial purposes. Tending these machines were men whose job it was to load the spools of wire on the winding machines and thread them through the appropriate apertures and passages. The machines controlled the speed and tension of the winding. They also fed the bare, wound copper cables to another operator who cut them off at the appropriate lengths. Once the machines were loaded, or set up, there was some time for the worker to relax until a spool needed replacement or a snag developed in the winding process.

Some of the men who were working on these machines were fixing tangled wires and reloading spools. We saw others standing around, watching the process, and occasionally smoking a cigarette. The winding machines were tended exclusively by men. The workers' "expertise," lay in their knowledge of the machines. They had to make sure the wires did not become tangled or caught. Facility in keeping the wires moving earned them a standard hourly wage rate of $6.15 an hour. Because to a large extent, the winding machines controlled the speed at which they worked, the men did not work on a piece rate.

Upstairs on the second floor, however, women were employed insulating and coating the cords and cables. Then plugs were mounted on the ends of each cord. "Plugging" was a difficult job. The women who did this operation sat at molding machines. Working as quickly as possible, they inserted the cut end of each cable into a circular mold which made four plugs. When the wires were inserted, hot plastic rushed into the mold. After the plastic had cooled, the cords were removed and put on a conveyor belt to be tested, labeled and packed for shipment.

Some of the women who worked on the molding machines had thin strips of cloth wound around their fingers to protect them from the heat of the molding machines. Yet it was sometimes difficult for them to avoid being burned because it was necessary to remove the cooled plugs from the molds as quickly as possible. "Pluggers" worked on a piece rate. The base pay was $3.85 an hour, about twenty-five to fifty cents higher than the base pay of women who worked as testers or who labeled and packed the cables. But no plugger would be satisfied to take home $3.85 an hour. Nor would her supervisor be happy with her productivity if she only worked fast enough to make her quota. In order to be working up to capacity, in order to be "making their money," these women need to produce beyond the rate. On a good day, pluggers make between $4.50 and $4.75 an hour.

But if you are a plugger, if you want to have a good day, there is no time for a breather. Women who test and pack the finished cords have more space to talk to each other as they pull the wires in and out of the testing machines or stack them in boxes. But, regardless of the jobs they do, if they are doing one of the women's jobs, the "unskilled" jobs on the second floor, there is simply no time to do anything as time consuming as washing your face or stopping to have a cigarette without losing money. When women smoke in the workplace they do it on their own time.

The sexual division of labor at Cerulean Electric is typical of the sex segregation that is found in production work. The question is, how have these patterns come about and what do they have to do with skill? Recently researchers have begun to challenge earlier theories which justified the allocation of difficult, yet poorly paid work to women. Women, it was argued, had no skills. At the same time, it was pointed out that these jobs were suitable for women because women had greater "manual dexterity." The fallacy of this "logic" is clear. If manual dexterity were a special "skill" allocated to women it would be difficult to justify paying them lower wages for their greater talent.

In a renewed effort to understand the real basis for women's employment in difficult, low-wage jobs, researchers have begun to look at the labor process itself. Many see the development and maintenance of sex segregation as historically rooted in the process of "deskilling" and the subsequent growth of "segmented labor markets." In other words, they argue that management has always controlled the introduction of new technology in manufacturing processes. This has often allowed them to remove control of the production process from the hands of skilled, male craft workers.[1] In response to this, men have, in part through their trade unions, tried to secure a relatively favored position in the labor force and protect themselves against the competition of the female "reserve army of labor."[2] As craft skills have disappeared, the bargaining power of skilled workers has been replaced by men whose claim to "skill" is based on their control of machines.[3] Others have pointed out that "primary sector" jobs, those with high pay, job ladders, and job security, have been associated with capital intensity.[4] Jobs in the secondary sector, those relegated to women, which are lower paid and considered more unskilled, tend to be labor intensive.

Many of these theorists have come to realize that both men and women production workers frequently have jobs which require the rapid performance of simple repetitive tasks that are intrinsically "unskilled." But when men do these jobs they do them on more expensive machines and the work is subsequently defined as more skilled. Definitions of skill levels then may not be self-evident. They may be socially constructed in order to preserve higher wages for men. Historians have shown that both management and male workers have collaborated in defining certain lower-wage production tasks as the special preserve of women. At the same time, women have been willing to accept such wages because they haven't had "families to support." As a result, like at Cerulean Electric, they often must work harder for less pay because the work they do is defined as "unskilled."

Researchers are beginning to question the justice of these definitions. They note that if women workers do not require a long time to learn the simple repetitive tasks they do, it does take them a considerable amount of time and effort to learn to work at a consistently fast enough pace. Indeed, one researcher who has explored this issue in depth has written, "The ability to work at high speed is a skill inadvertently created by deskilling."[5] Indeed, it is certainly difficult to justify why women, who may be working more intensely and working harder and faster than the men who are employed in the same factory making the same product, are nevertheless paid lower wages for their greater effort.

If management has avoided learning this lesson along with male union officials and workers who would prefer to maintain the gender-based wage differentials, the pattern has long been recognized by the women themselves. The women we spoke to were intensely aware and very proud of the skills they felt they brought to their jobs. Seventy-eight percent of the women indicated that the skills they brought to their jobs made them "especially valuable" to their employers.

One of the crucial qualities women saw as making them valuable workers was their ability to work fast. Barbara Sowell was a "dual packer" in a firm which manufactured light bulbs. This is the way she described her job, "I pack light bulbs. They have this run, and the light bulbs come down into the sockets. You take it from whatever belt you're working on and pack it." Barbara has to work fast and says with pride, "If the machine is running excellent, you can pack over 1,000 bulbs an hour with no problem."

But speed is not the only skill the women have. Many women who do factory work take pride in the fact that their jobs are physically difficult, that their work requires strength, energy, and coordination. Martha Hanley, who worked in a plant that made electrical cords and cables was also a packer. She described her job in the following way,

> It was extension cords that would be on a rack—six, nine, twelve, and twenty-foot cords that we take and put on a rung on a hydraulic machine which wraps them. Then a sleeve comes up and staples them. As we are doing that we are supposed to inspect them, to eliminate any exposed wires. Then we pack them into a box as we are working with each cord, stamp them [with the company logo] and put it on a conveyor. So we are inspecting and packing at the same time.

In doing the tasks of inspecting and packing she had to lift heavy objects and, once again, move pretty fast.

Sylvia Montrose had a job which required not only speed, but coordination and concentration. She was a "finishing operator in a firm that made things like ball joints for cars, masks, respirators for hospitals, brake parts, and a lot of stuff for cars."

What does a "finishing operator" do? Sylvia said,

> That's hard to explain. The press room molds the parts upstairs. When they're done molding them, they are sent downstairs. We trim the extra waste of rubber by hand or by machine. Whether it's machine work or hand trimming your hands are constantly moving. It takes a lot out of you. And if the work comes in with thick waste material at the edges, you have to stay a couple of minutes longer to get it out and finish it properly. You know if you just zip, zip, zip the work would come back.

Trying to work fast enough and at the same time, complete the work with care is very trying and very difficult even for a woman like Sylvia, who has been working at this job for almost five years. For this "unskilled" work, Sylvia earned about $4.50 an hour.

Women who have worked in a particular firm or industry for a number of years often become very versatile. Like Cynthia Barden, who works in a garment shop making children's clothing, these women have often managed to acquire a wide variety of production skills. Cynthia's job is classified as a "sewing machine operator," but that title masks the wide variety of different jobs she has learned how to do through the years. As she put it, "I'm a pocketsetter now. But I have also been a zipper setter, a stitcher, an overlocker, and a bandsetter. As a pocketsetter you do a lot of different things. You don't just set pockets. Sometimes you make darts or topstitch."

Whether it's children's sportswear or men's suit jackets, making clothing is not a simple task. Those of us who have learned to sew ourselves know the time and effort involved in learning to make a wearable skirt or dress. Moreover, studies have shown that home sewers, even those of us who are somewhat proficient at setting a sleeve or a collar, do not have skills which are easily transferrable to a factory setting. It takes up to ten weeks to train a sewing operator to work up to speed in a garment shop. Further, even where experienced stitchers work on piece rates and with state of the art technology, operators still spend 80 percent of their working time moving and positioning the fabric.[6] It requires effort and concentration to get one's fingers to do what the mind tells it to. Sewing involves both conceptualization and execution.

Sally Howell, who has spent twenty-five years as a garment worker, describes her job in the following way. "It's a tedious, nerve-racking, painstaking job. You have to be really skilled with your hands, 'cause it's all done in your fingers. You've got to really want to do a good job. My job is a trade. I'm a trained, skilled operator. I learn new things on the job every day."

Sewing machine operators do some of the most skilled factory work. But sewing is "women's work" and the garment industry has historically paid some of the lowest industrial wages—even before the apparel industry began to suffer from import competition.

The Contradictions of the Piece-rate System

As we can see, women express their sense of being skilled workers in a variety of ways. Yet whether they felt their skill was in their speed, their versatility, or their ability to turn out quality work, their expertise and competence meant their time at work was never seen as boring. Instead, what they complained about most was the need to work fast. The pressure of the piece-rate system provided the focal point of virtually all our discussions with the women about their work.

It is virtually impossible to describe the way the piece rates were set in each firm or to determine whether they were set "fairly" from industry to industry, from firm to firm, or between jobs in a single firm. First of all, piece rates are calculated differently in different industries, because the operations workers do vary. Second, even within an industry, the way rates are set can vary from firm to firm because some firms are unionized and others are not or because firms are organized by different unions. Third, even when firms within an industry are organized by the same union, rates can still be set differently from firm to firm. Piece rates are set on a plant by plant basis. Management organizes the production process and brings in efficiency experts who time each operation and set the rates.[7]

One student of factory women who has worked in a garment shop as part of her research[8] argues that the piece rates are set up to confuse the workers. She describes the way rates were set up in one New England firm where children's clothing was made.

Here piece rates are based on the decimal system, so they are easier to computerize. But they are also calculated to baffle the workers, since garments are batched in dozens, and most sewers keep their eyes on a clock which ticks away in sixty-minute hours. In the official system, the hour is divided into 100 parts, so that ten minutes is really .167 of an hour. Thus, a piece rate of .073 means that an operation must be performed on a dozen garments in 4.38 minutes if the sewer was to earn $3.31 an hour in 1977 or $4.05 in 1979—both base rates on which the piece rates are figured.

Lamphere writes, "I always used a pocket calculator [at home] to figure out how well or badly I was doing. . . . I figured that if I was to earn the minimum in 1977 [$92 a week before deductions] and if I was working all day on the same T-shirts with a rate of .073, I would have to sew a dozen garments [setting two sleeves each] every 6.3 minutes, completing 76 dozen garments in a day."

As a novice garment worker she was impressed with the speed at which the experienced sewers could work, sewing not 76 dozen garments in a day, but 110 dozen. Indeed, most garment workers we interviewed worked over their base rate, reckoning their hourly wages not by the "minimum" they could earn, but by their "average."

Peter Lewis was the union president at Condo Electric, a firm that made electrical cords and cables. He described their piecework system to me. The wages were higher and the rules were somewhat less complex, but the principle was the same. As he put it,

> The lowest rate in the plant was $5.91 an hour plus piecework. That's $5.91 an hour they see until they start making 85 percent of task, let's say 85 percent of 1,000 pieces. Then they start receiving 25 cents an hour over the $5.91. The person who receives piecework has to start achieving 105 percent of task. A lot of these women are doing 120 to 130 percent. Some of these women are making $6.50, $6.75 an hour. And if they're on the off-shift [the second shift which is 3:00 or 5:00 P.M. to 10:00 P.M. or midnight] they are adding 10 percent to that. There are some who are making $8.00 an hour. But when they are making money like that they are making a ton of money for the company.

Therein lies the central dilemma for the woman who is a pieceworker. Working fast earns you "good money" but at the same time, whether you're making pajamas or auto parts, it's hard work and you have to work like a demon. Moreover, for every dollar you earn, you are enlarging the profits of the company. The women feel management will take advantage of every opportunity to "speed them up and bust the rates."

About 65 percent of the women in our study worked on a piece rate— some by choice and some by default. How did they feel about it? We expected strong hostility toward a system of payment which is intrinsically exploitative and inhumane. Yet, whether women worked on a piece rate by choice or not, about half the women were satisfied with the arrangement and the other half were not. Ultimately then, how the women felt about the piece-rate system depended in part on the skill and experience of the women themselves, on their financial needs, and their willingness to deal with the pressure. Finally, what mattered most was the jobs the women held. How good was the pay? How feasible was it, with a minimum of strain, by working on a piece rate, to "make good money"? Sometimes the extra effort needed to earn well was part of the trade-off that working in a factory entailed.

There are many women who, despite the pressure, have learned how to "make the rate" and who are pleased to be working on a piece rate. Sara Stromberg, a bundler at Condo Electric, was one of the women Peter Lewis described who was making about $8.00 an hour. Initially she told us that the rates were set fairly "on most of the jobs." But after some thought she qualified her remarks. "They decided to start retiming some of the jobs. They wanted more work for the same amount of money. When they first had the bundling, they were paying just to wind the cords. Then they decided the girls on the machines could pack them too. Combined two jobs for the same price."

Sara recognizes a speedup when she sees it. But the opportunity to make almost $60 a day made it worth it for her, a 42-year-old woman with four children, to make the extra effort. She also pointed out that it was not that difficult for her to make $8.00 an hour on her job and felt she had the freedom to work at her own pace. "It was up to you to set your own pace. As long as you made your quota which was your hourly rate, nobody bothered you. If you were out to make money, you pushed yourself."

But for many women, working on a piece-rate job can be a deep source of aggravation—even if you are making your money. Sophie Cabral was a pocketsetter in a clothing shop which makes men's jackets and winter coats. For her industry she makes good money, over $6.00 an hour. But she would much rather have a job which pays a standard hourly wage. She feels the pressure to work fast is not only internal. "The hardest thing about working is trying to make the rate. Piece rate is more nerve-racking. You gotta push all the time. The more you do, the more you want to do. We're exhausted at the end of the day. You have to make close to your money or he [the boss] will tell you something."

If the women's own feelings about working fast and their willingness to do so influences their view of the piece rate, what is even more important is the kind of job they have. What is crucial is how the rates are set and how their jobs are structured. Some jobs are "easy"; they permit women who have the knack and the experience to earn well, while others require that women "bust their tails" but still don't allow them to "make out."

In the garment industry, women who have jobs that require straight seaming find they have an easier time making money. Ellen Morrison is one of these women. She closes the seams on slacks. As she tells it, "This job has been in existence for the past twenty years. They can't change the rate too much. So that every raise that you are supposed to have, with your union increases and raises, you pretty much see it coming into the rate."

On the other hand, "blouse girls," women who set sleeves or women who do any of the detailed tailoring that goes into making a good quality dress or blouse, have a much harder time. Ellen worked on blouses at one point, but swears that she will never do that job again if she can help it. A business agent in the garment workers' union explained why blouse girls had such hard jobs. She told us,

> The blouse girls have variable changes because every style is a different style she has to learn. This we feel is the toughest department in the industry. They are handling so many different parts to put the thing together. An operation like a zipper; that girl can make good money, because she is on the same thing day in and day out. Sleeve setting may be a little variable but it is still sleeve setting. Where the big deal is is on the girl who has to do a lot of handling and a lot of changes. Five styles can come into a shop a day and you are still going to close seams. But the blouse girl's gotta learn five different styles. So that's really where the hard rock of it is.

Just as there are good jobs and bad jobs in the garment industry, there are also good and bad jobs in factories where women make light bulbs or assemble electrical fixtures. As Mary Washington put it, "There were some jobs that for some odd reason were very easy and the piece rate was very good. There were other jobs that were very complicated and required a lot of manual dexterity and did not pay well."

Indeed, in some firms, there were jobs where the rates were set so high that workers had a great deal of trouble just meeting the quota. Michele Garvano assembles clamp lights. "I put the clamps on a cord [of an electric lamp] and the rate is 170 an hour. The most I can put out is 120 an hour. And that is really taking it out of me." Michele admits that she is probably a little slow. Other workers apparently do manage to make the rate. But few seem to surpass it. She adds, "These rates on the clamp light have been there ever since the plant opened. Nobody ever made a penny as far as bonus. Nobody ever made a cent."

However, if women can't make money on assembling the clamp lights, the women who pack light bulbs in the next department seem to do all right. Not only do they manage to meet the quota, but they also make about a dollar over the piece rate on a regular basis.

The Piece-rate System in Declining Industries

Conflicts over the piece rate are an inevitable part of the tensions between workers and management in firms where women work, where both wages and profits are generally low. Such conflicts tend to intensify and the pressures of women's jobs increase even further under conditions of economic decline. When a firm or a whole industry must struggle to remain competitive, women experience more pressure at work, both in dealing with the piece-rate system and in maintaining their wage levels.

As we have already pointed out, women sometimes feel pride in their versatility, but piece-rate workers are more able to make money when they do the same job all day long. Yet, when business is slow, firms sometimes get small orders for different products and workers are switched from job to job in a single work shift. This pattern is typical in the declining garment industry, when contractors are forced to accept small orders for different kinds of clothing of various sizes and styles. Dottie Nardello complained of the pressure. "The girls have a hard time. You really have to hustle to make any money. They work so hard to make maybe a dollar or two over your money. And then they threw in so many different styles, so that the next day he'll [the boss] put you on something else so you lose all the money you've been fighting so hard to make."

The same thing happened to Mary Washington who worked in a firm making electrical cables.

> There were times when girls would have to go from one job to another. I have had eight to nine jobs in a night. They don't allow you time for setting up. They say they do, but to go from one bench to another, you are moving everything around setting up the job. You lose time. And they don't allow for it even though they say it is in the piece rate. But if you stayed at that job for even four hours, you would make your piece work. But you are at a job an hour here, three-quarters of an hour there—you can't. I myself have gone to as many as three departments in one night. So it is very hard to make your rate at those times. I told the company I was going to put in a voucher for travel. They laughed at me but you could spend a half hour a night traveling.

Another problem women face in declining industries is the failure of management to either repair or replace deteriorating technology. When machinery does not work properly, when it continually breaks down, women who work on a piece rate lose money. More than one woman complained to us, "There are days that your machine breaks a lot and you feel the drop at the end of the day. Like you're waiting for the mechanic—you move to another machine—all that time counts when you're on piece work."9

Yet even where management, in the hope of maintaining its competitive edge, has the option and the will to replace or update obsolete and deteriorating technology, workers may experience an erosion of their control over the piece rates. The introduction of new technology can threaten not only to reduce the number of jobs, but it also has the potential to "bust the rate" for workers who remain at work.

The potential for conflicts between pieceworkers and management over the introduction of new technology is exemplified by the discussions which are currently taking place within the Amalgamated Clothing and Textile Workers Union. This union represents workers in the men's clothing industry, where new, computer-controlled, cutting and sewing technology is currently being introduced. These new machines offer the possibility of increasing productivity in the fabrication of men's clothing, reducing its price and ultimately making it more competitive with foreign imports. Union leaders believe such trends could ultimately maintain or even increase the number of sewing jobs in an industry which has rapidly been losing ground in this country in past years. For this reason, the ACTWU is encouraging the introduction of new technology and is cooperating with management in getting the new machines into the shops.

Much has been written about the implications of introducing new technology, its potential for upgrading skills as well as for deskilling work. Many have argued that it is not simply the technology itself, but the uses to which management has put it, which has the potential to benefit workers or create unskilled, low-wage, detail work. In the men's clothing industry, workers are fearful of and resistant to the coming of these new cutting and sewing machines with flashing lights and multiple switches. But they are less fearful of the skill changes involved in the use of new technology than its potential as a tool of management to cut jobs and/or bust their rates.

We found few Luddites among the women we spoke to. Workers were impressed with the way the new machines could turn out work. First, they were amazed at the speed of the machines and were not opposed to making twice the number of suits in half the time. Second, they were surprised and impressed that an apparatus which didn't look at all like any sewing machine they had ever seen could produce tailoring of such high quality. Third, given the assumption that technology tends to make work more boring, the women saw the new cutting and sewing machines as improving the quality of their work. The new, computer-run apparatus was seen as simplifying operations these sewers and stitchers viewed as difficult, tedious, painstaking, and aggravating tasks, allowing them to produce more high-quality pants, suits, and jackets with less drudgery.

The new computer-controlled technology promises to increase productivity, thereby making the domestic men's clothing industry more competitive with cheaper imports. The hope is that not only will jobs be saved, but that new jobs will be created in response to increased demand for cheaper, domestically produced clothing. For this reason, the ACTWU has been cooperating with management in helping to integrate new technologies into plants where their workers are represented. In this industry union contracts include language which protects workers against job displacement when technological changes are introduced. Nevertheless, there is a friendly antagonism which characterizes relations between labor and management on this issue. Union officials and workers know that the new technology not only provides management with an incentive to eliminate workers but also with the opportunity to reduce wages. Even where a union is playing a fairly strong role in trying to make sure that workers receive a share in the increased productivity which should result from investments in new capital equipment, workers are fearful of the potential effects of this on their earnings.

The fear is engendered by the women's own experience. They know that the process of incorporating the new technology into the workplace can play havoc with the piece rates. This is because the changes that are made in the organization of production call into question the entire basis on which work is defined as either skilled or unskilled. The unions, accepting the traditional argument of management, point out that workers using more capital-intensive, "high-technology" equipment are more "skilled"; they are more productive and should share in the gains made as a result of their increased productivity. They should be paid more. Management attempts to resist this argument.

The conflicts which have emerged then, are over how wages and piece rates are to be set when new machines are introduced. The women are just as happy to produce twice as many pairs of slacks in a day, but they do not want to have to work twice as hard or earn half the pay. Another issue which has created tension is the decision about who will be trained on the new machines. If new hires are taught to operate the new technology, it should be easier to set the rates lower than if the women who are put on the machines are those with more seniority. A third issue involves decisions about how workers and management will share in the cost of training. How will it proceed and how will workers be paid until they can make the rate and/or the "bugs" are worked out of the new equipment?

The transformation of technology is making it increasingly difficult to make an objective determination about what work is skilled and what work is not skilled. On the shop floor, the anxiety is about earnings. The bottom line for women who have changed jobs and of those who expect to change them when new technology is introduced is the size of their weekly paychecks. Or, as one woman put it, the most important question an operator can ask is, "Are you making your money? Are you maintaining your average?"

The Struggle on the Shop Floor

Working in a factory in a traditional female production job is probably one of the most difficult and one of the least satisfying kinds of paid work a woman can do.[10] Researchers who have studied women who work in jobs like these[11] have described the quality of the exploitation they face as some of the lowest paid workers in industrial jobs—the pressure, the lack of autonomy, and the frequent failure of management to respect their dignity as human beings. At the same time, researchers have begun to make us more aware of the ways women find to resist the pressures—to "humanize" the workplace and to resist the efforts of employers to treat them essentially as objects for the creation of profits. [12]

Yet it would be inaccurate to characterize the women we studied as either cowed or defiant, passive or militant. Instead, we need to develop a fuller, more complex way of understanding their experience. Women's factory jobs mean pressure, but it would be a mistake to believe that such jobs never offer attainable rewards. Depending on the particular jobs they have, the firm they work in, and the place they are at in the life cycle, these blue-collar women often see their work as a way to carve out a life whose progress is measured in the achievement of basic satisfactions and reachable goals. Many women see these goals as the result of a diligent commitment to hard work. They believe that their efforts can be rewarded, that their speed allows them some control over their work as well as the opportunity to earn "good money." The conflict for these women then, is not only between acquiescence to the discipline of factory work or resistance to it. The intrinsic conflict between workers and management creates an internal conflict for these blue-collar women. Their desire to earn well coexists with the desire to resist the speed and pressure of the piece rate system. [13]

What often motivates blue-collar women to confront and struggle with their factory jobs is both the need and the felt opportunity to make more money than they could earn anywhere else. The decision to work in a factory then, as we have seen, is often a choice to live with the pressures of piece work and the assembly line and forego the social status or gratification that other kinds of work might provide.

There is no doubt, of course, that many women work in factories because it is the only thing they can do—like Penny Montolio who earns $3.85 an hour working as a stitcher. We asked her repeatedly what she liked about her job and what she disliked. She merely replied, "It was all right. It was a job. It gave me a living." When we pressed her to be more explicit, she answered in the same vein, "All I can tell you is that it was a living. You have to work. So! That's my trade."

Yet many other women feel they earn "good money," better money than they could earn in most other kinds of work available to women with comparable education and experience. While they know their wages are low compared to men, compared to women who hold comparably "skilled" jobs in sales and service industries, many feel they are doing well, that their hard work and speed are rewarded. The pleasures women get from their factory jobs are not to be counted in the comfort of air-conditioned offices or the womanly satisfactions of helping others. What gets these women out the door each morning, through the factory gates, up the gloomy flights of stairs, and ready to face the ancient lofts, grease, noise, and pressure is the belief that their efforts will produce a larger paycheck.

It is often believed that women are less interested in the financial rewards of their work than men are—that women prefer a congenial work environment, one which offers good hours, a pleasant work setting and opportunities for socializing with other workers, while men are more interested in earnings and opportunities for advancement.[14] Our research does not support this view. We presented the women in our study with a checklist of ten different "qualities" of a job and asked them to rank order the five they felt were most important to them. As we can see from figure 4.1, "good pay" was, by far, the most important—well ahead of opportunities for sociability and compatibility with family responsibilities.

Moreover, if women who work in the unionized factories of New England do not believe they work in sweatshops, our research shows that most do not work at sweatshop wages. Despite the fact that women operatives have lost ground in the past decade compared to women workers in other types of comparable jobs, by 1980, they had still not entirely lost their wage advantage. They still earned more than women in full-time sales and service work.

The median wage of the married women in our sample was $4.47 an

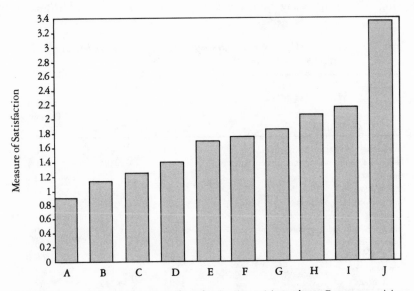

Figure 4.1. Important Qualities of a Job. A, chat with workers; B, opportunities for promotion; C, challenging work; D, good pace; E, good supervisor; F, safe place to work; G, no conflict with family; H, easy to travel to; I, job security; J, good pay.

hour. At this rate of pay, they could earn $156.45 a week if they worked a full 35-hour week. This figure is exactly the same as the median income for full-time women operatives in 1979, the year we did our interviews (see table 4.1).[15]

There were, of course, wide variations in the women's earnings. Many earned very little; indeed about half earned less than $4.50 an hour. Since we chose women deliberately because they had been laid off from their jobs, more than half were less than year-round workers. Yet, at the same time, almost one-third of the blue-collar women in our sample (32 percent) made $5.25 or more an hour. On a yearly basis a full-time worker earning $5.25 an hour could earn $183.75 for a 35-hour week. This was considerably more than the median earnings of a full-time woman worker doing sales, service, or clerical work. It is hardly surprising then that so many blue-collar women prize their factory jobs highly even with all the pressures they entail. Barbara Sowell, who packs light bulbs, described the trade-offs women make by working in factories when she answered our interviewer's question about whether she felt she had a good job. She first said, "No, it's very tiring. We pack about 1,000 to 1,200 bulbs an hour. I'm going to have to say it's tiresome." Then she added, "But it's also kind of good because it keeps you going. You don't have time to think. I feel if I have to put in forty hours some place, and you are going to get good pay. . . . I mean forty hours is going to take me away from my kids whether I'm sitting at a desk or

Table 4.1   *Median Usual Weekly Earnings of Full-time Wage and Salary Workers, by Sex and Occupational Group*

Occupational Group	Women	Men	Women's Earnings as Percentage of Men's
Professional and technical workers	261	375	70
Managers and administrators, except farm	232	386	60
Sales workers	154	297	52
Clerical workers	180	287	63
Craft and kindred workers	189	305	62
Operatives, except transport	156	257	61
Transport equipment operatives	194	277	70
Nonfarm laborers	166	220	75
Service workers	138	203	68
Farm workers	125	153	82
Average	$183	$295	62

Note: Preliminary data for the second quarter of 1979 for workers sixteen years of age and over.
Source: U.S. Department of Labor, Bureau of Labor Statistics, "Women in the Labor Force: Some New Data Series," 1979.

working hard, so I feel that the money makes it worth it. Yeah, it's a good job."

Social scientists usually assume that the tensions and pressures of low-paid, marginal work are somehow more bearable for women than for men because women, it is assumed, do not take their jobs so seriously. Work is peripheral but family life is women's "central interest." The assumption is that whatever a woman has to put up with at work—low pay, subordination, lack of autonomy—is presumably forgotten when she goes home to care for her family.

But if the relatively high wages of a full-time, unionized production job keep New England's blue-collar women at their benches, if the opportunity to make "good money" motivates the trade-offs they make, it is frequently because the women recognize how much their families need them to do so. In talking with the women who work in factory jobs, we came to realize that the needs of families do not always limit but can also enhance women's feelings of involvement and commitment to their jobs. Indeed, women make a commitment to full-time factory work because of—not in spite of—their families. Like men, many see themselves as having families to support. If blue-collar men feel obligated to confront the toil of factory work, women confront the realities of production jobs for the very same reasons. [16]

Because their jobs are needed, because they are important to the family, managing the workplace can become an issue of central importance to a blue-collar woman. Indeed, because these stressful factory jobs are seen as offering the most highly paid work available, blue-collar women know they must develop the coping skills and strategies they need to manage the tensions of the factory floor in order to continue earning "good money." Women's daily survival lies not in ignoring the tensions at work because they care more about what happens at home, but in developing ways of protecting themselves against the pressures of their jobs.

Women who hold factory jobs learn very quickly that the social relations of the work process are a direct embodiment of management's efforts to get them to work as hard and as fast as they possibly can—and for the least amount of money. The pressures of the assembly line and the tensions of the piece-rate system confront the women with their own exploitation each day in a very immediate way and inevitably lead them to become aware that their interests are opposed to those of management. In that sense they are class-conscious. Women know they are being exploited and find ways to resist and defend themselves against employers' continuing pressure to get the most work from them at the lowest possible wages.

Other students of women factory workers [17] have made the same observation, showing that blue-collar women do not respond to their work experience with passivity, but develop active strategies of resistance to protect their welfare at work in response to the pressures of the piece-rate system and the assembly line. They carefully document how essential it is for the women to keep track of how many pieces they produce each hour; if you haven't been vigilant, the payroll clerk can make a "mistake" in calculating your pay at the end of the week. To protect themselves from bosses and supervisors who play favorites, women develop informal ways to cooperate with their co-workers so that the "good work" and the "bad work" is shared. While women work hard to "make their money," they also bring informal pressures to bear on those who work so fast they threaten to "bust the rate." Finally, in certain industries where it is possible, women make attempts to improve their situation by moving from job to job and firm to firm until they find a situation which is suitable.

But class consciousness and resistance to the exploitive nature of the work process is not expressed on a daily basis in militant efforts to challenge or undermine the piece-rate system. Instead, women have learned to live with the piece rate. One of the things they do is to make attempts to develop positive relationships with supervisors and establish friendships with co-workers which keep the shop floor from becoming an armed camp. Most of these blue-collar women feel they have been able to carve out a sphere of autonomy and a network of interpersonal communications which make the workplace livable. The strategies women devise make it possible for them to keep returning to the shop day after day so that they may continue to earn as much as they do and, at the same time, retain their dignity. Ultimately then, women's resistance may best be described as a form of self-protection.

Women who have not been able to work out a *modus vivendi* with supervisors have some of the worst complaints about their jobs. Immediate supervisors, after all, can constantly be "on your back" or "breathing down your neck." Michele Garvano was the woman who assembled clamp lights but couldn't seem to make the rate. Her inability to do so took its toll on her paycheck, but what really became a source of deep bitterness was her relationship with her supervisor. She told us, "It's not only that the rates are high, it's the supervisor, I had an argument with her. I didn't care, at that point, where it was going to take me. She sounded like she owned me. I was her slave and she was my master."

Sylvia Montrose also described a particularly oppressive situation between workers and management. "Sometimes everyone would be silly. They would laugh and joke. It would break you up. The company didn't like it sometimes. They would say, "cool it" or start timing us. But you know it shouldn't be a gestapo. It's not supposed to be run like a prisoner of war camp. If it wasn't for the workers they wouldn't be getting their money or business." Situations like this may tend to encourage women to leave firms where they feel the boss is a martinet and makes the workday unbearable.

Women also recognize that the pressure they get from supervisors emanates from the pressures the supervisors get themselves. In understanding the structure of the workplace, they learn to cope with the pressure more effectively. Mary Washington, who packs and wraps electrical cables, talked about her own supervisor in the following way. "You know, the supervisors . . . they get funny. They have a lot more pressure than we do. A lot of times if the machine isn't running they take it out on the girls. Then you get your women who are frustrated and grouchy, but everyone tries to make the best of it."

Barbara Sowell, who packs light bulbs, sees the same problem in her own job, but like Mary, accepts the chain of command with a certain degree of equanimity. "Jim is our foreman," she says. "Then we have a supervisor in our department. He tells Jim what to do and Jim tells us. And he must get orders, too. Our boss is good enough. He doesn't come over and breathe down your back." But Barbara knows that the boss will leave you alone only as long as you make the rate. As she puts it, "I'm not a company girl—like you are for the boss and everything the boss says goes."

She is a committed union member and knows she owes the job she has to the bidding system that was negotiated many years ago. But she also recognizes an obligation to accept the pressure of the assembly line. She sees this as keeping up her end of the bargain, adding, "You have to show that you can produce for them. You are there to work . . . and to earn a week's pay. I have to work and that's what I'm there for. I wouldn't be mean. I wouldn't cheat them out of anything. The girls do the work and it gets out."

Blue-collar women, like all workers, understand the *quid pro quo* between themselves and their supervisors. The garment factory where Ellen Morrison works as a stitcher is a good example of a situation in which this works very well. It is a firm of about two hundred workers, many of whom she says have been there for more than twenty years. She describes the women she works with in her department as a family. "We really take care of one another, we worry about one another."

She describes her supervisor, who has also been there for some years, as "a peach." He knows the women will get the work done, that they will stay late to get out a rush order and do repairs on work which they don't always get paid for. He appears to be very flexible and relaxed. Ellen says of him, "Our foreman is just the easiest going fellow in the world. You can have your radios going, your fans going, you can get up and talk to one another. Very, very relaxed atmosphere. He spends half the day laughing but he gets more done." Women don't always talk about their bosses in such glowing terms, but when they do they are just as likely to mention their own commitment to doing a good job in the same breath.

One thing which is very important and was mentioned frequently was the potential to come in late or leave early for a personal or family emergency. This was particularly true in the garment industry where individual and small firms are the norm rather than multinational conglomerates. Sally Howell told us, "If I have an appointment, all I do is tell the supervisor, and he is very reasonable about that." Cynthia Barden, a garment worker with two small children, mentioned how much she appreciated being able to have flexible working hours. "I have a small baby and a small boy. You can more or less keep your own hours. You can go in later and work later hours. That's the understanding we have in our shop. The boss is really nice."

Such relationships have been characterized as paternalistic—and indeed, when they are the outcome of informal arrangements like these, they can bind women to employers in ways that do not ultimately serve their interests in getting better wages and working conditions. As Ferree has pointed out,[18] women often try to work out their own personal solutions to the work-family dilemmas they face because no public policy guarantees them the flexibility they need to do two jobs. A policy of staggered working hours has been introduced in large, highly bureaucratized firms. "Flexitime," as it is called, has proven a very effective way of serving workers needs and increasing productivity. There would certainly be more equity if flexible work hours were formalized in these manufacturing firms. However, when a woman gets a phone call telling her that a sick child is waiting for her at school, she will be just as ready to leave her work, whether or not her option to leave is fully institutionalized.

If good relationships with supervisors are important for the quality of working life, so are good relationships with co-workers. Indeed, there is a mystical, almost sentimental quality to what has been written about the close friendships that women form with their co-workers in both office and factory work situations where there is a preponderance of women.[19] Women share family events, provide each other with mutual support, and create a working community which sometimes involves deep emotional ties. Friendship ties in the workplace can be seen as serving a very instrumental function for these women. Liking one's co-workers, or at least getting along with them, was an essential aspect of feeling integrated into the work situation. It is important to stress that the strength of workplace friendships varied considerably. For some of the women we interviewed, relationships with friends and relatives at work went well beyond the shop floor. They were an extension of community ties. For other women, friendships at work stopped at the factory gates. In other cases women saw their relationships with co-workers as peripheral to the main values their work has for them.

Yet regardless of the salience of workplace friendships, those women who didn't get along with their workmates, who said they kept to themselves, or who reported that others were uncooperative were often individuals who were unhappy with their status as factory workers and/or were making plans to leave.

Gloria Richards is a 38-year-old married woman with three children. She works in a firm which produces lighting fixtures where she packs light bulbs. Working the second shift, from 3:00 to 10:00 P.M., Gloria is currently in school, training to be a paralegal. The money she is earning, about $7 an hour, helps to pay her tuition at the local state university. When our interviewer asked her if her co-workers were cooperative she replied, "On the surface yes. But really, underneath, I would say no."

She keeps pretty much to herself—seeing her job as a means to an end—and offers some of the classic responses that scholars say describe the "alienated" worker. Unlike most of the women we spoke with, she says about her job, "To me it is sort of degrading. You don't feel like a person when you are doing the work, you just feel like a part of a machine. If you do a good job, nobody ever gives you credit for it."

Loretta Towers is a 45-year-old mother of five children, the youngest of whom is a dyslexic son. She works in the same plant as Gloria Richards, but in a different department, making the filaments of light bulbs. She worked on the "graveyard shift" from midnight to 7:00 A.M. so she could be at home with her son during the day. Loretta said at the beginning of our interview, "I went to two and one-half years of business college and I am a business secretary by choice." Like other women in her firm, she feels she earns well, but she feels there is a gap between her status and that of her co-workers. Loretta is not pleased with her job. What does she dislike?

> I think working in a factory. There are so many different life-styles. It is very difficult to be with people who have no manners, who have no morals, who are crude and cruel. And I don't choose to mingle with them. I see it every day. They have what they call cliques in shops. If you don't belong to the clique, you just don't belong. And these girls can be really tough. The language is atrocious. And their attitudes! They are always trying to rip the company off. You are paid to go in and do your work. I just don't like them.

Other women who did not get along with their co-workers were those who had been laid off and reemployed in a new production job. These women spoke nostalgically of the loss of good working relationships as one of the disasters that had accompanied the job loss. Valerie Delos says of the new garment factory where she has recently obtained work, "It is not a friendly place. The most difficult thing is trying to adjust to the girls. They can be nice to you but then they are not. It is a difficult thing. At [her former firm] we helped one another more. Here they are all looking out for themselves."

As we mentioned before, some have argued that women seek out the opportunity to socialize at work because they are unambitious and gregarious. It has also been argued that women's nature allows them to accept paternalism from employers and supervisors. Other analysts play down women's acceptance of paternalism and see women's concern with sociability as a way for exploited women workers to express their solidarity. Indeed, both of these perspectives embody part of the truth.

Women are concerned with establishing good relationships at work. Despite their class consciousness, however, they are just as interested in establishing good relationships with supervisors as they are with peers. This is because the development of a *modus vivendi* in both spheres softens the sharp edges of what are implicitly impersonal, competitive, and exploitative social relations. While women know there are deep and intrinsic conflicts that are embodied in the workplace, they are not anxious to fight these battles every day on the shop floor. Instead they try to establish interpersonal obligations, a workable *quid pro quo* among individual workers as well as between workers and supervisors which can mitigate some of the worst conflicts of factory work.

Unions

Some of this *modus vivendi* is worked out within the framework of the union contract. In administering the contract, women are concerned with establishing norms which govern the ways they can be treated in the plant. Unions negotiate wages and piece rates for each operation. The union contract, then, is an arbiter of how piece rates are administered and how conflicts about piece rates are to be adjudicated.

It is not my intention to be overly sanguine about the power or the justice of contemporary trade unionism, particularly in declining industries. The women we spoke to were certainly aware that the overall power of their unions to protect their jobs was becoming increasingly limited. They realized that their unions are not always models of democracy; nor do they always look out for the best interests of their women members. Most of the women have minimal input into the politics of even their local unions and have little to do with the contract negotiations which determine their wages and piece rates. Finally, even with a union contract, there are always things management can do to circumvent the rules, which sometimes makes it difficult for these women to "make good money."

Yet if rules can be bent they cannot be arbitrarily changed. They can serve as a benchmark of what is legitimate and what is not. To the extent that workers are educated about these rules, and some of them are, to the extent that unions are willing to go to bat for their members, enforcing the contract rules or filing grievances when violations occur, unionized workers do have some protection in the workplace. Women's concerns sometimes do filter up to union officials through the shop stewards and business agents who deal with their problems on a daily basis. Many of the women do believe that their unions protect them from some of the worst abuses of factory work and the piece-rate system.

Women believe their unions make some difference in their wages. Being in a union is no guarantee of having a high-wage job these days, especially in declining industries. Yet, many of the women who did earn well believed they owed their good wages to working in unionized plants. As Susan James, who earned $7.50 an hour packing light bulbs, put it, "It's the wages that keeps us in factories. I'm sure that if the shopping center up here paid even $5.00 an hour I would be very inclined to go there and seek employment—but they don't. It's the wages that keep us in the factories. And the reason we have the wages is because of the union."

Her co-worker and friend, Martine Lewis, said the same thing. "Right now I get $7.25 an hour—that's counting my 10 percent [for working the night shift]. And we are due for a raise in September and then in March. We get at least two cost-of-living raises a year. We have a good union!"

Rose Dubois earns much less than either Susan James or Martine Lewis, slightly more than $4.00 an hour. She had worked as a nurses' aide in a nursing home for nineteen years. Feeling she was losing her patience with the elderly people she was helping to care for, she quit and went to work in a garment shop. She commented, "I liked taking care of old people, but the nursing home was terrible. First there was no union. They could do what they pleased. They were paying $2.50 and I was lucky to get that. I like the job I'm in as far as convenience. The pay now is double for less work and less hours. And there I had to work weekends."

Yet not all blue-collar women are as optimistic about the benefits their unions have to offer. Sometimes they feel that the leadership is "in bed" with the bosses. Maria Caros ran for union chairperson of her garment shop, but felt the existing union leadership there undermined her efforts. She saw the leadership as threatened by her grass roots organizing efforts on behalf of a group of women who felt their rates were too low. As she put it,

> I don't like working in a union shop because the union doesn't do anything for you. They all stick by the bosses. They go by what the bosses say. She [the incumbent union chairperson] used to be upstairs on the second floor and she didn't know what was going on. When she found out I would stick up for the girls, she went against me on the day they were voting.

There is no doubt that union leadership is often weak and vacillates in its efforts on behalf of members. Yet even at their worst, unions can protect women workers from some of the worst abuses of authority. Sylvia Montrose, the finishing operator who trimmed the excess off molded plastic parts, was one of the few women in our sample who worked on a piece rate but was not in a unionized firm. The company she worked for made a lot of different products and the rate changed for each product. The workers had no recourse. Sylvia told us, "There were times we would get bad work . . . toward the end of the day you get all bad baskets, they would lower the rate. We would bitch for a new time [a new rate]. Like there were days we worked and worked and you couldn't keep the rate. And times when you couldn't keep the rate you would be called in the office."

Sometimes unionized women have no recourse either. Workers in all kinds of firms, from those that fabricate cords and cables to garment shops to plants which make bread and candy, complained of being moved from job to job, despite the fact that contracts carefully stipulate that employees with specific job titles may only do certain operations. Cynthia Barden offered a detailed description of a similar problem in her garment shop, where the problem is particularly severe because lots are small and styles change frequently. She says,

> I don't say you shouldn't do two or three jobs, but when you do five or six in a day, it's impossible to make money or even make your minimum. At one time, you either did your own job or you did what was called your second operation. So the odds were that you were going to make out a little bit better. Today that's not true. And it's the union's fault, because they don't stop it.

The union doesn't stop it because, in a declining industry, they try to make it a little easier for the employer to stay in business. If there is no work on a particular operation, the supervisor, who in this case is the owner, simply refuses to lay off the women. If they were laid off, they could collect unemployment insurance, as many would prefer to do rather than working and being unable to make the usual amount of money. As Cynthia puts it, "This way he gets to use you any way he wants."

The process is certainly a violation of the women's union rights. Yet at the same time, the existence of the rule, even in its abrogation, continues to protect the workers to some extent. First, no one is humiliated by being called on the carpet for not making the rate. Second, there is some sort of a compromise made. In this situation, Cynthia's boss pays the workers who are asked to switch jobs on a standard rate. Therefore, no matter how slow a woman is on a job she is not familiar with, she is still guaranteed some sort of a safety net. But Sylvia Montrose was summoned to the office when she couldn't make the rate and was completely at the supervisor's mercy. She said, "When you tried to prove to them that the work was bad and you needed an adjustment, sometimes you would get it and sometimes you wouldn't. So that caused bad morale."

Women expressed a good deal of anger at unions and at particular union leaders they felt had not done enough to protect their rights; this was especially true for those women who lost jobs due to plant closings or employment declines. Yet if unions are weakened and allow bosses to violate workers' rights, women feel, in their justified anger, that even in the breach, they do have rights. Even in the context of declining wages and job losses, they often feel a sense of security; the union gives them the right to express their anger when they feel they are not being treated with justice or dignity. Should they have a problem the union will be there to back them up.

Mary Washington, who packs and wraps electrical cables, feels the union is partly responsible for the good relationship she and her co-workers have with the supervisors. In fact she thinks her job is better than that of the supervisors, who she sees as "the guys under pressure who aren't in the union. They have a lot more pressure than we do . . . [because] if anything goes wrong [with the machines], we have the union to back us up."

When our interviewer asked Ellen Morrison whether the union made her job more secure, she answered, "It depends . . . I do feel a little more secure having the union there. Ted [her boss] doesn't follow it [union rules about recall after layoffs] to the letter. I've seen him try to get rid of some girls he didn't want . . . and he can't. I think there is some security there."

There is no air-conditioning in garment factories. There is also a union rule that if the weather gets too hot, the women may simply go home. Dottie Nardello described what happens in her shop. "In the summer, the union states that up to 90 degrees you work and then you can go home. But they [the business agents] tell you if you're warm at 80 degrees and you can't stand it, you go. This is what the girls do. He [the boss] doesn't like it, but there's nothing he can do about it if a girl thinks she's going to be sick."

Carol DiFazio told us of a dispute she had with her boss over the money she was earning. "Once we had a big fight because I was making $8.00 an hour and my boss said he was going to cut my pay because that was too much. But I fought it and told him I would go to the union if he did." He didn't cut her wages.

We did not hear much ideological support for the principles of trade unionism or for the justness of the "workers' cause." Though the women felt their interests and those of their employers often diverged, the women also felt it was their obligation to put in a full day's work, to "give good production." In exchange they wanted to be treated fairly. Many felt that in a dispute, even if they didn't always win, the union chairperson or business agent would be forced to confront the issue and to adjudicate the conflict in conformity with the union contract. There was therefore some buffer, some protection against the arbitrary or capricious judgment of the boss; ultimately there were some rules.

The desire for as much unbiased equity as possible was expressed by one woman who had been a union chairperson. When our interviewer asked her what had been the most common complaint she instantly replied, "Prices, naturally, they are always complaining about the prices. You hear, 'He's never fair' or 'The prices should be better.' But get them the extra penny and everything is rosy." Of the boss, she said, "He doesn't keep his records straight. He'll forget from day to day what he gave you on the last one." And of the conflict between the women and the boss, she said, "I felt I was under a lot of pressure from the girls and from him. Of course you never please them. You try to please them, but then you don't please him. Every once in a while you make out for both of them. I always felt as chairlady that there were two sides to every story. He had his rights and the girls had theirs."

She believes workers and management should play by the rules, rules determined by the union contract. She adds, "I think the union's wrong in that they don't teach the people the rules. They really need some sort of classes, not just for the chairlady but for everyone, so they understand what the rules are. A chairlady always has a contract."

Reckoning the Costs of Factory Work

The dynamics of women's factory work in the mill-based industries of New England are formed by the requirements of the piece-rate system. It is an inherently exploitative system. Management continually strives to increase production and tries to avoid sharing the fruits of increased productivity with the women who do the work. These simple facts are not lost on the workers, as evidenced by the fact that the "rates" continue to be the primary bone of contention between the women and their bosses.

Yet blue-collar women also accept the pressures of the piece-rate system. Many feel they can earn better wages in factories than working in the alternative jobs that are available to them. Further, the piece rate offers some women a feeling of being able to control their earnings through their own efforts. If making the rate means sewing 75 dozen collars in a seven-hour workday in order to earn $4.10 an hour, it is hard work to sew eighty-five or ninety-five dozen—even if you can make $4.75 or $5.00 an hour by working that much faster. But it may be even harder work being a chamber-maid in a hotel or serving hamburgers in a fast-food restaurant at the minimum wage. Moreover, these jobs do not pay more if you vacuum more thoroughly or serve more hamburgers.

Women who hold factory jobs then, learn to devise strategies to protect themselves from the exploitation that is an intrinsic part of their work. They figure out ways to manage jobs that are difficult and demanding but are also seen as valuable. They learn how to protect themselves on the shop floor through negotiations with supervisors and workmates and, wherever possible, by mobilizing the support of their local unions. Blue-collar women have learned to establish a *modus vivendi* which softens the harshness of exploitation and allows them to return to their factory jobs day after day, week after week, and hopefully, year after year.

5 Coping with the Pressures

AFTER EXPLORING THE STRUCTURE of the workplace and the response of blue-collar women to the pressures of subordination at work, it is time to take a closer look at the interaction of women's work and women's needs. There are commonalities in the way women who work in factories view their work, cope with its pressures, and defend themselves against its worst abuses. Yet, jobs are not randomly distributed; patterns of labor market segmentation influence the way good jobs and bad ones are allocated by age and ethnicity. Older women, younger women, and Portuguese women often have different jobs and therefore respond to their work in different ways. But the strategies women develop for dealing with the demands of their jobs are not only related to what is happening on the shop floor. Women's response to their work is related to their needs as members of families and to their needs as women of different cultures who are at various stages in the life cycle.

As I have tried to show, women, in choosing factory work, often feel they trade hard work and low status for more earning power. But under what circumstances and at what wage levels are the pressures of piecework justified? How do women in different job situations and life circumstances see the value of working hard? Where are there worthwhile trade-offs between higher pay and hard work and when are women "stuck" with pressure and nothing to show for it?

In what follows, we will explore and compare the job experience of three groups of blue-collar women. First we will look at the jobs held by Portuguese immigrants, (the married women between twenty-five and forty-five with dependent children). Then we will look at the work experience of American-born, older women (married women between forty-six and sixty-five, whose children tend to be older or have left home). Finally, we will look at the work experience of American women in the central childbearing and childrearing years of their lives (married women with dependent children between the ages of twenty-five and forty-five). We will examine, in some detail, how each group responds to the work and wage opportunities they have, and how each group deals with the pressures of the piece-rate system. Then we will be in a better position to understand more clearly what working-class women want from their jobs.

To understand how women cope with working in factories and to know more about what women want from their jobs, we focused our analysis on the dimensions of work satisfaction. We were not concerned with how satisfied the women were with their job. As we have pointed out, levels of work satisfaction among blue-collar women tend to be low; the women in our study were no exception.[1] What we wanted to know more about was the way in which different qualities of a job were linked to work satisfaction. What was it about an "unskilled" factory job that could make a woman's work experience more or less gratifying, more or less satisfactory, despite the limits of factory work itself? We needed to isolate the correlates of work satisfaction for each group of women in order to understand how particular dimensions of jobs were related to earning well and to working on a piece rate.

The Trade-offs

Portuguese Immigrant Women

Researchers and casual observers alike recognize that the Portuguese immigrant women who have settled with their families in the small industrial cities of eastern New England are committed to a life of hard work in the region's mills and factories.[2] Sometimes the efforts of these immigrants are lauded by the more "enlightened" employers and tradesmen in the community, who often stand to benefit from their efforts. Community leaders point, with civic pride, to the fact that decaying neighborhoods have been transformed by Portuguese immigrants into streets with neat rows of newly renovated homes, each with its own carefully tended garden. Yet there is also prejudice against the newcomers. The American-born women they work with often view their efforts with scorn and pity, describing the immigrants as "greenhorns" willing to work for low wages and thereby undercutting the wages of American workers.

Hard work is required from every woman who works in a factory in a piece-rate job. When you work on piece rates you are expected not only to make your quota, but to go beyond it. All women who work at these jobs are constrained in this way, not only by the structure of the jobs and the bosses' demands, but by their own internalized motivation to "make money." Yet Portuguese women are noted for doing more than just the respectable number of pieces. They are frequently accused of working so hard and so fast that they undercut the rates and spoil jobs for their co-workers.[3] We also found this attitude among the women we studied, mixed, no doubt, with a good deal of prejudice that was in part motivated by the fear that the Portuguese women might take their jobs. Sandra Tomasso, a cable packer in a cord-set plant said of her Portuguese co-workers, "They'll work night and day. They'll take your job. They gotta work, but I don't see why the government doesn't stop it."

If the history and culture of this immigrant community encourages hard work for low wages in the interests of promoting the upward mobility of the family unit, the women's efforts are reinforced by the kinds of jobs they hold. First of all, Portuguese women earned significantly lower wages than their American-born counterparts. When we compared the average hourly wage of Portuguese- and American-born, married women with children, we found the average hourly wage for Portuguese women was $4.58 an hour while the Americans earned $5.35.[4]

Portuguese women were also concentrated in some of the worst jobs, jobs which put a lot of pressure on them to work hard. Though there were no differences between wage rates for pieceworkers and standard-rate workers for the sample as a whole, Portuguese women were concentrated in low-wage, piece-rate jobs. First of all, they were somewhat overrepresented in piece-rate jobs. While only 60 percent of the American-born women worked in piece-rate jobs, 76 percent of Portuguese women did. But by working on a piece rate the Portuguese women could earn over a dollar an hour more ($4.81) than their immigrant sisters who worked on a standard rate ($3.75).[5] Only by working on a piece rate could they earn more than the minimum wage. Portuguese women had jobs which required that they work hard if they were to earn a decent wage. But even when they worked harder, as a group, they did not surpass the wages of their American co-workers.[6]

Portuguese women, as we will see, get a lot of pressure from their families to work hard. But the pressure, which the women internalize and feel as an obligation, is also reinforced by the demands of the work they do. In this context their strategy is to push themselves hard. The calculus is that even if the base rate is low, by pushing they can earn twenty-five or fifty cents more an hour. That can mean five or maybe ten dollars more in one's pay envelope at the end of the week, which is sometimes seen as an important contribution to a family economy where every extra penny counts, where each additional dollar is something that helps the family get ahead. Maria Cordeiro described her piece-rate job in a garment shop in the following way, "You know that if you work hard, at the end of the day, you're the one who is going to profit. If you were standard, it would be just the same monotonous job."

Yet, there is also a down side to this optimistic view. While few blue-collar women have any illusions about the "intrinsic satisfactions" their jobs offer, some of the blue-collar women who were born in this country, especially the older women, expressed pride in the work they did. Some felt they were skilled, that they had a "trade." The younger American women said they worked in factories for the money, suggesting they had sized up the alternatives and, given their needs for more earnings, benefits, full-time work, or perhaps the convenience of a night shift, had made their decision.

But what the Portuguese women had to say revealed their feelings of having little choice about their work. The women said things like "I took whatever job they gave me"; or "I decided on this factory because they taught me how to operate the machines"; or "I needed a job."

The Portuguese women know that, in coming here, sometimes with as little as four years of schooling, without even being able to speak, let alone read or write English, they had to take whatever jobs they could get. Delores Fernandes is a poorly paid garment worker who came to this country at the age of thirteen. She said she quit high school at the age of sixteen because her father required it. When we asked her how she felt about her job, she said, "When I was sixteen years old, my parents didn't believe that a girl should have an education. Therefore, they told me that I should go to work. That was the only job that didn't require training or anything other than just stitch." When we asked her what she liked most about her job, she replied, "That I have a job. We should be thankful every day that we have a job. If we haven't got a job, we got no income."

What then, within the constraints of low pay and hard work, are the qualities of a job which make work most bearable, most "satisfactory" for the Portuguese women? The results are depicted in table 5.1. We calculated the partial correlations between women's overall sense of work satisfaction and the women's ratings of four aspects of their jobs. We calculated the partial correlation for each independent variable, holding the other three constant.[7]

As we can see, Portuguese women do not value their jobs because of the opportunity to socialize with other workers. Surprisingly, they *do* value their jobs when their work provides them with a sense of accomplishment. What is most significant to these women, however, is satisfaction with wages and comfort. Portuguese women are happier with their jobs when they feel they earn well. They are also happier with their jobs when their jobs are physically comfortable.

These results suggest a double bind for Portuguese women, who find themselves in an unfortunate situation where they face two equally unsatisfactory alternatives. We will remember that immigrant women who work at piece-rate jobs earn better wages, although they do so at the cost of intense pressure. Women who work at standard-rate jobs, however, earn on average less than $4.00 an hour—the lowest of any group of women in our sample. These women are more likely to say that they have comfortable

Table 5.1   *Partial Correlates of Work Satisfaction: Portuguese Women*

Overall work satisfaction with "a chance to chat with other workers"
   controlling for:
      1. a sense of accomplishment
      2. comfortable work
      3. good pay
$r = .079; n = 62; p = .267$

Overall work satisfaction with "a sense of accomplishment"
   controlling for:
      1. a chance to chat with other workers
      2. comfortable work
      3. good pay
$r = .222; n = 62; p = .039$

Overall work satisfaction with "good pay"
   controlling for:
      1. a sense of accomplishment
      2. a chance to chat with other workers
      3. comfortable work
$r = .305; n = 62; p = .007$

Overall work satisfaction with "a comfortable job"
   controlling for:
      1. a chance to chat with other workers
      2. sense of accomplishment
      3. good pay
$r = .335; n = 62; p = .003$

---

jobs. Those who said they had comfortable jobs were more likely to be working on a standard rate than a piece rate.[8] The dilemma is apparent; Portuguese blue-collar women who feel they get comparatively good pay sacrifice comfort, while those with comfortable jobs clearly sacrifice earnings. As we will see when we look at the work/family connection, the pressure women get from their families to work hard along with the pressure they get from their jobs makes for a good deal of stress.

Older Women

Older blue-collar women experience the options and limits of their work differently than their immigrant counterparts, largely because they hold different jobs. Their jobs are not different in terms of wages,[9] but older women are much more likely to work on a standard rate. Forty-one percent of the older women in our sample worked on standard time compared to 24 percent of their Portuguese counterparts. What is most significantly different for older women is that they get paid better for easier work. More than half of these women, 51 percent, earned at least $5.25 an hour on standard-rate jobs compared to only 6 percent of Portuguese women. Among older women it was those who worked on piece-rate jobs who earned poorly—$4.48 on piece rates compared to $5.44 on standard-rate jobs. [10]

As we can see from table 5.2, older women, like their Portuguese counterparts, also want comfortable jobs and jobs which pay well. Though older women don't earn significantly more than their immigrant counterparts, given their priorities, they certainly do have "better" jobs. They are more likely to have easier jobs—to be paid a standard wage. On standard wages they earn more money. Their greater work satisfaction may lie, in part, in the fact that they tend to earn more doing work which is more comfortable. For older women, work satisfaction is significantly linked to the opportunity to chat with other workers as well as to a sense of accomplishment.

Despite the fact that many of these older women have been working in factory jobs twenty and thirty years, they did not earn as well as their younger, American-born colleagues. In jobs where speed is skill, older women, women who have probably slowed down, see their earnings suffer. Yet, there nevertheless seems to be a mechanism whereby some older wom-

Table 5.2   *Partial Correlates of Work Satisfaction: Older Married Women*

Overall work satisfaction with "a comfortable job"
   controlling for:
     1. a chance to chat with other workers
     2. a sense of accomplishment
     3. good pay
$r = .388; n = 86; p = .000$

Overall work satisfaction with "good pay"
   controlling for:
     1. a sense of accomplishment
     2. a chance to chat with other workers
     3. a comfortable job
$r = .335; n = 86; p = .001$

Overall work satisfaction with "a chance to chat with other workers"
   controlling for:
     1. a sense of accomplishment
     2. a comfortable job
     3. good pay
$r = .287; n = 86; p = .003$

Overall work satisfaction with "a sense of accomplishment"
   controlling for:
     1. a chance to chat with other workers
     2. a comfortable job
     3. good pay
$r = .195; n = 86; p = .035$

en can still be rewarded for their long years of service. The older women who managed to get standard-rate jobs earned some of the best wages. While they were no more likely than younger, American-born women to have such jobs (40 percent in both age groups), if they worked on a standard rate they got paid more than if they worked on a piece rate. Only 38 percent of younger women who were standard-rate workers compared to 51 percent of older women who worked standard time earned $5.25 an hour or more.

Older women reported higher levels of work satisfaction than either of the other two groups of women. Forty-nine percent of older women reported being "very satisfied" with their jobs, compared to 33 percent of young, American-born women and 34 percent of Portuguese women. Older women were more satisfied with their jobs even at low wages. Twenty-one percent of older women who earned less than $4.25 an hour, compared to 4 percent of younger, American-born women and 12 percent of Portuguese women reported they were very satisfied with their jobs.

Though older women evidently prefer to earn the best possible wages at a standard rate when they have the choice, most opt for comfortable jobs even if it means earning less money. They recognize clearly that speed is skill. As they get older, however, many begin to have difficulty working at the breakneck pace that is required to "make good money." As Tina Catoli said, "Let's face it, we do slow down at a certain age. We can't work like we used to when we were younger."

Or, as Mary Florence put it, "Sometimes you get awful tired, especially as you get older. You know I'm 57. It's not like when you are young."

One might expect that older women would be bitter about declining earnings as they age and that they would consider not being rewarded for their long years of service with increased wages to be unjust, but many of these older blue-collar women were willing to acknowledge their age as a liability. Few women seemed angry that their younger colleagues who could still work fast earned more money. As the older women saw it, younger women, women with growing families to support and heavy mortgages, needed more money. Sarah Fantes was a 54-year-old garment worker who had worked in her industry for more than thirty years and had been employed in the same shop for the past fifteen. She continued to work on a piece rate earning $4.50 an hour. Sarah's response to her job exemplified the way older women factory workers often feel about the piece rate and their jobs in the context of changing family needs. As she put it, "Yes, I like working on piece rate, but I would take standard now because my working days are over. My family is all grown up, and I don't need to rush anymore."

Carol Doherty feels the same way as Sarah does. She says, "I would prefer to work on a standard rate—$3.50 an hour would be enough. You could get up in the morning, get washed and dressed, and say, 'Oh, I'm going to work and no hassles.' And you are only going to make $3.50, but you know you get it every week."

Yet, most older women don't want to stop working entirely; they just want easier jobs. Carol Doherty, a garment worker, would prefer to work, "in the cutting room or the shipping room—something not with the machines. You can make better money on the machines, but it's nerve-racking. If you have an upsetting day you come home and take it out on your husband." Though she likes working, she would be glad to have less pressure. She adds, "And if you have a good day you could just work around the clock."

But if some older women accept their lower wages with a degree of equanimity because their needs for earnings aren't as intense as they used to be, if others enjoy working more than when they had small children at home, many women begin to feel the pressure of working in a factory more acutely. Connie Cabrallo remarked that if she could afford it, she would prefer to work in a store than a factory. What she wants is "a job where you are there enjoying it and no pressure—something in a store—but they don't pay." The conflict between financial need and the difficulty of working is particularly severe for the women who have to remain on piecework because, despite the low pay, they still need their jobs. Connie adds, "On piecework you have to make sure you make your money. And you are always on nerves."

As we will see in the following chapter, blue-collar women cannot afford to retire. When we asked her if she felt she and her husband would have enough money for retirement, Carol Doherty replied, "I am, truthfully, not looking forward to it. We have a pension. We've taken out retirement insurance and have been paying on that. But, one day to another, you never know."

Ultimately, what keeps so many of these women in factories until they reach sixty-two or sixty-five are their hopes of collecting their full pensions. [11] The unionized blue-collar women we interviewed were among the small minority of working women who expect to receive private pensions when they retire. Further, the longer they work, and the higher their wages when they retire, the larger their monthly pension checks will be.

We estimated that full pension benefits for women production workers who retired in 1980 at age sixty-five were between $125 and $250 per month, hardly enough to pay the maintenance fee on a fancy condominium in Florida. Nevertheless, most of the women we spoke with saw their pensions as an important part of the financial cushion that would enable them to maintain their economic independence and security in old age. Their unions had negotiated the company contributions to the pension fund. Pensions were viewed, then, as another benefit they got from the union. But even more important, the women felt they had worked hard for their pensions. Therefore, a monthly pension check at retirement was something the company owed them.

Younger Women

The blue-collar women who earn some of the best wages in the traditionally female, unionized jobs are married women born in America, between the ages of twenty-five and forty-five. These women worked to support their growing families and, to some extent, they did this quite well. The average hourly wage among this group was $5.48 an hour. Women who earned this much money per hour and worked full-time earned, in 1979, more than the median wage for a female clerical worker and about the same as the median wage for a female craft worker (see table 4.1). As I have already pointed out, the potential to earn "good money" has provided an incentive for many of these women to abandon cleaner, physically easier, and somewhat higher-status jobs in order to work on production lines. Such women are prepared to work hard to earn the money they need for their families at this financially demanding time in their lives.

However, when they are happiest with their work, what makes them happy is not greater wage satisfaction nor opportunities to socialize with other workers. These younger women are happier with their jobs if they feel they have comfortable jobs. But what is most important in generating work satisfaction is a sense of accomplishment. It appears then, that the high wages these women can earn *may keep them on the job*—but neither earnings nor opportunities to socialize make them happier with their work (see table 5.3).

What could there be about simple factory jobs, jobs which were physically difficult, tedious, and demanding, that could enable these younger, American-born women to get the most satisfaction from their work when it provided them with a sense of accomplishment? Was there something unique about the jobs they held, or did their response have something to do with the women themselves? To explore this very complex issue, we first looked at the quality of the jobs these younger women held. How were they different from the work done by the other two groups? We found that younger, American women shared piecework and standard-rate jobs in the same proportion as their older counterparts, though unlike the older women, they earned about the same wages regardless of how they were paid. Among this group there was no earnings difference between pieceworkers and standard-rate workers. [12] Moreover, the nature of the work these women did was no different from the older women or the immigrant women. They packed light bulbs, bundled cord sets, and hemmed skirts. Ultimately the only difference we could find in the jobs they did was their higher pay; but this higher pay was not associated with more work satisfaction.

We found then, that the nature of their jobs was no different from

Table 5.3   *Partial Correlates of Work Satisfaction: Younger, Married Women*

Overall work satisfaction with "good pay"
controlling for:
  1. a sense of accomplishment
  2. a chance to chat with other workers
  3. a comfortable job
$r = .135$; $n = 68$; $p = .133$

Overall work satisfaction with "a chance to chat with other workers"
controlling for:
  1. a sense of accomplishment
  2. a comfortable job
  3. good pay
$r = .083$; $n = 68$; $p = .248$

Overall work satisfaction with "a comfortable job"
controlling for:
  1. a chance to chat with other workers
  2. a sense of accomplishment
  3. good pay
$r = .214$; $n = 68$; $p = .038$

Overall work satisfaction with "a sense of accomplishment"
controlling for:
  1. a chance to chat with other workers
  2. a comfortable job
  3. good pay
$r = .434$; $n = 68$; $p = .000$

those held by the older or immigrant women. Nor, can we emphasize too strongly that these younger women did not report that their jobs gave them a greater sense of accomplishment than reported by women in other groups. What the data does tell us, however, is that the opportunity to get a sense of accomplishment from one's job is most significant in producing work satisfaction among the more highly paid, younger, American-born women factory workers.

How does one get a sense of accomplishment from hemming skirts, packing light bulbs, or bundling electrical cords? What is there in jobs like these that provides gratification? Or, what do the women bring to their work which allows them to feel pleasure in the work they do? Ultimately we could not "boil down" the answer to this question to a series of variables in a statistical analysis. Only the women themselves, in their own words, allow us to understand the variety of ways in which factory jobs allow the women who do them a sense of purpose and accomplishment.

There are some women, though not many, who take pride in the work they do. Like Laura Lafleche, a garment worker who was also very active in her union. She volunteered the following without even being asked,

"What's important to me in a job is if it's what I like to do. I like to sew for
one thing. I think you have to work at something you like, whether it's
stitching or cleaning house. I like to see that what I'm doing comes out
well. I have pride in what I do."

But for most factory women the pleasures are more indirect. Some
women have a high energy level and like doing physical work. Barbara
Adams is one of these women who likes her job because it gets her out of the
house and gives her a sense of competence. She works in an electrical wiring
plant and earns $7.50 an hour. She told our interviewer, "A lot of people
say you work because you need the money, but I think if I didn't have to I
would. I work because I enjoy it. I could never sit home day after day. You
know you can only do so much housework. I would go crazy if I didn't
work."

Sonia May, who works on the line with Barbara, describes her feelings
about her job in much the same way. But these women, in talking about
why they work, express more than just the "need to get out of the house."
Both in their late thirties, each married with two children in grade school,
they not only have the energy but the need to do something meaningful
with their lives that goes beyond raising children. Erik Erickson has called
this "generativity." As Sonia May puts it, "I need to work myself. I would
not be in the house twenty-four hours a day, seven days a week. I need the
outside company—the need to know you are capable of doing something
else than cleaning a house and taking care of children."

In a world where earnings are a measure of self-worth, jobs which are
perceived as paying well may be experienced as a more meaningful activity
than those which pay poorly. As Sonia put it, "I would leave my children
for $8.00 an hour, but not for $3.50."

It's important to realize how valuable it is for women to be able to
contribute to the financial well-being of their families, especially in a world
where women, especially those without education, earn so little. In such a
context, a woman who holds down and manages a demanding job has good
reason to feel a sense of personal efficacy and pride. When women work
primarily for the money, a blue-collar job, indeed any job which pays well,
contributes to a woman's sense of power and control. She feels she can
enhance her family's well-being by her own efforts. Sarah Candinski earns
$8.25 an hour packing light bulbs. Her husband also does well as a skilled
worker in the shipbuilding industry. The Candinskis have a boy who is
twelve and a girl who is eight. As Sarah puts it, "If I didn't work we would
not starve to death, we would not lose our home, but we would not have the
extras. Like right now we are going to Florida. We would not have these
trips. My kids would not have a lot of things my working has provided for
them. I enjoy the freedom that comes with having extra money." She adds
with a sense of irony, "I spoil my children rotten. They have the best

clothes. They have not done without much of anything materially. They are much better off than I was."

Sarah Candinski is certainly not complaining that her work destroys the intimacy of her family life, as some argue is the case in similar situations. Instead she is proud that her own efforts have contributed to her family's well-being. Because of her efforts her family can participate in the mainstream of American economic life. What is at issue here is not merely her "willingness" to put up with the pressures of a factory job, to make the required trade-offs for the financial rewards. What is more important is that the ability to meet the challenges her work demands contributes to her sense of mastery, the feeling that she has had a measure of success in being able, through her own efforts, to meet life's challenges.

Choosing Blue-Collar Work

What then, as Pat Sexton asked almost a decade ago, do working-class women want from their jobs? Blue-collar women want a variety of different things. What they want—and what they get—depends on the jobs they hold, their cultural backgrounds, and their stage in the life cycle. Moreover, even within the context of what seems to be a very narrow range of occupations, the labor market in these older, mill-based industries seems to allocate "good" jobs and "bad" jobs on the basis of age and ethnicity.[13] Inevitably then, blue-collar women respond differently to what is available in the workplace, partly because they have different jobs available to them.

Younger women, with physical energy and growing families to support, often choose factory work over the higher status, easier work alternatives available to them because of the wages they can earn. Indeed, what gives them a sense of accomplishment is earning well and supporting their families. If older women do not have the opportunity to earn as well as their younger counterparts, neither do they have the energy or the need to continue working so hard. They do, however, continue to need their jobs. In order to continue working until they retire, older women choose a different strategy for coping with the pressures of the factory system than do younger women. Some simply slow down while others manage to get easier jobs. Portuguese women, immigrants with no other work alternatives, must take whatever jobs they can get, regardless of the pressure and the low earnings. These are the women who are "stuck" with the worst pressure and the least to show for it. Yet, we must not see their seemingly relentless efforts to work hard as a sign of passivity or acquiescence. Their efforts to make the rate and "make money" are ways of coping with some of the worst factory jobs available to women in New England today.

This research also refutes the commonly held belief that women in low-paying "unskilled" jobs like to work primarily because they are "isolated" housewives who are dying to get out of the house and talk to other adult women. These women are not *primarily* concerned with sociability on the job. Certainly the opportunity to chat with other workers has an impact on how happy the women are with their jobs and is an important component of blue-collar women's work experience, especially for the older women. Nevertheless, deriving a sense of accomplishment from one's work, having a comfortable job or satisfaction with one's wages are frequently more important to blue-collar women than opportunities for sociability.

This research also suggests that when women work, not for fulfillment, but primarily for the money, they are often willing to put up with a wide variety of work pressures when they need the money and have the chance to earn it. Joyce Miller, who is a member of the Executive Council of the AFL-CIO, spoke recently at a New York conference on the needs of women moving into traditionally male, skilled craft jobs. She told the assembled researchers and policy makers, "It may be that no woman wants to work in overalls, but no woman wants to starve."

It is evidently not only women in skilled craft jobs who are willing to do this. It is not only women who confront penury; indeed it is not only women who head families who are likely to make such trade-offs. Even married women, women with husbands to prevent them from "starving," need and want good wages. By developing the capacity to manage their work, women take some control of a basic working-class dilemma—the pervasive problem of financial insecurity. In that context, well-paid jobs can become a real source of gratification.

Finally this work shows that the distinctions social scientists often make between "intrinsic" and "extrinsic" work satisfaction may not be warranted. It demonstrates that women themselves don't see their employment as an either/or proposition. They don't see their jobs as solely a vocation, an opportunity to seek "fulfillment," but neither do they work "just for the money." It is certainly true that blue-collar women work primarily "for the money," but it is important to understand that the money they earn also has a variety of meanings for them. It has important psychological as well as material benefits which cannot be separated from each other. Given the low wages available to the "ordinary" working women in America, women without professional or technical training, a chance to earn well evidently goes a long way toward increasing women's "intrinsic" satisfaction with their jobs.

Today the threat of losing one's unionized, blue-collar job hangs like a sword of Damocles over the heads of many of New England's women factory workers who earn a living in the region's mill-based industries. Are these jobs worth saving? Some argue they are, claiming the alternatives are non-unionized, part-time, more poorly paid sales and service occupations, jobs which are often without stability, benefits, or pension plans.[14] Others envision a happier future for women than working in factories. They put their hopes in the promise of new, high technology occupations or in the increased education of women for work which is cleaner and more highly skilled. The dilemma is a thorny one.

What does the future look like for blue-collar women who have lost their jobs? This issue will be addressed in a later chapter. But before we explore the consequences of job loss and unemployment for blue-collar women, we need to understand how women's factory jobs affect their families. It is to this subject that we now turn.

6 Beyond the Factory Gates: Blue-Collar Women at Home

AT 3:00 OR 3:30 IN THE AFTERNOON the machines stop. In garment shops and wire plants and candy factories women leave their benches, hurrying to locker rooms where they wash up, comb their hair, or change their clothes. As they put on coats and punch out, the women stop to chat with a friend in another department or maybe someone in the neighborhood who is just arriving to take their place on the second shift. The women on the first shift, which started at 7:30 in the morning, are finished for the day. They are going home.

But most are not going home right away. First, there are a few stops to be made—at the babysitter's house to pick up the children, at the supermarket to get the quart of milk or the loaf of bread that was forgotten from the weekend shopping, at the dry cleaner to get a husband's suit for a family wedding on Saturday night. Nor are the women done working. There is laundry to be done, clothing to be ironed, supper to be made, and dishes to be washed before bedtime, then sleep and another round like this one tomorrow.

Angela Shane, a garment worker, described her day to us. What stands out is the rush and the hurry, the pervasive lack of time. She told us, "I take them [her two children, ages two and four] to my mother's at 7:00 A.M. I pick them up at 4:30, quarter to five, and if I have to run an errand, 5:00. I have no time, really, to spend with them. By the time dinner is done . . . they have dinner, they are tired themselves. So there is no time there. During the weekend I have the chores to do, I have the house to clean. There is really no time."

Sarah Bellows works the second shift at Condo Electric, where she packs light bulbs. She chose the night shift so she could be at work when her husband was home to take care of her two school-age children. Sarah has the same dilemma. She told us, "I worked 3:30 to midnight. By the time you get to bed it's 1:20. Then I get up early to get the kids to school. Then back to bed for a few hours and then I get up to do my housework, and then it's time to go to work—and I have absolutely no time for self."

Angela Shane and Sarah Bellows know full well what is meant by women's "double day" of work. They know what it means to come home from paid jobs to dinner, dishes, cranky children, and tired husbands; to work all week and spend much of the weekend doing laundry and cleaning the house. How do these women who work full time and year-round manage their double day of work? What is the impact of their full-time, year-round work schedule on the fabric of their marriages and the quality of their family lives?

These days, TV programs and magazine articles extol the women in high-status jobs, in professional or business careers, who have learned to manage the demands of work and family life. Successful women are lauded for their extraordinary strengths. Their efforts are justified by the sense of achievement and pleasure they get from mastering the demands of their "dual role."[1] But if glamorous careers are valued by middle-class women, what about the 80 percent of women who work, not because they want to, but largely because they "have to"? As married women have entered the labor force in record numbers, the debate about the family wage has re-emerged once again.

Traditionalists, from members of the Moral Majority to male Marxists, have defended the virtues of higher wages for men and the benefits of stay-at-home wives for the working-class family. Many on the left have defended the "family wage."[2] They blame "stagflation" for the fact that two paychecks are now needed to keep working families in the mainstream of American economic life and argue that women bear the major burdens of living in a two-earner family, coming home from "paid work" to shopping, dinner, dishes, childcare, laundry, and cleaning the house. Even feminists recognize that a paid job doesn't overturn women's obligation to do the lion's share of housework. Most working women then, are seen as "exploited" by capitalism in the workplace and "oppressed" by patriarchy at home.[3]

There is certainly more than a grain of truth to this view. At the same time, as Ferree[4] has pointed out, such theoretical abstractions vastly oversimplify the complexity of women's lives. Women do not see themselves simply as victims of "patriarchy" and "capitalism." While they see the advantages of having financial support from husbands and staying home to care for their families, they also appreciate the importance of working and earning money. The major problem is the poor quality and low pay of most of the jobs available to them.[5] Yet despite sex segregation in the work force and low-paying women's jobs, many working-class women enjoy their jobs and find ways to manage their dual roles.[6]

Working-class women weigh the "costs" of working against the benefits to be gained. A woman's decision to work or to stay home is influenced by her family's need for more money, by the ages of her children, her husband's earnings, and also by her husband's attitudes about having a working wife. But if working-class women take jobs "for the money" rather than for "fulfillment," the value of paid employment and the strength of a woman's commitment to her job will also be a function of the quality of work that is available to her.

Moreover, even if paid work confronts women with a double burden, women see advantages in accepting the overload of the double day. Researchers have found that women's ability to earn and provide for their families can create the opportunity for them to create a more equitable balance of power in marriage and lead to a greater sharing in their family lives.[7]

We would expect then, that in working-class families, women who are "providers" rather than just supplementary earners should be able to translate the resources from their jobs into more efficacy and control at home,[8] but a woman's ability to transform her efforts at work into more influence in her family is always circumscribed by her ability and willingness to provide and by the way she and her husband understand their obligations to one another.

In what follows we will move from the factories to the triple-decker apartments and ranch houses which characterize the working-class neighborhoods of Milltown, New England. We will explore how unionized factory work shapes and defines the family lives of blue-collar women. What are the conditions in which playing a provider role allows blue-collar women to translate the resources of their paid work into a more equitable division of labor at home and into a greater sense of personal efficacy and control? In exploring these questions we hope to more fully understand the dynamics of the two-paycheck, working-class family.

As I have tried to show, the wage advantage of New England's unionized, blue-collar women has begun to erode. Today it is virtually impossible for a woman to support herself and her children on a woman factory worker's salary. Yet, these blue-collar jobs do allow many of New England's women factory workers to play a significant provider role in their families. When we compare these working-class women to others who are full-time housewives or to women who are more marginally employed, the consequences for women and their families will become apparent. These factory jobs allow some of the women to create a more equitable division of family labor and improve the quality of their family lives. Such a view flies in the face of long-held beliefs that working-class men are inevitably authoritarian and "oppress" their wives by their patriarchal behaviors and attitudes.[9]

To examine these issues we will first compare the family lives of younger, American-born women factory workers with other research on women in working-class families. Then we will compare these younger factory women with their older counterparts. Finally, we will explore the differences between women whose families' cultures are rooted in American life and those who are Portuguese immigrants. The comparisons will show clearly that the adjustments men and women make to the demands of a wife's paid work are never automatic. They represent the results of role bargaining and marital negotiations which take place within the context of demands created by one's job options, one's stage in the life cycle, and a particular cultural framework. Ultimately, all of these factors shape the adjustments working-class families make to a wife's blue-collar job.

It is indeed unfortunate that our research did not allow us to speak with the husbands of these blue-collar women. What follows then is perhaps, more an expression of how these women feel about their lives. One researcher has called this "wives' family sociology" and argues that it prevents an "objective" picture of family dynamics. [10] If there is bias here, so be it. Yet we listened very carefully to what the women told us, what gave them pleasure and what gave them pain. There is consistency here between what we know about women's lives and what we heard. If we cannot provide an "objective" portrait of their family lives, we can nevertheless understand how these women see themselves and what they want from their lives.

Portraits of Life in the Blue-collar Family: A Historical Perspective

If there are many who wax nostalgic for the time when men could presumably support their wives, when working-class families could get by on one paycheck, we need only recall the lives of the women in working-class families in the affluent 1950s and 1960s to be quickly chastened. Intellectuals in these affluent postwar decades[11] may have rejoiced at the new level of prosperity enjoyed by American factory workers and their families. Yet the wives in these families apparently led lives few would envy.

Described as pitiable and subservient, the daily routines of working-class housewives were largely circumscribed by the demands of their husbands and the needs of their children. Social life was limited to the neighborhood and the company of extended kin. In the words of one analyst, such women led lives of "quiet desperation," worrying about "junior's whooping cough, the week's ironing, the plugged sink, the runny nose, the paycheck that can't cover expenses, the kids who won't stop yelling and fighting, and the husband who offers little affection or attention in payment for her drudgery." [12]

This portrait of the working-class wife was echoed in other major studies of working-class family life during this period. Apparently, after the

second World War, Rosie the Riveter had retired to the working-class sub-
urbs to raise her 2.3 children. But instead of the family paradise she longed
for in the trying years of the war, she found herself isolated, "cooped up"
and "tied down" by the monotonous rhythms of housework and childcare.

Many working-class wives who were beneficiaries of the hard-won
family wage understood full well the financial constraints of living on a
working man's salary in a period of touted affluence. Not only was it hard to
make ends meet, but many paid the family bills from an "allowance" doled
out to them on a weekly basis by secretive husbands who often refused to
divulge just how much they actually earned. Blue-collar wives were depen-
dents in the true sense of the word. Many felt they were caught in a limbo in
which they had total responsibility for serving their families and managing
the family budget but had virtually no control over the resources with which
to accomplish these goals. Some chose to work, but most were loath to defy
husbands who wanted them at home.

Working-class Wives and Mothers Enter the Labor Force

By the early 1970s, many of the wives of working-class men had
joined the labor force, essentially to ease some of the "stagflationary" financial pressures their families faced as they struggled to raise children and pay
their bills. In one of the best treatments of life in the working-class family,
Rubin's *Worlds of Pain*, 58 percent of the wives of working-class men held
paid jobs outside the home. Most were employed in part-time sales, service,
and clerical work.

However, Rubin found that wives' employment did little to change
their limited control or satisfaction with family life. A job outside the home
simply created an added burden; it failed to alter the traditional division of
household labor or minimize their husband's authority. She concluded that
class rather than gender, particularly the inadequacy of the husband's income, was the most important limiting factor in the women's opportunities
for satisfaction, experience, and freedom. The working-class family remained a central location of women's oppression. Rubin's conclusions echo
the words of Pat Sexton, who noted the same experience more than a decade
before. Of the women Rubin studied, she writes that there was "no way,
short of years of nagging or divorce, to defy her husband's authority and
dicta about what she may or may not do with her life."[13]

Though Rubin's excellent portrait of working-class women and their
families broke new ground in exploring the working-class family from the
women's perspective, it continued a long sociological tradition of seeing
working-class men and women as victims. Husbands, struggling and humiliated at work, are seen as jealously guarding their self-esteem by limiting the freedom of their wives at home. Wives feel compelled to participate

in their own subordination, supporting their husbands' authority, in part because they feel that, as women, they ought to and in part because their husbands are indeed the essential and primary providers.

Rubin's work suggests that holding a job and bringing home a paycheck are not effective ways for working-class women to increase their autonomy or their authority in the family. Yet, as she also points out, the jobs these women held were low-paying and marginal. They did not enable the women to be providers. As one of her subjects points out, "I work three days a week, but it's different. The family doesn't depend on my working; it does on his." Not surprisingly, the women she talked with had a fairly minimal commitment to their jobs. Rubin writes, "The wife is likely to move in and out of the labor force depending on the husband's job stability, on whether his overtime expands or contracts, on the exigencies of a family—a sick child, an aging parent."[14]

Research has shown, however, that when women become providers, that is, when wives earn a substantial portion of the family income, women increase their authority in the family.[15] The blue-collar women I studied, who work in unionized factory jobs, have a very different approach to paid work than the women Rubin studied. The differences between these two groups of working-class women, situated at opposite ends of the country, may have a lot to do with the jobs they held or the paid work that was available to them.[16]

If the women factory workers we talked to (native-born women with husbands and dependent children who were between the ages of twenty-five and forty-five) felt their families depended on their employment, it was because they earned so much of the family's income. While Rubin calculated that the women she studied earned 25 percent of the family's annual income, we found that the women in our study in comparable life situations earned almost half, or 45 percent of their family's income. A full 83 percent of the seventy-three younger (between the ages of twenty-five and forty-five) American-born married women with children agreed strongly with the statement "women today need to work to help their families keep up with the high cost of living." As we have seen, married women with young children worked year-round and full time and made arrangements for their children's care so they might continue to work irrespective of their husbands' employment situation. Indeed, their commitment to work largely resembles that of blue-collar men. Like their husbands, they worked to support their families.

If, as Rubin argues, so much of the "pain" of working-class life is created by the lack of resources, the contribution blue-collar women make to the family purse goes a long way toward alleviating that pain. Rubin estimates that only 30 percent of the families in her study had incomes at or above the "intermediate" level of living for an urban family.[17] Most of the higher-income families had husbands who moonlighted or worked a lot of overtime. The men were the breadwinners.

This earning pattern is in sharp contrast to the families of women who worked in New England's unionized factory jobs. In these families, the women's paychecks substantially raised the family's standard of living. The blue-collar women we studied, like the women Rubin interviewed, were not married to men who could support their families well on one paycheck. Their average yearly earnings ($14,692) were slightly less than fifteen thousand dollars a year, well below what the Bureau of Labor Statistics calculated as an "intermediate" level of income ($20,517) for an urban family of four in 1979. However, because blue-collar women earned almost half the family income, 80 percent of the families, compared to 30 percent in Rubin's study, had family incomes above the intermediate level of living.[18] The comfort level these blue-collar women shared with their families was a direct result of their own employment. It was not a result of their husbands' earnings. Their families fared as well as they did economically only because the women worked year-round and full time at relatively well-paid jobs.

The women who worked in New England's unionized factory jobs could raise their families from poverty and keep them living in modest comfort. Inevitably, their families have come to depend on the women's factory jobs to maintain their standard of living. If women work at factory jobs because their families need the money, the jobs themselves have come to bind the women to the labor force, creating a work commitment which persists and which has a profound impact on the women's families.

The "Extra" Money: Its Impact on the Family

When we first began our research, many of our interviewers expected that women who worked in factories would tend to be poor. Indeed, some of the homes we visited were shabby by middle-class standards. There were women who lived with their families in third-floor, walk-up apartments, in decaying tenements in deteriorating sections of town. Other women had furniture that resembled what Rubin described as "a collection of hand-me-downs and cheap Ward's or Sears' specials." Yet many others found themselves facing women in comfortable suburban homes with spacious yards, wall-to-wall carpets, and fully applianced kitchens. A majority of the women, 59 percent, said they owned their own homes and 77 percent told us they had savings.

The tenets of radical chic often disparage the value of consumption as the be-all and end-all of "alienated labor." Yet those who downplay the value of carpeting or microwave ovens as crass materialism fail to recognize the "pain" that is caused by the absence of consumer comforts in a society where these things represent achievement and success. Just as important as the use or comfort value of these possessions is their symbolic meaning. The tangible material benefits employed women can acquire for their families are a testimony to the women's own powers; because such acquisitions are physical representations of personal accomplishments, the thought of losing them generates a great deal of fear. At the same time, the carpets and microwave ovens are valued because they represent so much hard work.

It would not be inaccurate to say that what keeps these blue-collar women on the job is the hope, and often the ability, to provide microwave ovens and wall-to-wall carpeting. Even though most of what they earn is not spent on such luxuries, these women see their jobs as a means to helping their families "get ahead." Since the women earn almost half of the family income, their wages are more likely to help pay the mortgage and the gas bills. Nevertheless, depending on husbands' income, full-time, unionized factory jobs allow women to make sure their families escape poverty or achieve a standard of living that would simply be impossible if they held more marginal jobs or did not work at all.

Yet, despite the relative comfort in many of their lives, these "blue-collar" women frequently experienced a profound sense of financial insecurity. There was an underlying anxiety, not unrealistic for blue-collar workers, that despite the progress their efforts had wrought, the house, the car, and the microwave ovens could disappear. We asked the women who agreed to talk with us whether they felt economically secure. Most replied as Myra Billings did. "Right now I guess I am. I don't have a high mortgage. I do have a little in the bank. I'm pretty well secure . . . but we don't splurge. And you really never know in my opinion. Heaven forbid, if I got sick or something like that. Money just goes. From one day to another, things can change. You are never secure for anything . . . it can tumble."

Not only did many feel a certain tenuousness about whatever level of comfort they enjoyed, they also felt that the quality of their material life had eroded in a period of inflation. Virtually everyone complained about the high cost of living and the increasing difficulty of making ends meet. Perhaps it is not surprising that Mary Ellen Dunn, a garment worker with two children and a husband who is poorly paid, should feel this way. She said; "To me sometimes you get a raise and it is gone on the groceries. And sometimes you lose when you get a raise because they just take out more taxes."

Yet, her friend and co-worker, Judy Channing, is married to a well-paid, skilled worker. Her complaint is much the same. Judy said, "We've got two pays coming in and we used to save much more money. When he [her husband] started carpentry about fifteen years ago he got $3.19 an hour. Now he gets $10.00. But then the money used to go much further. Now I go to the grocery and come out with a little bag with nothing in it and it is $15.00. If either of us lost our jobs I would be nervous."

Blue-collar women married to blue-collar men are not likely to feel a great sense of economic security. Yet, while there was a fearful sense that, indeed, "everything could tumble," the women we spoke with did not feel that their security rested only on the security and stability of their husband's job. He alone was not responsible for putting food on the table or a roof over their heads. If women work in factories to pay the mortgage and the gas and electric bills, at least they feel the homes they own belong to them as much as to their husbands. As Myra Billings told us, with both pride and anger, "Everything I own, my husband and I have worked for. No one has given us anything."

This attitude on the part of blue-collar women is in sharp contrast to the findings of other research on working-class family life where husbands both earn and control the money. In other studies wives were often ignorant of how much money their husbands earned. Some simply received a weekly allowance for the household expenditures. Without money of their own, the economic dependence of housewives was virtually complete. Even when wives held jobs, their employment and earnings did not allow these working-class women much control in deciding how money was to be spent or how family purchases were to be made. [19]

However, when the wife's earnings have helped the family put a down payment on a house or continue to help make the monthly payments on the family car, the authoritarian working-class husband may simply fall by the wayside. Despite repeated probes by our interviewers, few of the women we spoke with indicated or expressed resentment that their husbands had veto power over family purchasing decisions. The women felt, by and large, that they made their voices heard.

Sarah Bellows and her husband are both providers. They put their paychecks together and budget for the week. As she describes it, "We put our money together and pay the bills out of it. He [her husband] gets paid on Thursday. I get paid on Friday. We pay the bills and put what's left over in the bank."

What emerged from our interviews was an insistence that major purchasing decisions be made together. Women had pacts with their husbands not to spend money without the consent of the other party. As Myra Billings said, "We never go off and just buy something on our own. That's one decision we make together . . . since we got married nineteen years ago."

The same is true for Mary Ellen Dunn and her husband. Who makes the decision in the Dunn family about a major purchase? "Together! That's very important for us to do it together. I don't come home with something and he doesn't either."

These agreements do not mean that decisions about what to buy with the family's money are made without conflict. At times he transgresses. Sophie Donato and her husband live on a tight budget. Sometimes she resents it when he goes out drinking with his friends. But she also feels torn. "Tony's a man and men like to spend money. As a woman knows, she runs the house and knows it can't be. We have bills. And if you make an agreement to pay that bill you gotta pay it. But he has to relax with money sometimes."

Yet, if husbands transgress, wives also transgress. Millie Barnes is thirty-seven years old and has two little boys aged seven and nine. Although the Barnes' are saving to buy a home, Millie admits she spends too freely sometimes. "Sometimes I'm a sneak when it comes to that [buying things]. Like I bought a couple of rugs before that were a good buy. Like wall-to-wall rugs, on sale. I didn't tell him—and when I finally did, he got mad. And I said, 'Gee, if I were to ask you about it would you let me buy them?' He said, 'No!' I said, 'Well then, what's the point?' If it were big, like a bedroom set, we made it [the decision] together."

Paying the Bills

Some researchers have assumed that the person in the family who is responsible for paying the bills (usually the husband) has the most control over the family purse.[20] Others argue, however, that in working-class families, writing the checks and paying the bills are simply additional chores that fall to women in the context of their daily round of homemaking and childcare.[21] In having to balance a frequently insufficient budget, women are forced to juggle the creditors and shield their husbands from the painful truth that they are not earning enough to make ends meet.

Paying the bills can be both a chore and a reflection of real power. But whichever it is and however it is experienced, blue-collar women share the job with their husbands. Sometimes he pays the bills—sometimes she does. Only 48 percent of the women said they were primarily responsible for paying the bills. Thirty-six percent of the women said it was the husband's job and another 16 percent said it was a task they shared with their husbands.

The women often do see balancing the checkbook and paying the bills as a burden, but not one they have to bear alone. When we asked Millie Barnes who paid the bills in her family, she said, "I used to pay it all the time, but now he pays them sometimes, because it was too much on me."

Mary Ellen Dunn told us, "I hand it [her paycheck] to my husband. He does all the marketing and pays all the bills." Tom Dunn pays the bills, according to his wife, because that's the way he wants it. But, according to Mary Ellen, it's all right with her. She adds with a sense of relief, "He can handle it! He can have it!"

Myra Billings, on the other hand, takes care of all the money in her household. "I do all the bills. Our money kind of goes all together. I pay the rent. I do the food shopping. I pay the charge accounts and the bills. I do it." But when her husband expressed some discontent about the way she was managing, she told him, "Honey, you want to take over, you take it over."

The Balance between Work and Family Commitments

The financial contributions blue-collar women make to their families create a greater level of material comfort for their husbands and children. Their hefty paychecks are also a source of increased autonomy at home. Yet whatever gains the women make are ultimately purchased by their commitment to long hours of hard work away from home. Such two-paycheck blue-collar families, then, are hardly models of domestic paradise. Moreover, even if husbands adjust to their wives' employment and recognize and support such efforts on behalf of the family, the hefty paychecks of blue-collar wives are nonetheless often viewed as a challenge to the traditional roles upon which working-class marriages are usually based. Male authority, founded primarily on the husband's role as "breadwinner," is still an integral part of most working-class family relationships.

Although we did not speak with the men directly, we did ask the women how their husbands felt about their working. In response to an open-ended question, 30 percent of the seventy-three women told our interviewers, in no uncertain terms, that their spouses were not happy about their wives working, saying things like, "He doesn't like it!" or "I know he'd rather have me home." Another 34 percent were less forthright and perhaps more ambivalent. These women would repeatedly answer the question by saying things like, "Well, he doesn't really mind it" or "I don't really know—he doesn't say anything about it."[22]

Husbands' attitudes about their wives' jobs varied in response to the earnings of each spouse. Women reported that husbands who were better earners (earning more than $15,000 a year) were less accepting of working wives than men who were poor earners (earning less than $10,000). Wives of more "affluent" men were more than twice as likely to say, without hesitation, that husbands disliked their working than the wives of poor earners (41 percent compared to 16 percent). Aside from acknowledging the needed income of working wives, the wives of lower-income husbands reported their spouses as more likely to feel that working was good for them. Likewise, husbands were seen as less accepting of working wives when women earned higher wages. Sixty-three percent of the women who earned $5.25 an hour or more said their husbands saw them as "nervous, tired, and cranky" as a result of their jobs, while only 39 percent of the women who earned less than $4.25 an hour said as much.

These responses come from the wives rather than the men themselves.

Yet it is important to note that they reaffirm what we know about the needs of working-class men to see themselves as providers. Though a husband with poor earnings may adjust to the fact that his wife contributes to the breadwinning, and ultimately may be grateful for her efforts, a man who is a better earner is more likely to feel his prerogatives challenged by a working wife, especially one who earns well herself. A man's ability to provide is, after all, a source of self-esteem.

According to Rubin, one of the major sources of tension in working-class families comes about when the husband's income can't provide well enough. Yet for blue-collar women who earn well themselves the conflicts are more likely to emerge between a husband and a wife who both earn relatively well. He wants her to stop working, while she, because she is earning well, may not want to. At the same time, however much he earns, husbands are happy to have the extra money. We asked the women in our study, "What are some of the things your husband likes about your working?" In one form or another, 91 percent of the women mentioned the money they earned. But if there are conflicts between husbands and wives where both spouses earn relatively well, blue-collar women have found a way to manage the underlying tensions. They do this largely by deferring to their husbands as the "major" provider. Regardless of a woman's real contribution to the family, the husband is defined as the main breadwinner. There is a shared belief that he is the one whose income "really supports the family." The husband's income is for "essentials"; it goes into the bank to pay the mortgage and the other inevitable monthly bills—fuel and electricity, insurance and car payments. The wife merely works for "extras" like gas, groceries, things for the children, or savings.

Claire Sweeney worked at a high-wage, blue-collar job. She was earning $8.00 an hour as a packer in a wire plant. She and her husband had worked out the following division of their earnings. She told us, "I would take my pay and save $80 of it. I used to take every raise that I got and put it in the credit union. I started with $50 a week. This is how we bought the house. And I would take the rest—between $90 and $100—and I would go to the market. I would buy anything I wanted—steak, sirloin patties, anything. And I would buy the children clothes, buy myself something, or take the money and go where I wanted to. And Fred [her husband] would pay the mortgage."

Claire is clearly a provider. According to her own words it was, literally, her salary that put food on the table and provided the down payment for the roof over the family's head. Moreover, when we asked her, she told us it was she who made most of the financial decisions in the family. Yet, at the same time, she made a strong assertion that it was her husband who really supported the family.

Sara Talbot earns considerably less than Claire Sweeney and her husband earns less than Fred. Yet she and her husband have worked out the same modus vivendi in their marriage. She sees herself as a secondary earner who is only "helping" her husband fulfill his obligations. She said, "I feel that when I'm working I bring home a good pay. It helps out. I wouldn't say I'm working just to spend. Today you need to work. A woman needs to help out her husband."

Like Claire Sweeney and Sara Talbot, many blue-collar wives recognize that their husbands' sense of manhood is contingent on the shared belief that his paycheck is "supporting the family." Even while they work and intend to continue working, wives feel they don't want to encroach on a role which gives a man his pride. Despite the fact that couples know they have come to depend on the wife's paycheck to sustain the standard of living they have carved out for themselves, women continue to define their work as "helping" husbands; they *define* their earnings as "supplementary."

The fiction eases tensions and serves a variety of functions in these working-class marriages. First of all, it allows the women to keep working and maintain harmony at home. This surely requires a trade-off—long hours of hard work. But the ability to achieve this balance allows these working-class women to avoid some of the anger and powerlessness other working-class women have felt in the difficult attempt to stretch a single, sometimes barely adequate, paycheck.

Second, support for the notion of "separate spheres"—she the homemaker, he the breadwinner—is also a way of reinforcing a husband's obligation and willingness to continue providing support for his wife and children. This is crucial to working-class women who, even when they work year-round and full time, can barely earn enough to support themselves and their children. Blue-collar women don't expect to be fully cared for by their men, but they know the financial problems divorced women face. Our interviewers heard time and again that "every woman is only a husband away from welfare."

Third, women's deference to their husbands' primacy as breadwinners is more than a subterfuge. It is not simply a way of placating husbands who suffer inadequacies about their ability to support their families on their own. The "help" they offer their husbands engenders an obligation on the part of the men for the help received, an obligation for "reciprocity." Men who get help often feel it is only fair to return the favor at home. Fairness requires that if she helps him, he should also help her.

Even in the context of real limitations on their time and energy, and even though they bring home a sizable part of the family's resources, it is not a matter of principle for blue-collar women that husbands be enlisted to do an equal share of the housework. If breadwinning is a husband's role, domestic work is seen as a women's responsibility. However, while women did not make ideological demands for an equal sharing of childcare and housework or overtly challenge their husbands, they did make demands for a quid pro quo. Negotiations with husbands were conducted to minimize confrontation, to invoke cooperation, reciprocity, and a sense of fairness. What the women considered important was creating a division of labor at home which was workable for them in the context of demanding jobs and the needs of their families. So that if Sara Talbot feels she needs to "help out her husband," she also feels that, "My husband helps me a lot too. That's one thing I told him. If you want me to help you out then you'll have to help me. That way we can help each other. So far it's been working pretty good."

Housework and Childcare

If he works and she works, who does the housework? Much has been written about women's "double day." Studies show that even though husbands "help" with the housework, women still take responsibility for the lion's share of domestic labor. Moreover, even when they help around the house, they don't increase what they do in response to their wives' employment.[23] Is it really possible that the men who are married to women who work in full-time factory jobs do not respond to the needs of their wives who, just like themselves, spend thirty-five to forty hours a week on an assembly line?

As we can see from table 6.1, women who work in factory jobs, like women in other walks of life, also report that they take responsibility for the

Table 6.1   *Wife's Reports of Husband's Participation in Domestic Chores*

	Employed Women (*n* = 50) (%)	Unemployed Women (*n* = 23) (%)
1. Preparing meals	18	5
2. Grocery shopping	38	30
3. Washing dishes	47	19
4. Doing laundry	35	9
5. Cleaning the house	43	26
6. Paying bills	52	30
7. Doing minor repairs	87	91
8. Car maintenance	85	90
9. Errands	51	48
10. Childcare	63	21
11. Bathing, washing, feeding preschoolers	56	15
12. Yard work	88	94

Note: Calculations are based on wives reporting husbands as being fully responsible for task *or* that the task is shared equally between spouses.

majority of domestic labor even when they are working full time. According to the women, there is a very traditional division of labor in these families. Men do the outside work, yard work, home repairs. They look after the family's car. Women do the "inside work."

Nevertheless, as other in-depth studies of two-paycheck families are beginning to show,[24] the women report that their husbands do make a sizable contribution to a wide range of household chores in response to the women's employment—men apparently contribute to doing even those chores which are typically considered to be women's work. Many of the women in our study who were working when we interviewed them told us that their husbands took primary responsibility for or shared responsibility for the everyday tasks of preparing meals, shopping, washing dishes, doing the laundry, and cleaning the house.

Our inability to speak with the men means, of course, we can say nothing about the men's view of their domestic roles. Moreover, we know nothing of the actual time and/or the amount of responsibility men took for domestic work. What is clear, however, is that these blue-collar women *do see their husbands as responsive to their needs at home* when the women are holding down a full-time job.

Husbands apparently vary their involvement in domestic chores in response to their wives' employment status. When the wives are working, husbands do more; when the wives are unemployed, the wives reclaim the responsibilities. Almost three-quarters of the women who were working (72 percent) told us their husbands shared at least one or more of these "inside" tasks as compared to 35 percent of the women who were out of work.[25] The women feel that their husbands are responsive to their increased needs for help when they are working. Moreover, helping a working wife did not mean a man abandoned his own household tasks. Though women reported men took on more "inside" tasks when their wives were working, these husbands continued to be responsible for the "outside" jobs like home repairs, car maintenance, and yard work (see table 6.1).

Susan Jameson, who is thirty-five years old and has two children, five and ten years of age, works the second shift at a nearby plant that produces electrical wires and cables. While her husband, Ted, needs some direction, she describes him as quite responsible about doing work around the house when Susan is working. Susan says, "He's really good. He feeds the kids supper. I leave meals once in a while. He's not big on meals. He doesn't like to clean up and do the dishes. I leave easy stuff—sandwiches, soup, hot dogs. But he's terrific. I have no complaints. I'll leave him a note, 'Honey, take the clothes off the line.' I'll come back and everything is folded and put away."

Sarah Talbot's husband also does a fair amount of work around the house. "He's always done the laundry. He can vacuum; he washes the dishes, he dries them and puts them away; folds the clothes, takes care of the children. He's always been very good as far as that goes."

As others have pointed out,[26] a large part of the help husbands provide at home is directly related to taking care of children when wives are working. As we can see from table 6.1, almost two-thirds (63 percent) of the women said their husbands shared childcare responsibilities. More than half said their husbands shared in the feeding, bathing, and dressing of preschoolers when wives were working.

Sometimes women chose to work the second shift (3:00 P.M. to midnight) because fathers were home to take care of children at night. Families sometimes prefer a family member to a babysitter. Moreover, families avoid the costs of childcare in this way. Madeline Alberts clearly made the point of how important a father's childcare contribution was to her own blue-collar family. "I don't know what I would do if I were, say, divorced or didn't have a husband. If I didn't have a husband I'd have to have day care. I couldn't live on what welfare gives you. And to pay out $30 a week for a babysitter. There should be a cheaper place you can go."

Many women told us that initially husbands felt awkward with young children and were reluctant to take responsibility for them. Yet they said that in caring for their children the fathers had been drawn into closer relationships with their sons and daughters. Sonia May, an electrical worker, told our interviewer about her own husband and children. "Not putting him down, but I don't think he would have taken the responsibility he did with his children if I were home. He had to bathe them, feed them, dress them. I didn't have to ask him to do it. It was forced on him. And it made him a little bit more responsible, a little more aware of his children."

Other women had the same reaction, stressing the fact that fathers became closer to their children, and more mature themselves, because their wives were working and they had to take responsibility for their children on a regular basis.

In many ways then, the fact that blue-collar women are providers shifts the balance of women's power and autonomy in their working-class families. The work they do gives them the ability to contribute extensively to the family purse. Though some would view the need for two earners in working-class families as an added burden, the women don't always see it exclusively in those terms. Though their work is hard and the hours long, blue-collar jobs may also be perceived as an opportunity for women to help their families get ahead. As such, they function to legitimate women's right to work in the eyes of men who, as we have seen, would prefer to maintain their own roles as full providers. Working for the family welfare also justifies the women's time away from home and children. It permits women some control over the family finances and requires husbands to commit themselves to housework and childcare. As the women see it, the value of a wife's domestic labor is recognized by husbands who are willing to "pay" for their wives' earnings by contributing to the domestic work.

If women's earning power makes the family more of a joint enterprise than it might otherwise be, men do not do the housework or take care of their children in direct proportion to their wives' earnings. Wives with high earnings report husbands who share an average of 1.59 "inside" tasks. Wives with low earnings report husbands who share an average of 1.58 "inside" tasks.[27] A husband's efforts at home then, may reflect his sensitivity to the burdens his wife bears, or it may be a response to family decisions for husbands and wives to work different shifts to save money on childcare.[28] Whichever, men are willing to increase their share of the housework because their wives are helping the family "get ahead." Likewise, wives view their husbands' help and support as substantive demonstrations of love and concern. A woman's happiness with her marriage is not enhanced by a husband who earns a higher income;[29] however, her marital satisfaction does increase *marginally* as her husband does more housework, as he shares more of the "inside" or women's work.[30] Women who reported that their marriages were either extremely happy or very happy compared to the other responses were more likely to report that their husbands shared the housework.[31]

Role Strain and Blue-Collar Jobs

If having a husband who shares the housework increases a woman's marital satisfaction, it doesn't reduce the conflict she is likely to feel about work and family life.[32] Having a husband who shared more of the housework could not reduce the conflict women felt between working and caring for their homes and families.[33] Yet women who were more satisfied with the wages they earned reported that they felt significantly less tension coping with the competing demands of jobs and families.[34]

These findings suggest that, within limits, it is not only how hard women have to work but how they feel about working hard that influences the perceived level of "overload." Indeed, the same phenomenon seems to occur among women who are employed in higher-status jobs, such as among women who work as professionals, administrators, or in managerial positions.[35] Apparently, women who are more satisfied with their work lives are better able to cope with the heavy demands of the "dual role." Baruch, Barnet, and Rivers found that for women with families, "role strain" was least severe for those who were employed in high-status jobs. Among blue-collar women "role strain" is least severe among those who feel they are getting paid decently enough for the hard work they do.

Surely, working in a factory cannot provide the same "intrinsic" rewards as professional jobs. Yet, within the class context of their social aspirations, blue-collar women who feel they have "good" jobs are probably more willing to accept the increased efforts they need to make in order to help their families get ahead. The benefits of "good" jobs, those regarded as jobs which pay well, justify the additional efforts these women make at home. At the same time, blue-collar women who are earning poorly feel they are on a treadmill; they work hard without being able to see the fruits of their labor.

Older Women

As blue-collar women grow older and children grow up, there are major shifts in the balance of work and family life. Even as financial responsibilities for children diminish and mortgages get paid off, the women continue to be providers. The pressures and benefits of blue-collar jobs continue to influence the way older couples manage financially and the way they negotiate the later years of their lives together.

One of the most profound changes that aging brings is having one's children grow up and leave home. As other studies have shown, the transition from a family to a couple creates the possibility for women to forge a new intimacy with their husbands. The older women in our study were no exception. American-born women over forty-five years old reported higher levels of marital satisfaction than their younger counterparts. Among older women, 66 percent reported being extremely happy or very happy with their marriages, compared to 53 percent of the younger women and 42 percent of the Portuguese women. Indeed, among older, American-born women, those with no children living at home reported being even happier with their marriages than women who did have children at home.[36] Evidently, husbands and wives found the space to draw closer together as their sons and daughters became adults. Many times women said that working was easier now that their children were grown. Mary Florence told us, "When you have your children all grown up it isn't that bad working."

Connie Cabrallo, who is fifty-one years old and has two grown children still living at home, echoes the same sentiments. When she was young she worked largely because her family needed the money. "We had just bought this house. As I got a little older there was no one [to take care of]. . . . You know, Barbara goes to high school and George [her son] just started working. There is no real reason to stay home. So I work now because I want to work."

Grown or departing children can reduce the conflict between work and family life, but they can also generate a sense of loss. Yet the "empty nests" of older, blue-collar women may be filled by their work or the "girls in the shop" who in some ways become a surrogate family. Older women who have long years of tenure in a single firm develop strong attachments to the women they have worked with for so many years.

As we have seen, for older women opportunities to socialize are important contributions to their work satisfaction. There is a rich female work culture which tends to develop in workplaces where women have spent years working together. A business agent for one of the unions we worked with eloquently described the importance of this culture in the following way. She said, "How many girls have said to me, you know, I don't have to do this for a living. There are girls who have been friends eighteen, twenty years. They've spent their lives in the shop. They talk about their kids from the day they saw their fanny to the day they got married. And they cry together and they laugh together and they are happy together."

The culture contributes to the women's sense of identity as workers, to their feelings of having a "trade." Perhaps even more importantly, in sharing their joys and sorrows, blue-collar women affirm to one another the value of the factory woman's struggle to provide for their families.

Ironically, it was when women talked about their children that they provided us with insight into the way work had given meaning to their lives. These women saw their factory jobs as a means to being providers. Working long hours and taking care of their families, which had been a source of enormous stress and tension in earlier years, had now become a source of pride. The women spoke about how difficult their lives had been when their children were young. But many saw their efforts justified in the successes of their children. The lives of their children and grandchildren became a tribute to their years of hard work.

Mary Bart, who has been a factory worker for more than thirty years, has five grown daughters. When her girls were little, she worked the graveyard shift (11:00 P.M. until 6:30 A.M.) in order to be home during the day. She remembers, "I used to make sure they were bathed and fed. I used to take and do twenty-five dresses a week. I would wash and starch and iron so the girls would each have five dresses. I used to make sure my kids were washed and clean and their hair combed. I'd be home [from work] at ten minutes to seven. Then I would get the girls off to school. . . . Each had her own. Like when Sharon graduated [from high school]. I never made Barbara wear her dress. I felt that the day—that is your first and only day— and everything should be yours. I worked hard to make sure they had." Today, Mary's five daughters are all married with families of their own. One daughter is a nurse, another has her own hairdressing business, and the others are comfortably married. They are raising their children and have chosen not to work. With pride, she reminded our interviewer, "I have ten grandsons and five granddaughters."

But if older women get psychic income from their factory jobs, the main reason they need to continue working is financial. We asked the oldest cohort in our sample, women fifty-five years of age and older, ($n = 43$) if they wanted to quit working now, presumably before they became eligible for Social Security or pensions. Only 16 percent said they wanted to stop working. Another 36 percent said they wanted to continue working because they liked their jobs. Yet, almost half, (48 percent) said they could not afford to retire.

Though most no longer have to provide for children, they must continue to provide for themselves—and for their husbands. The men they are married to earn substantially less than the husbands of their younger counterparts, a function of the men's declining wages, disability, and retirement. While the husbands of younger women earned almost $15,000 a year, the average yearly earnings of the husbands of older women were substantially less—only $8,884. While 44 percent of the younger women had husbands who earned $15,000 a year or more, only 22 percent of the husbands of the older women earned as much. As a result, older women, even with their own generally lower earnings, brought home on average fully half (51 percent) of the couple's total annual income. Ultimately then, most older women who work in blue-collar jobs must continue to play the provider role. Even though their children have grown up, even though most older blue-collar women are willing to accept lower wages with a relative degree of equanimity, they cannot afford to be without their jobs.

Mary Florence is one of these women. She is fifty-eight years old; she and her husband now fully own the house they bought thirty years ago. They also have some savings. She continues to insist that she only works for extras now that her children have grown up. But her husband has retired early from his job at the post office because of a heart condition. In order to continue to "enjoy life," Mary feels she needs to work—even though she would like to retire and enjoy her grandchildren. As she puts it, "Right now I don't really have to work, but it makes it easier. There are things you want to do to your house and the yard. My husband doesn't get that much from his pension. We could get along. But it makes it easier to have another pay to get the extras."

Moreover, as women age, their husbands not only retire, but many also become ill or disabled. Then a woman's paycheck no longer goes for "extras." Her factory job may become the major source of income for the elderly couple, a source of income a woman cannot afford to relinquish nor one her husband can manage to ignore.

Women who can afford to do so, whose husbands earn enough or who have enough money from other sources, may simply stop working, doing what Mary Florence can only wish for. As we have seen, when women age it gets harder and harder to work. Older, blue-collar women feel that it would be nice to sit back, relax, and be taken care of themselves. As Carol Doherty said, "Sometimes the hardest thing about working is knowing you have to get up every morning and get out."

Though she likes having the "extra" money, Mary Florence feels the same way. She said, "Sometimes you wake up and it was easier to get up when you were younger. You have to get up, catch the bus. Some mornings you don't want to get up."

But if you have to work, a comfortable job and a workplace relatively free of tensions can make the responsibility of providing easier to bear. As Mary Bart put it, "If you have an upsetting day, you come home and take it out on your husband. And if you have a good day you could just work around the clock."

However, for those who remain employed, aging itself appears to improve the overall quality of life for blue-collar women. As noted previously, older women report being happier with their marriages and happier with their work. The physical effort required to work becomes harder, but apparently the pressures decline. At work, older women certainly earn less. Yet, at this stage in the life cycle, many women feel they can afford to earn less. On the home front, grown children and husbands, who continue to help with the contracting amount of housework,[37] reduce the length of the double day to some extent. There is also a considerable reduction in the amount of work-family conflict older women feel as compared to their younger, American-born, blue-collar peers.[38] There is simply less work to do at home.

Yet, if blue-collar women have to work, even in their later years, if the reduced physical strength of aging makes factory work more difficult to do, the women's ability to provide still heavily influences the way they live at home. While blue-collar jobs no longer give women a sense of accomplishment born of earning well for their families, and even though aging reduces the extent to which they can find satisfaction from hard work, better jobs can still make their lives easier. Unlike their younger counterparts, older women who earn higher wages report that their husbands do more housework than older women who earn lower wages.[39]

The Portuguese

Good jobs have the power to transform the quality of life for blue-collar women. Yet the patriarchal and authoritarian culture of Portuguese family life has the potential to neutralize some of the benefits even good jobs can have. As we will see, for these immigrant women, the burdens of oppressive work are intensified by the pressures imposed on the women by their families. Indeed, in many ways the immigrant women come closest to the scenario described by those who advocate the family wage. These are the women who would rather stay home and be supported by their husbands. Only 24 percent of American-born women agreed that "men should get most of the higher paying jobs because they have families to support"; 74 percent of the immigrant women said as much. Only 39 percent of the American women agreed strongly that "it was better all around if a woman can stay home and take care of her family instead of having to work"; a full 79 percent of immigrant women agreed.

But why, one might ask, is the life of a factory worker so much harder for Portuguese women than it is for women who are born here? The stresses these women experience and the pressure they get from their families to earn well are not the results of a greater impoverishment experienced by Portuguese families. Immigrant families did have slightly lower incomes than their American-born counterparts, just as we had expected. But the differences between the Portuguese families and the families of American women were not so large that the lack of material resources could account for the differences we found in the women's attitudes.

The Portuguese women earned lower incomes than the women born here, as was the case with immigrant husbands in comparison with the husbands of American-born, blue-collar women. Portuguese men earned an average yearly income of $12,701 while the husbands of American women earned about $2,000 more—$14,692. However, the average yearly income for the Portuguese families was $25,593 and the average yearly income for the American-born families was $27,122—a gap which is not very large. Moreover, the earnings contribution of Portuguese women to the family purse were not negligible, representing an average of 40 percent of the total family income, compared to 45 percent for the younger, American-born women.[40] Moreover, the immigrant women we interviewed were just as likely to own their own homes (young, American-born—59 percent; Portuguese—65 percent) and just as likely as American families to report having savings (young, American-born—77 percent; Portuguese—70 percent).

It is certainly true that Portuguese women have some of the worst factory jobs, a fact which contributes to the stress they experience. But as we will see, the origins of women's work motives are not to be found exclusively in their jobs. What is the source of the added burdens which afflict these immigrant women? To what extent are they to be found in work and to what extent do they emanate from the Portuguese immigrant culture and the women's family life?

To explore the interplay between work and family life among immigrant women it is crucial to understand the patriarchal nature of their families. While others have documented the strong element of "machismo" in the men's attitudes,[41] this alone cannot explain the dilemmas their wives face. It is necessary to understand the larger cultural context in which the men's attitudes are formed—attitudes which are then integrated into the cultural goals of the Portuguese peasant families that have emigrated to America.

What became clear in our analysis was not only that Portuguese men expect to dominate women or that they are more "macho" than the men who were born and raised in this country. What is important is that the masculine authority they claim is not legitimated primarily by their ability to support a family, but by custom and religion. The deference and obedience owed to a Portuguese husband and father is sanctioned by tradition and the Portuguese Catholic church, not by virtue of his role as primary breadwinner.

While wives born in the United States claimed their husbands were happier about their employment when the men earned less, Portuguese women did not report the same pattern. Among the younger, American-born women, 41 percent of the wives of husbands with high earnings said their spouses disliked their wives working as compared with 16 percent of the husbands with low earnings. Among the Portuguese women, 38 percent of the wives of high-earners said their spouses disliked their working as compared with 47 percent of the wives of low-earners. Among the Portuguese then, there was no relationship between a husband's income and his wife's beliefs about her husband's desire to have her at home.

The good father and husband in the Portuguese family, however, is hardly a man who sits back and allows himself to be supported by his wife and children. He is a man who works hard for his family. As a factory worker or fisherman, he puts in long hours on the job. On weekends or on evenings when the weather is good, you will find him painting or repairing his house, or perhaps tending to a lush and elaborate garden. But if he works hard himself, it is also his business to assure that the rest of his family—at least those who are able to—do so as well. It is his duty to ensure that his wife and children work for the welfare of the family. His authority is used to that end.

Improving the family's welfare resides in the acquisition of property. Moniz, in her study of the Portuguese community, describes the pattern in the following way.

"The desire to save for a home is paramount. The quest for home ownership is probably attributable to the status linkage with land acquired through a long history of feudal relationships. The oft mentioned desire for one's own car and TV is merely an artificial result of an industrialized and technological age. Although achievement has replaced property in an era of egalitarian society, the Portuguese still seek status through the older vehicle—the land which was longed for in the age of traditional authority.[42]

Owning a house in a working-class neighborhood of a mill town or small industrial city is certainly not the same thing as being a landowner in a semifeudal society. Yet as Moniz argues, it can serve the same function and fulfill many of the same needs. As we have already seen, an impressive number, 65 percent, of the immigrant women we spoke with said they owned their homes. The initial down payments on these modest houses, and the continued ability to pay the mortgages, depend on the efforts of husbands and wives who both work in factory jobs.[43]

However, by working in factories, Portuguese women, wives and mothers, are contributing to the fulfillment of the peasant families' dream. Yet the transition from agricultural work to factory work is particularly difficult for women. Much has been written about the experience of "first generation immigrants" in industrial society. Historians have shown that becoming a factory worker means not only leaving the land, but learning to "sell" one's time.[44] Industrial time is regulated not by the natural rhythms of the day, but by the clock. Time at work is time which is not one's own. The time one owns begins when the workday is over.

As the wives and daughters of tenant farmers, Portuguese women certainly know what it means to work hard. Most have grown up working and seeing their mothers work. Few have the idea that getting married and having children means becoming a "housewife," staying home, and bringing up their children while husbands support the family. Yet coming to America changes the way these women must make their contributions to the family. As Luisa Pires put it, "In America, women have to work in a shop."

For women this means that work doesn't end when the factory whistle blows at the end of the day—it simply begins anew at home. Indeed, even the Portuguese men we talked with in the course of our research, community leaders and union officials, were likely to say that work is especially hard in America for women.

But why, we must ask, is it especially hard for Portuguese women to work in factories? After all, blue-collar women who were born and raised in America also suffer from the double day. They, too, must cope with the fact that work is divided into separate spheres. In part, the greater tensions of Portuguese women lie in their harder jobs and lower wages. But most importantly, immigrant women are more stressed, not only because they are doing a double day of work, but because they get less support at home. They get less support at home because the old values prevent the women from developing effective strategies for coping with the double day.

It is certainly true that American and Portuguese women both work to earn money for their families. But the way they understand their responsibilities is quite different. By working at factory jobs and doing all the housework, Portuguese women are doing no more than fulfilling their obligations as dutiful wives and mothers. On the other hand, American-born women do not think of their employment as an enjoined responsibility. As I have pointed out, they define their paid jobs as a way to "help out" husbands, who, for one reason or another, can't earn enough to support the family at an appropriate standard of living. While women work because they "have to," a paid job is not something their husbands are likely to require by force of their authority. In fact, as we will remember, husbands who earn well tend to object more strenuously to their wives' employment. In this context, a woman's paid work, though limited by what the labor market offers, is to some extent, a woman's choice, a choice occasionally made in opposition to her husband's sense of manliness and sometimes against his deepest wishes.

Further, when American women work hard at their factory jobs, the effort is often experienced as a response to an opportunity. By earning a large portion of the family income they can help their families "get ahead." Good wages are an incentive to a woman's efforts, allowing her a sense of accomplishment on the job. However, fewer Portuguese women have the same incentives, since the work they do does not pay as well as comparable work done by their American peers. Portuguese women then, more frequently face the dilemma of feeling obligated to work hard for lower wages—a situation which produces less satisfaction and more tension.

Even in the face of low wages, the strong cultural prescription Portuguese women feel to defer to the family by making a financial contribution reinforces the pressure they feel to work so hard. It probably accounts for their extraordinary efforts on the shop floor. Indeed, the data show that it also accounts for some of the tensions immigrant women feel about coping with the pressures of paid and unpaid work. Portuguese women report a much higher level of work-family tensions than comparable women born in America.[45] To be certain, some of this difference might be explained by the fact that American women had better jobs. But even when we control for wages, by comparing the low-wage Portuguese and American-born women (those earning less than $4.25 an hour), the work-family conflicts among Portuguese women factory workers were still significantly higher than those reported by the younger women who were born in this country.[46] As we have seen, greater satisfaction with ones' wages tends to reduce work-family conflicts for American women. Greater wage satisfaction also seems to have the same effect on Portuguese immigrant women.[47]

Immigrant women feel such intense pressure because, despite the high value men place on their earnings, wives get very little help at home. According to the data, Portuguese men do substantially less around the house, particularly with respect to the "inside" chores like cooking, cleaning, laundry, dishes, and food shopping, than the husbands of American women. While others report that Portuguese men take care of their children in order to make it possible for wives to work, their wives say they do substantially less than the husbands of women born in America.[48]

The failure of Portuguese men to help wives with housework can be understood in the way men and women understand their obligations. American women expect their husbands to be breadwinners. A man's inability to earn enough to fully support his family then, requires that he get "help" from his wife. However, as we have seen, this engenders a need for some reciprocity on his part, to help her with her job at home. Portuguese couples do not have the same expectations of one another. Masculine authority is not defined by the ability to support one's family alone and men are not reluctant to have their wives work. When a woman works thirty-five or forty hours a week in a factory job, she is merely seen as fulfilling her obligations as a wife and mother rather than helping her husband. When she also shops, cooks, cleans, does the laundry, and takes care of the children by herself, again she is just doing her job. Concomitantly, there is little obligation on her husband's part to reciprocate or to help his wife do her job.

In making the adjustment to the separation of work and family required by industrial life, Portuguese women simply have more work to do. Yet despite the fact that some men recognize their wives face a "double burden," despite the fact that some agree that "life is hard for women in America," many immigrant husbands have a hard time transforming their attitudes or behavior. When we asked the women in our study what their husbands disliked most about their working, 51 percent of American women said their full-time jobs put strains on the quality of marital relations, 23 percent said it interfered with family work. Women said their husbands felt there wasn't enough time to spend together or that women were often tired or cranky and this interfered with the quality of intimacy. Forty-one percent of Portuguese women, however, said their husbands felt a wife's job reduced the amount of domestic work she could accomplish. Only 26 percent said their husbands felt their work interfered with family relations.

However, if the earnings of wives and mothers in Portuguese families are valued so greatly, if women are strongly encouraged to contribute to the family's finances, Portuguese husbands may subtly reward their wives for earning well. Portuguese wives reported they were happier with their marriages when they were more satisfied with the wages they earned.[49] Yet, if affirmation comes with earning well, there may be serious consequences at home for earning poorly.

A union official told us the following story about a woman who had been temporarily laid off from her job in a garment shop, an event which is fairly typical in the apparel industry. The union business agent vividly remembered a distraught Portuguese woman who showed up one afternoon at the union hall.

> I thought she was going to have a stroke. I couldn't understand a word she was saying so I got [a fellow business agent] to translate for me. The whole thing was she was being sent home. She was saying, "How am I going to go home and tell my husband I am not working this afternoon? He'll kill me." I

said to Pete, "What can we do for her?" He said, "I can't do anything for her. Everybody goes home at one point when there is no work." We tried to calm her down. When she left here she wasn't crying, but I don't know what happened to her when she got home.

This story is not offered to suggest that layoffs typically generate such strong reactions. Men and women eventually learn that bouts of unemployment are an inevitable part of working in the garment industry. Nonetheless, it does provide us with a glimpse of the way in which Portuguese couples see the rights and obligations of men and women.

The Value of Earning Well

My initial purpose in writing this chapter was to explore the way blue-collar jobs affect the family lives of the women who do them. My goal was descriptive as well as analytical, to offer some images of the life experience of women who work in New England's mill towns and pass their days going back and forth between home and factory. Yet, the cultural and life cycle differences I unearthed went beyond the purely descriptive. Comparisons among the three groups illuminated several important theoretical issues which have informed discussions about women's work and women's family lives.

First, in comparing the needs of older and younger women it became clear that if women at different points in the life cycle have different requirements of their work, factory jobs remain important for women throughout their lives. Older women need to continue bringing home a paycheck to counteract the effect of their husbands' declining earnings. But what is perhaps most interesting is the fact that both work and marriage become more rewarding as women age and their children grow up. Life apparently gets better for blue-collar women as they age, even in the face of diminished earnings and work which is stressful and physically taxing.

What is perhaps most illuminating, however, is the way in which comparing the work and family lives of American and Portuguese women sheds light on the importance of well-paid jobs for the autonomy, if not the leisure, of working-class women. Most importantly, it shows how much male authority or "patriarchy" in American working-class families is dependent on the husband's role as breadwinner. The findings suggest that if male authoritarianism in American working-class families is to continue, it may depend on the continued allocation of well-paid jobs to men and their denial to women. A woman's opportunity to hold a job outside the family in itself may do nothing to change traditional family relations. However, women who have the chance to contribute a more equal proportion of resources to the family have the opportunity to develop more egalitarian relationships at home.

There is no doubt that the combination of full-time jobs piled on domestic work is enormously demanding and creates a real strain on the women's time and energy. *If they had the choice,* many of the women we spoke to, especially the Portuguese, would opt for their men to earn more money so they would not have to work so hard. Some women would not work at all and would use their time to be with children or do things they enjoy. Other women, without needing to worry so much about money, might find easier, interesting jobs. Women with small children might work part time, while older women would stay home and enjoy their grandchildren.

But the women who work in factories don't have a choice; they have to work to earn the money they and their families need. Yet, even without the choice, their jobs still offer some important trade-offs. Many women, particularly American women, feel a sense of accomplishment and pride in their improved standard of living. Some appreciate the greater autonomy and equality at home. But most women know these are purchased at the cost of hard work. Ultimately, the trade-offs are not made intentionally; women don't choose to work in factories because they expect to gain power at home. Nevertheless, the demands of these jobs inadvertently shape the quality of their marriages and the dimensions of domestic life.

The chance to work in a unionized factory job is hardly a rapidly expanding option these days. Nor is the prospect of spending one's days on an assembly line an opportunity that most women would relish. Yet for many of those who have spent their lives at benches doing factory work, the opportunity to contribute to the prosperity of their families has represented a worthwhile choice. As we will see in the next chapter, the demise of this work, the loss of these jobs, is hardly an event that fills the hearts of New England's blue-collar women with pleasure at the benefits of progress.

7   Layoffs and the Women's Labor Market

E ARLY ONE MONDAY MORNING IN early March, Laura Lafleche drove into the parking lot behind Cutogs, the garment shop where she worked as a stitcher, making children's clothing. As
she parked her car she noticed a small group of women she worked with
crowding around the door. Why, she wondered, were they standing there in
the cold instead of going upstairs to work? Laura locked her car, hurried to
join the group, and soon found out why they were standing there. The door
of Cutogs was locked and bolted. Stuck to it with masking tape was a
handwritten note saying only, "Closed until further notice" and signed by
the owner.

What could this mean? How long was "further notice"—a few weeks,
a few months, indefinitely? Laura Lafleche had left the shop on Friday,
tired, glad to be going home for the weekend. She returned now, on Monday morning, relaxed and in good spirits from her niece's wedding on Saturday night, only to find herself, and apparently all her co-workers, without a
job. Laura joined her friends who were huddled around the steel door, sharing with them the pain of shock and disbelief.

Everyone knew, of course, that work had been slow in the past weeks.
The women had seen some layoffs, but layoffs were typical in the clothing
industry. This year, of course, the layoffs had been worse and their shop,
like others in the community, had contracted considerably. Other firms had
closed their doors. Increasing imports were hurting the whole industry.
Yet, the workers at Cutogs had never believed, or despite the rumors, had
not wanted to believe, that their shop would close permanently—and certainly not so suddenly, without even a warning.

After exchanging phone numbers so as to remain in touch about this
crisis, the women, wearying of the cold and the approaching downpour,
slowly drifted back to their cars. Millie Barnes, the union chairperson at
Cutogs, was delegated to call the main office to find out what had happened
and relay the information. How long would the layoff continue? Was the

shop closed permanently? Many of the women had left things in their lockers they hoped to reclaim. But Cutogs never reopened its doors again.

On that fateful March morning, Laura Lafleche, along with the other women who worked with her, joined the ranks of the approximately five million workers that the federal government estimated were "displaced" between 1979 and 1983. As I have already pointed out, in January 1984 the Bureau of Labor Statistics defined a displaced worker as one who has lost a job "because of the closing down or moving of a plant or company, slack work, or the abolishment of a position or shift."[1]

The survey reported more than a third of the displaced workers, a full 35 percent, were women. Not all of these women were factory workers, but a third of all workers displaced from manufacturing jobs (33 percent) were laid off from jobs in nondurable goods industries where women are heavily represented. As I have already pointed out, job displacement is not simply a problem that affects male workers. Indeed, the following chapters will look at the experience of New England's blue-collar women as they lose their jobs and begin to confront a variety of increasingly difficult choices.

In preceding chapters I have tried to show how valuable factory jobs are to New England's unionized, blue-collar women. But as we will see, the potential loss of these jobs is a major part of these women's work experience. In this chapter I will explore the dimensions of the job loss experience in the context of the women's work lives. How do married women respond to the events that catapult them into the ranks of the unemployed? How much can they rely on husbands to provide a cushion against the exigencies of being without paid work? How does a husband's earnings buffer their options in an inhospitable labor market? Can they get new jobs and what kinds of jobs do they get? How do women's family situations and their stages in the life cycle generate the strategies they develop to cope with the employment choices they face? Finally, how do the options and limits in the work lives of blue-collar women compare with those of displaced men?

The Scenario of Women's Job Displacement

When one thinks of job displacement, a prototypical plant closing scenario comes to mind. The president of a well-known national or multinational corporation makes a public announcement of hundreds, perhaps thousands, of layoffs. The event may become a national story as major TV networks broadcast it on the six o'clock news and reporters from *The New York Times* and *The Wall Street Journal* write stories which reappear on the front pages of major city newspapers throughout the country.

The blue-collar women we studied in New England, however, did not lose their jobs in so public a way. Nor did they always become unemployed in the same dramatic fashion as Laura Lafleche and her friends at Cutogs.

Indeed, the events which signaled the loss of their jobs explain, in part, why the plight of blue-collar women has not entered the public consciousness. The women production workers we studied in New England's declining industries lost their jobs by fives and twenty-fives and fifties. They were displaced from countless, publicly undistinguished companies that few people, except those in the local community, have ever heard about. Indeed, sometimes the women didn't even know they were losing their jobs.

The following stories illustrate how varied women's layoff experiences can be. When Carol Ponti, as assembler at Condo Electric, lost her job, she knew about it six months beforehand. The president of her union announced the news at a meeting. The company was planning to shut down the whole cord-set operation and move production to Mexico. Three months later, the phasing-out period began. The layoffs of more than two hundred workers took place on a staggered basis until only a skeleton crew remained to dismantle the machinery and ship it away.

But if Carol Ponti was notified about the plant closing well before she "hit the streets," when Barbara Taylor got the news of her layoff she didn't even realize it would be for good. She was a packer, along with fifty or so other women, in a firm which made baked goods. When her shift, the graveyard shift, from midnight to 7:00 A.M., was eliminated, she was put on "temporary layoff." Her supervisor told her the shift was only being closed for a month or two because business was slow and would probably be reopened for the Christmas season. But when we spoke with her, she had been out of work for seven months. The new year had come and gone. She had been calling the union for a month now to find out when she could expect a recall notice, but the union people could not tell her anything. She was beginning to panic. She said, "At first, it didn't bother me at all. I figured I'd have time to rest. But now I'm worried about money. If I don't go back to work we could lose this house."

Sometimes temporary layoffs are, indeed, temporary. In many industries where women are heavily employed in production work, temporary layoffs occur with regularity. There is a slow season every year, especially in the clothing and garment industries, when women are put on "temporary layoff." Usually they are recalled in a few weeks, perhaps after a month or two. Because most are able to collect unemployment insurance, women are sometimes glad to have what they feel is a needed vacation. But in an era of industrial decline, "temporary layoffs" like Barbara Taylor's often become permanent.

However, if temporary layoffs can become permanent ones, it is also possible for permanent layoffs to become temporary. Plants close and reopen, recalling some, if not all, of the original workers. Penny Follett worked as a stitcher in a shop which made men's sportswear. The firm, which initially closed about six months before Cutogs, opened again only six weeks later, "under new management." As one of the women who was laid off described it, "He closed his books and he opened up as a new shop. Even though it's the same name."

When the shop closed there was the same shock and panic as there was at Cutogs. There were rumors about whether the shop would reopen. Tara Medeiros, the union chairperson for the shop, described the scene as, "Panic! It was like the end of the world. My phone never stopped ringing all day. At all hours people would call and ask, 'Have I got my job?' I'd be down at the plant trying to find out if the place was going to open. And then, after I found out that we were really going to open again I called everybody and asked them who wanted to come back to work."

The women were called back a few at a time. While we don't know how many of the original three hundred workers returned to their jobs, Tara believed she contacted everyone. However, even if everyone who wanted to got her job back, the women had no way of knowing how long they would continue to be employed in the future. Six months, a year, or two years later, the shop might close for good.

The women's stories also reveal the chronic job instability they face. Their employment situation is chaotic and precarious. There were certainly many women we interviewed who had stable jobs and worked in the same plant for long periods of time. A few of the older women had worked in one firm for twenty or thirty years. But others had succeeded in staying employed only by going from a job in one closing firm to a comparable job in another company. Indeed, at every age group, the women in our sample had experienced an average of between three and four layoffs during the past ten years. Some of these had been temporary but just as often women had lost their jobs "for good." Moreover, this was true not only for the job losers in our sample but also for the women in our control group who remained employed.[2]

The women who have managed to stay in production work, then, are survivors. Yet, even for those who are lucky enough to have jobs in relatively stable firms, or have managed to find new jobs when they were laid off, most have lived with a good deal of job insecurity. Job displacement for New England's blue-collar women is not a once in a lifetime event but a perpetual threat. Moreover, as these stories suggest, one never knows if the layoff that has just been announced is a "temporary" or a "permanent" thing. You may get your job back again, but then again you may not.

Ultimately, the outcome of a layoff is only as good as the toss of a coin. Among the women job losers we interviewed, we found that only 51 percent of the women who told us their layoffs were "temporary" were recalled to their jobs after six months.[3] At the same time only 46 percent of the victims of plant, shift, or department "closings" had been recalled at the time of our interviews, and we had no way of knowing how long the recall would stay in effect. Only 68 percent of the "temporary" job losers said they had expected to be recalled when they were laid off. (An expression of their pessimism?) But 69 percent of the plant closing victims also said as much. Ultimately, the women's initial expectations were totally unrelated to whether they eventually got their jobs back.

Women's Responses to Job Loss—Anger, Betrayal, Powerlessness

Although workers rarely got much notification, it is very unusual for layoffs to occur as a complete surprise. Well before that awful March day when the workers arrived at Cutogs only to find the shop had closed, there had been ominous signs of the impending disaster. As Laura told us, "Well, there were a lot of rumors that it was going to close. You know how rumors start. And then when he did close, we figured that he was just going to close because the work was slow—our orders were slow. . . . But we assumed we would be called back and we never were."

What was so appalling to Laura and her co-workers was not only the layoff but the way her boss had handled it. He had never told them he was closing for good. The women found out that Cutogs would not reopen only when they went to collect their unemployment insurance. "About four weeks later we went to the job center and he said, 'They are not going to call you back. He is closing for good.'"

One of the most painful things the workers felt about the layoffs was the bosses' failure to be honest with them; the women felt betrayed. Many of the women felt they had not been treated with the respect, which they felt they deserved as loyal workers. Marcia Penvert, a good friend of Laura's, expressed this sense of betrayal eloquently. She said, "He didn't even talk to us about it. He could at least have the decency to tell us he was closing. I wouldn't work for him now if I had to. That's what I think is wrong. That an employer can do that to us."

Unlike the owner of Cutogs, most employers do give their workers some notification of a layoff or tell them when the plant is going to close. Yet, it is typical for management to give employees as little notice as possible.[4] Among the laid-off women we interviewed, 75 percent reported that they were told of the impending layoff less than a week before they "hit the street."

If the women at Cutogs were angered by the failure of their employers to be honest, the women at Condo Electric felt the same sense of betrayal, even though they knew they would lose their jobs well in advance. The women felt that the company had violated an important trust that existed between workers and management, a trust which, in part, had made their jobs valuable.

After her layoff Carol Ponti realized that her company (a cord-set factory) had been making plans to move for years but had been denying it to the workers all along. With great precision, she described their long-term failure to reinvest in more productive machinery. She told our interviewer, "At the end, the last seven years before they moved, the handwriting was more or less on the wall. I went to one of the unit managers and I asked him, 'Why aren't you fixing those machines? Why aren't we putting money into them?' That's where the loss was. It wasn't in the high wages that they tell everybody. They knew exactly what they were doing." Later she added, "We had a Tampa-Guard machine come in that puts safety caps on the connectors. That machine sat downstairs in the department in the way for a full year and it was never used. . . . But yet, they'll tell the public that our wages put us out."[5]

The sense of anger and betrayal so many of the women expressed when they knew they had lost their jobs was part of a deep sense of powerlessness many felt, a new inability to control some fundamental aspects of their lives. By working in factory jobs these women had made their greatest efforts to enhance their own lives and the lives of their families. Somehow, these efforts had nevertheless come to nought.

In the course of our interviews we asked the women to put into words the feelings they experienced when they realized they were out of work. Some of the words they used in answering our question communicated that sense of powerlessness and despair. The women felt defeated. They said they were "heartbroken," "stunned," "dazed," "depressed," and "disgusted." As Penny Follett put it, "All these years and I've lost everything."

Sylvia DeNiso, who worked with Carol Ponti, said the layoff was "A sure loss. Part of your life seems to come to an end . . . you worked there for so long. Sometimes life seems to be going backwards."

Eliza Mather put it this way, "I was disgusted. I was so many years in one place and I knew I would have to start over. In fifteen years I never missed a day of work. I even went in when I was sick. Now I have lost everything."

Married Women's Ambivalence

There is uncertainty, anger and feelings of betrayal in the experience of losing a job. But in the aftermath women must face the more pragmatic concerns and worries that come from finding themselves without work. What do they worry about? How do they respond to the prospect of waking up each weekday morning and knowing they are not going to work, that on Friday afternoons, at least for a while, there will be no paycheck coming in to help make the house payments or to put a roast on the table for Sunday dinner?

To begin to answer this question, we asked the women in our study to describe in detail, the feelings they had when they knew they had lost their jobs and found themselves out of work. In response to this open-ended question, the women mentioned a wide variety of issues which colored their responses to unemployment. We expected the vast majority of women to tell us how unhappy they were. But, if the women worried about money, if they were concerned about reemployment, there were also some pluses associated with not having a job—at least in the short run.

The multiplicity of answers the women gave us could not easily be categorized. In order to systematically treat their responses, the answers they gave were coded as either positive, negative, or ambivalent. The American-born women were evenly split between positive and negative responses (36 percent to 38 percent among younger women [$n = 44$] and 35 percent to 36 percent among older women [$n = 58$]). As one might expect, given their attitudes about work, the Portuguese women were most unhappy about their layoffs (56 percent unhappy to 26 percent happy [$n = 40$]). What was most surprising, however, was the extent of ambivalence.[6]

What were some of the things women liked about the layoff? The greatest pleasure was having time—time for oneself and some freedom from the constant rush of the double day of work. It meant being able to have some time to oneself, to spend more time with children, to catch up on undone housework, or work in one's garden. More than three-quarters of the women in all groups agreed with the statements, "After I was laid off, I was happy to have more time to take care of my home"[7] and, "After I was laid off, I was pleased to have more time for myself."[8] But at the same time the women worried about lost earnings. Sixty-four percent of the younger women, 45 percent of the older women and 70 percent of the Portuguese women agreed with the statement, "After I was laid off, I was very worried about how my family and I would pay the bills."

To Sally Deniro, a laid-off garment worker, the layoff meant she could be home with her children while they were out of school during summer vacation. She described her feelings about the layoff in the following way. "It didn't make any difference to me because I was collecting enough [unemployment insurance] and I was home with my kids."

Tina Bologna has children who are grown and living away from home. But she was also happy to have the time off to catch up on things she wanted to do around her house. She said, "I cleaned and wallpapered. I worked in my yard and took it easy."

But underlying the sense of relief at a respite that is welcome, and acceptable precisely because it is out of one's control, there is always an underlying fear and tension about the family's lost income. Despite the fact that all the women had husbands and almost all collected unemployment insurance, lost earnings were the major source of the women's anxiety. As

Mary Lewiston, a breadpacker who was laid off when management closed her shift, described her feelings about the layoff, "Personally, it couldn't have happened at a better time. I was drained from work. I needed the rest, but I still worried about the money."

The ambivalence these married women feel about being laid off is an inevitable response to their real situation. Married women, as we have seen, do not see themselves as the primary breadwinners in their families. As we have seen, most felt that, ultimately, it was a husband's obligation to "support the family." Unlike unemployed men, these unemployed women feel comfortable in accepting their spouse's support as a "cushion" against the vagaries of an uncertain labor market. As Ferree has pointed out, their domestic roles are perceived as a partial escape from the exploitation of paid work. At the same time, blue-collar women know their families need the money they earn.

Blue-Collar Women—Married and Single

Conventional wisdom suggests that married women are financially protected from the impact of unemployment while female heads of households are most vulnerable to it.[9] Indeed, there were sizable differences in the family resources of displaced married women in our sample and job losers who were female heads of households. The average family income of women who lived alone or lived alone with their children was only $8,971 or about 45 percent of the average family incomes of married women with families. Single women had family incomes which varied between $5,000 and $13,000.[10] One would think that these single women, widows, and mothers supporting their children, would be much more emotionally devastated by the loss of their factory jobs than women with husbands.[11]

As is to be expected, married and single women responded to the layoffs in different ways. As a group, female heads of households were significantly more worried about their continuing ability to pay their bills than were married women.[12] Single women, however, were significantly less likely to say they were happy to have time to take care of their homes and be with their families.[13] Inevitably perhaps, without husbands, women do not see family work as an alternative to paid work. However, their different worries and concerns did not have much of an impact on their job search behavior. Female heads of households were no more likely than married women job losers to say they looked for work than were married women.[14]

Further analysis of our data suggests that what stage blue-collar women are in in the life cycle has more to do with the way they respond to layoffs than whether they were married or single. When we compared the way single women responded to job loss with the way the other three groups of married women did, we found important differences in the way each of the

four groups felt about (1) the opportunity to have more time for their families, (2) worries about their capacity to keep paying bills, and (3) their
decision to look for work. Our findings indicate that we need to modify the
way we think about the cushioning effects of husbands' earnings on working-class wives to really understand how blue-collar women think about the
trade-offs between reliance on family resources and paid employment[15] (see
Table 7.1).

Table 7.1 confirms our initial findings that married women, regardless of their age or cultural background, are happier than single women
to have time to stay home and care for their families when they are laid off.
However, when it comes to worrying about their continued ability to pay
the bills after a layoff, younger, married women, whether they are Portuguese or American-born, are no more likely than single women to worry
about money. At the same time, older married women (those born in America) are *less* likely than single women to worry about money.

Table 7.1 shows quite clearly that just because women have husbands
who are likely to bring home another paycheck, they do not necessarily

Table 7.1   *Comparison of Three Groups of Married Women with Single Women:
Response to the Loss of Their Jobs*

	Kendall's Tau	Sig.
*Likes time for home**		
Younger, married women and single women[a]	−.368	.001
Older, married women and single women	−.228	.001
Portuguese, married women and single women	−.242	.007
*Worries about bills**		
Younger, married women and single women	.110	.129
Older, married women and single women	.278	.001
Portuguese, married women and single women	.134	.089
*Looked for work after layoff**		
Younger, married women and single women	.086	.208
Older, married women and single women	−.028	.210
Portuguese, married women and single women	.158	.078

[a]Single women were defined as those who were unmarried. They either lived alone, most often as
widows or divorcees, or they were female heads of households living alone with dependent
children.
*These questions were measured by the women's response to the following statements: (1) After I was
laid off, I was pleased to have more time to take care of my home and family; (2) After I was laid
off I was worried about how I (and my family) would continue to pay my (our) bills. The
responses were measured as follows: (1) agree strongly, (2) agree somewhat, (3) disagree
somewhat, (4) disagree strongly. "Looked for work after layoff" was measured by the women's
response of yes or no to the question, "Did you look for work after you were laid off?"
Younger, married women (*n* = 44)
Older, married women (*n* = 58)
Portuguese, married women (*n* = 40)
Single women (*n* = 48)

worry less than single women about being able to pay their bills when they lose their jobs. The data suggest that financial worries are caused primarily by concerns about meeting the material needs of growing families. While the younger, American-born women and the Portuguese women who lost their jobs are just as worried about losing money as are the single women, older, married women are less worried than single women about the financial aspects of losing their jobs. These women have husbands who bring some money into the family. Since they do not have dependent children, they probably feel they need less money to get by.

Certainly one can argue that the feelings and sensibilities of women who have lost their jobs do not reflect the women's actual needs. Worrying about bills may be common to both married and single women when they are laid off, but without the cushioning effects of a second income it is reasonable to assume that single women without jobs tend to experience a more desperate situation than do their married counterparts. Single women, divorcees or widows, and female heads of households with dependent children are likely to confront a layoff with nothing to live on but unemployment insurance and, hopefully, some savings. Single women then should be more likely to look for jobs than their married counterparts who have another income in the family and who are more likely to enjoy staying home. Yet as we can see from table 7.1, this is not the case. Regardless of whether they are older or younger, American-born, married women are no more and no less likely to look for work than their single counterparts. Portuguese women, perhaps because of the greater pressure put on them by their families to be employed, are marginally more likely than American-born, single women to look for work.

Displaced Women—A Brief Vacation?

In the course of this research I happened to speak with a male union official. I spent some time explaining to him that the research was designed to learn about how women and their families cope with the experience of job displacement and unemployment. He simply smiled and said incredulously, "They take care of the children."

He presumably believed that married women are less vulnerable to the effects of losing their jobs than men who "have families to support." He saw the recent layoffs of fifty women in one of his plants as merely a brief vacation.

Economists and policymakers have often shared this view, arguing that the unemployment of married women in today's two-earner families presents few serious financial problems for the women or their families. They believe that today's unemployment rate is swelled by housewives returning to the labor force or seeking work for "extra money." They point out that much of today's unemployment is of fairly short duration and does not lead to impoverishment. It ought not be viewed today with the same seriousness as it was during the Great Depression when there was long-term unemployment among male breadwinners. Further, unemployed women can be economically productive doing domestic work at home as well as doing paid work. [16]

Martin Feldstein is among those who share this view. He notes that changes in the tax law mean that today's working wives who get unemployment insurance can receive as much as 80 percent of their net family income for twenty-six weeks when they are unemployed. [17] According to Feldstein, since one spouse is still employed, such circumstances provide little incentive for unemployed workers in two-paycheck families to look for work. Because women can rely on a combination of alternative forms of income (earnings and her husband's income), working wives will be marginally more likely to refuse jobs and/or purposely postpone reemployment until their benefits are exhausted. Feldstein sees this as a potential for abuse of the unemployment insurance system. His work led to "reforms" through which unemployment insurance was subsequently taxed.

Other researchers have examined Feldstein's contentions and have disagreed about his conclusions. Some [18] have verified that unemployment insurance increases the duration of unemployment, reporting a fairly strong positive relationship between these two factors. Yet they also find the relationship to be weaker among women workers—single or married. Others [19] suggest that the effect of unemployment insurance in postponing reemployment is minimal.

The absence of strong conclusive findings about this relationship suggests the weak theoretical underpinnings of Feldstein's argument. In fact, a close examination of his assumptions reveals deep gender biases. His approach assumes a model of labor market behavior which seems "rational" for both men and women but does not consider how women make decisions when their unemployment is caused by job displacement in a declining labor market. Feldstein, and even those who criticize his work, fail to understand what displaced blue-collar women want from paid jobs, how they view the options between paid work and family work, or how the constraints of a low wage and a declining women's job market shape their choices.

Economists often assume that men's pattern of labor market behavior is and ought to be the normative pattern. For them unemployment is a problem that can only be resolved by reemployment. But women cannot respond as men do to paid work, in part because the labor market offers them wages which are only about three-fifths of the wages the job market offers men. At the same time the society legitimates women's economic dependence on men in exchange for domestic labor. Feldstein, like other economists, downplays the way incentives in the family and marketplace motivate women's choices. He would condemn any delay unemployed workers make in seeking jobs as illegitimately seeking a paid "vacation" at government expense.

Feldstein is certainly correct in assuming that almost fully replacing the wages of unemployed women will have some effect on the women's job search behavior, inducing them to postpone looking for work, to refuse jobs, or to prolong the duration of their unemployment. Almost all, (96 percent) of the women who lost their jobs received unemployment insurance, but a full 40 percent said they didn't look for work. Of this 40 percent, however, 82 percent were waiting for recall. This means ten of the 142 displaced blue-collar women said they did not look for jobs and did not expect to be recalled, preferring to take some time off before resuming the double day. Among the 142 married women who had lost their jobs, 17 percent refused jobs they were offered and six women, or 4 percent, said they turned down jobs because the wages were too low. Seven women in the job-loser sample exhausted their benefits before going back to work.

But blue-collar women do not always view the world through the eyes of economists. As we have seen, the ambivalence they feel about losing their jobs reflects the fact that displacement and unemployment reduce their earnings but also free them temporarily from the double burden of working full time and taking care of their families. For married blue-collar women, then, unlike men, neither full-time, year-round work nor being without work at all are adequate ways of resolving the tensions of their condition. Instead they utilize whatever options and resources are available to them, family income and unemployment insurance, to optimize their welfare. Taxing unemployment insurance further constrains these options.

Moreover, the women do not see the weekly unemployment checks they receive as handouts but as legitimate solutions to the irresolvable tensions in their lives: the women do not see themselves as "ripping off" the government, but as receiving a justly earned compensation. Unemployment insurance, after all, is financed by a payment made by the very individuals who have benefited from their cheap labor and willingness to work in jobs where layoffs are endemic. The ability to "collect" is seen as a fair exchange for working in jobs which are unstable. At the same time, unstable work is a mixed blessing, allowing the women some respite from the constant pressure of the double day.

Unemployment insurance does indeed shelter the women and their families from their loss of earnings. We calculated the proportion of family income that unemployment insurance "replaced" on a yearly basis in 1980 (the year the women were interviewed)—what Feldstein calls "replacement wages" (see chapter 8). Their families lost approximately 15 percent of the annual income they would have had if the women had worked a full year without being laid off. These blue-collar women replaced even more than the 80 percent Feldstein calculated. Unemployment insurance does cushion the blow of women's lost income quite substantially. That indeed, has been the intention of the program.

Feldstein has also suggested that unemployed workers, especially those who have alternative sources of income, will delay their reemployment in the hopes of finding better, higher-paying jobs. Such a strategy seems like a rational and purposive response to unemployment in a labor market where there is full employment. However, in a labor market where wages are falling and jobs are disappearing, added time spent in a job search may not enhance one's future earnings. Blue-collar women do not delay their reemployment in the hopes of finding better jobs.

When we look at the wage differentials between the jobs the women had lost and the new jobs the women had taken on during the six-month period after they were laid off, it becomes clear that blue-collar women did not enhance their reemployment wages by postponing their reemployment. As we can see from figures 7.1, 7.2, and 7.3, women who went back to work earlier did not gain or lose any more wages than women who went back to work later in the six-month period.[20]

The women generally lost wages, an average of twenty-five cents an hour. Yet, as we can see from the data, there was no wage advantage to be

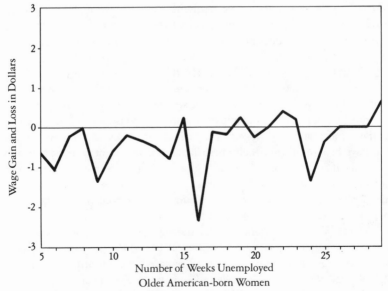

Figure 7.1. Wage Gain and Loss among Job Losers: Between Old Job and New Job

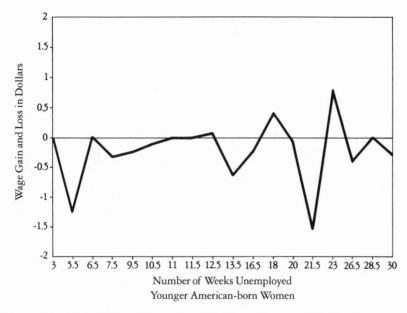

Figure 7.2. Wage Gain and Loss among Job Losers: Between Old Job and New Job

gained by postponing or delaying reemployment—for any of the three groups of women.

What is at issue for most of these displaced blue-collar women is not the immediate months ahead. Most are willing and able to live on unemployment insurance for a few weeks—or even a few months. They are willing to reduce their levels of consumption temporarily in exchange for a respite from the double day. But they hardly see themselves as cheating the system. Moreover, they know that whatever "vacation" they get, they cannot stay home permanently; the women must either get recalled or find work again. They must look beyond "collecting" to the next job.

Many of the women we spoke with said they enjoyed the time they had after they were laid off, time to rest, to catch up on their neglected housework, to be with children. But the length of time they spent between jobs was not something most could control. If most could afford a few weeks without working because they were collecting unemployment insurance, at the same time they were beset by anxiety about when and how they would find new jobs, anxiety which tended to offset any pleasure they got from the involuntary time off. Ultimately there are few "cushions" that save these women from having to go back to work; neither husbands' earnings nor unemployment insurance can provide that. Sooner or later they have to find

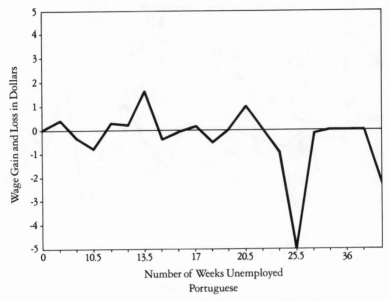

Figure 7.3. Wage Gain and Loss among Job Losers: Between Old Job and
New Job

jobs. Either they must be recalled or start over again somewhere else—as
soon as possible and at whatever wages are available.

Twenty Years Ago and Now

If women factory workers ever had the opportunity to benefit
from layoffs, to take the much vaunted brief vacation, it may have been in
the affluent twenty-year period after World War II. Though there is little
research that explores the lives of displaced factory women during that time,
one study, *The Job Hunt,* done in 1964 by Sheppard and Belitsky,[21] stands
out by making comparisons between displaced men and women. Most importantly, the findings of this research highlight the increasing importance
of paid jobs to married women factory workers today, showing how much
times have changed in the past twenty years or so.

The data collected by Sheppard and Belitsky is not strictly comparable
to the work done in this study. Nevertheless there are enough similarities
between New England and the small industrial towns of Pennsylvania of
two decades ago to make comparisons between the studies worthwhile. Perhaps most importantly, when the research for this book was done, Erie
County was a medium-sized industrial community which had in the pre-

vious ten years or so, like New England today, experienced a decline in its manufacturing base.

Sheppard and Belitsky interviewed 146 women displaced from both white-collar and blue-collar jobs. First of all there were differences in the two studies between the numbers of displaced women who looked for work. Almost 60 percent of the women in the 1980 New England study looked for work compared to only about 40 percent of the Erie County women in 1964. The authors of *The Job Hunt* concluded that the married women who lost jobs simply did not want to go back to work: "About 70 percent of the women not employed at the time they were interviewed gave the reason that they 'preferred to stay at home.' "[22]

But what is most striking are differences between the behavior of married and single women in the Erie County study, differences which do not exist among the contemporary New England women. In the 1964 study, married women were much less likely to be reemployed at new jobs when they were interviewed after their layoff than women who were single and supporting themselves. Women with more dependent children were also less likely to be reemployed.[23] There were no such differences in our 1980 study. Married women were just as likely to find jobs as single women.[24] Women with preschool children were no more likely to remain unemployed than women with older children.[25] Women with dependent children eighteen years old or younger found new jobs as readily as women without dependent children under eighteen.[26] Evidently married blue-collar women today feel they need to work just as much as their single counterparts.

Reemployment

How well do displaced women fare after being laid off? Do many get recalled? If not, do they find new jobs? Are they successful in finding the kind of work they want? Finally, which women are most successful in achieving a satisfactory reemployment outcome?

As we have already seen, blue-collar women would very much like to have their old jobs back, hoping, sometimes against their better judgment, to eventually be recalled. But when hope dies, they look for other full-time, unionized factory jobs, jobs much like the ones they have lost. When we asked them what kinds of jobs they would look for, more than three-quarters of the women (77 percent) said they wanted full-time jobs. A full 77 percent said they wanted factory jobs.

Compared to other recent studies of displaced women factory workers, New England's unemployed women factory workers fared well. According to the national survey of workers displaced from their jobs between 1979 and 1983, done by the Bureau of Labor Statistics, women were less likely than displaced men to have returned to work and more likely than displaced men to have dropped out of the labor force.[27] In a study of a plant closing in western Pennsylvania, Snyder and Nowak found that 60 percent of the displaced women in their sample were unemployed about a year and a half after their layoff.[28] Perrucci et al. found that 74 percent of the women were without work eight months after their RCA plant closed.[29]

The majority of our displaced women workers in New England found work and found it relatively soon. Moreover, most seemed to find just the kind of jobs they looked for. Of the 142 displaced married women we interviewed, 110 or 77 percent of these women had worked again when we interviewed them about six months after they had been laid off. Of those 110 who had worked at all, 87 were still employed.[30] These 87 represented 61 percent of all those who had lost their jobs; so, more than three-fifths of the women who lost jobs were working six months after their layoffs. About half of the 110 women who had worked (58, or 53 percent) had been re-called to their jobs while the other half (52, or 47 percent) had found new jobs.

Moreover, despite their initial fears of not being able to find new production jobs and their anxiety that they might have to settle for non-unionized or part-time jobs, there were relatively few women who found themselves in this situation. Only four women (3 percent) took jobs in the sales and service sector. Just seven women were employed part time, or less than thirty-five hours a week. What is most disturbing is that almost 20 percent or 10 out of the fifty-two women who found new jobs were not working in unionized firms.

These transitions do indeed represent serious losses to the women who had to take sales and service work, part-time and nonunion jobs. Yet the findings hardly present a scenario in which the majority of women were relentlessly and unsuccessfully looking for work, only to face despair and impoverishment at the exhaustion of their unemployment insurance benefits. Indeed, as I have already mentioned, only seven women of the 142 ran out of benefits from unemployment insurance. Most of the women appear to have found new jobs that were quite similar to the ones they lost. This "good news" is largely a function of the historical industrial mix of employment in the region. As mentioned previously, New England has always had, and continues to have, a relatively large number of traditional, female production jobs.

Results like this seem to lend credence to the arguments of those who would downplay the seriousness of job displacement for women workers. But if these findings do not seem to be dramatic indicators of pain and suffering, it is important to take a closer look at who obtained jobs and what kinds of jobs they received before concluding that only minimal damage was done. It is necessary to probe deeper, to look further than simply at the numbers of women who found work. In doing so, we will discover the serious problem of underemployment which New England's blue-collar women confront today.

There were no significant differences between the three groups of married women—younger, older and foreign born—with respect to who was recalled to jobs.[31] Presumably being called back had more to do with whether one's old job became available rather than with the characteristics of the workers. Since the firms we dealt with were, for the most part, unionized, our findings suggest that seniority rules were probably operating. But there were large and significant differences between the three groups in terms of who obtained a *new* job. Among the women who were not recalled, Portuguese women were by far the most successful in finding new jobs (84 percent). Older women were a close second in finding new work (69 percent). But the younger, American-born women were, by far, the *least likely* to get new jobs (31 percent).[32]

Why do those women who appear to be in the most advantageous labor market position (born in America, with youth and education) have the worst time becoming reemployed? Why do those with the worst circumstances—Portuguese women—get new jobs most often? The answer is related to the kinds of jobs that were available, namely, factory jobs which paid significantly lower wages than the ones the women had been forced to leave. Women who were recalled to their former jobs managed to retain their wage levels, a fact which probably accounts for the women's decided preference for being recalled. But women who took new jobs lost wages. Further, women who had higher wages lost more when they went back to work at new jobs[33] (see table 7.2).

The women who had higher wages to begin with suffered the largest decline in their wages. The wage loss among average earners was twenty-five cents an hour, or only a 5 percent drop. But the overall 25-cent drop masks

Table 7.2   *Wage Gain and Loss[a] Results of Multiple Regression Equation*

	B	Beta	F	Significance
Hourly wages[b]	− .4331	−.5612	49.888	***
Recall/new job[c]	−52.4792	−.2943	13.800	***
Apparel workers[d]	29.4965	.1690	1.897	
Electrical workers[e]	16.5354	.0910	0.560	
Constant = 222.80; N = 108; R^2 = .3785; F = 15.6834				

[a]Dependent variable measured in cents.
[b]Wages of pre-layoff job measured in cents.
[c]Recall = 0, new job = 1.
[d]Apparel workers = 1, nonapparel workers = 0.
[e]Electrical workers = 1, nonelectricl workers = 0.
(Outgroup is workers in other industries.)
***$p < .001$

the difference between workers who were called back and those who took new jobs. Workers earning the average wage who were recalled managed to maintain an even wage level; their hourly wages did not increase or decrease. But those at the average wage who had to take new jobs lost an average of fifty-five cents an hour, or about a 12 percent loss. Women who earned one standard deviation ($1.14) above the mean hourly wage of $4.51 lost an average of $1.05 an hour. They suffered a 19 percent drop in wages.

For these blue-collar women, then, getting a new job was hardly an unmixed blessing. It should hardly be seen as a positive outcome. Actually, the women who took new jobs may have been those who felt most desperate. Such women were willing to return to work even if it meant a considerable decline in wages. What this suggests is that in an era of disappearing jobs and declining wages, settling for a low-wage job may be the only way to keep working. The only alternative may be continued unemployment. Indeed, this is the bitter choice confronted by today's blue-collar women.

It is not that the women fail to understand the economic and political dimensions of the economic decline that is occurring. Almost two-thirds (64 percent) said it was difficult to find a good job these days; almost half of this group, or 53 percent, said it was difficult because of industrial decline (the disappearance of jobs) or declining wages. There is deep anger. As Carol Ponti, an electrical worker, put it, "The people are getting hurt and the government is letting them get away with it. I don't think companies should be allowed to go out. I consider us people—the small people—we work, we help keep America going. We depend on the government and our representatives to take care of us while we do our work. But it doesn't work that way."

At the same time, the anger cannot prevent the problem from being experienced as an immediate personal tragedy. Ultimately, each individual woman must find some way to deal with the job situation. Millie Barnes, the union chairperson at Cutogs, described the painful experiences faced by one of her former co-workers when Cutogs closed. She said, "We had one girl who has already gone to five jobs. She couldn't get the money she wanted. She went to about four or five shops and no one would give her $6.50 an hour. I think she's trying to find the same atmosphere and the same money. Every plant she went to she couldn't find either one of those. Right now she's doing nothing." Then she summed up the problem in one sentence. "When you go somewhere else you are going to start at the bottom."

The pattern of wage declines associated with recall or taking new jobs goes a long way toward explaining why these women prefer waiting for recall to searching for new jobs. The hope is to stay in the same firm and retain one's seniority and earnings. These patterns also explain why the women one would expect to have the best labor market opportunities—

younger, more educated women—are most likely to remain without work. Because they earned more they had the most to lose from taking new production jobs. For the short run at least, many of these women remained without work.

Labor Market Opportunities and Life Situations

Another important thing this analysis shows is that it is not possible to understand how "women" as a generic group deal with displacement and unemployment. Women make choices about work and unemployment not only as women, but in the context of differential labor market opportunities and life situations. Younger women, older women, and Portuguese women make different choices about reemployment and continued joblessness—at least in the short run.

We asked the women in our sample why it was difficult to find a good job. About half were concerned about declining wages and disappearing jobs. Thirty-five percent of the older women, however, said they feared age discrimination. But as we have seen, older American-born women did not have more trouble than their younger American counterparts finding new jobs. On the face of it they had more success, but their "success" meant losing wages.

Older women with husbands who are disabled, retired, or looking toward retirement are evidently willing to take lower-paying jobs. They feel their life situation allows them to do this. Such women, however, not only need to continue supporting themselves, sometimes they must also support ailing husbands whose earnings are diminishing with age. It is essential that they work until age sixty-five when they can begin collecting Social Security. For women in the clothing and apparel industry, continued employment, even at lower wages, can still mean holding onto their pensions. These women search for and are often likely to find jobs in shops that are organized by the same union. By doing this, older women often retain their pensions and continue accumulating benefits toward retirement. Penny Follett, an older woman who was called back to the shop that made men's sportswear after it closed and reopened, told us, "If he didn't open up, I would try to get a job in the same union."

Portuguese women also choose to go back to work as soon as possible. Only three out of the forty women who lost their jobs had not found any work when we interviewed them; thirty had found new jobs and were currently reemployed. As we have already seen, the family pressure on Portuguese women to earn is strong. Moreover, because they have typically been employed at low wages to begin with, they don't face the problem of wage loss as intensely as women born in this country. They earned poorly to begin with and therefore haven't as much to lose from taking another low-wage job.[34]

It is the younger, American-born women who appear to face the worst dilemma. As we will remember, these are the women who had high-wage jobs—the women who had benefited most from the wage gains blue-collar women had made in the postwar period. Ironically, this wage advantage, the reason many had decided to work in factories, becomes a disadvantage when they lose their jobs. Many of these once fortunate women face the prospect of taking some of the worst wage cuts. Because many have young children at home and husbands at the peak of their earnings, a majority of these women have decided to stay at home for a time. This "choice," however, is in no way a long-term solution. Ultimately, they will have to find new jobs. Only a small minority of women refused jobs. But it is interesting that this group was twice as likely as the other two groups of women to say they had refused jobs they could have had (26 percent compared to 14 percent of the older women and 13 percent of the Portuguese women).

Like Sylvia Deniso, the woman we met at the beginning of this book, these women, who are at the height of their productivity and who have heavy financial obligations for young children, are finding themselves at a major crossroads in their lives. They worked at factory jobs because they could earn good wages, and few are prepared to accept large wage cuts. Carol Ponti, an electrical worker, whose plant closed and moved to Mexico, said, "The way things are in this state, it will be very hard to find a job. I don't think anyone should take a job for $3.70 an hour unless they desperately need it."

Her friend and former co-worker, Sonia May, said that without unemployment insurance, "We'd be in a lot of trouble. I would have to go to work for $3.00 an hour. I wouldn't have a choice."

For the moment, then, these young women are simply pulling in their belts and living on unemployment insurance. But when their benefits run out the women know they will have to make a career change.

Many would like some help in making a decision about new kinds of employment. We asked the women in our sample if they would like to be retrained for a different kind of work. Among the younger, American-born women, 78 percent of those who remained without work said "yes," compared to only 65 percent of the older women and 50 percent of the Portuguese women. But what kinds of work will they be retrained for? The problems they face are perhaps best highlighted by their responses to the question, "What would be the ideal job for you?" Carol Ponti replied, "To tell you the truth, right now that is something I am trying to figure out for myself. When my unemployment runs out, and perhaps even sooner than that, I would like to find something to do. What that is I don't know. I will take a typing course at night. I did work in a hospital before. I have thought about going back to school. Probably part time. I don't know if I could handle being a full-time student after all these years." Then she adds, "But if I want to go back to school, where would I get the money?"

Her answer speaks for itself.

Men and Women

It has been a standard assumption (one, no doubt, that is difficult to quarrel with) that male breadwinners in high-wage jobs are the primary victims of job displacement. For that reason, until quite recently, researchers have excluded women from studies of job displacement on the assumption that the nature of women's job loss experience was essentially contingent on the men they had to support them. In studies of plant closings, firms which employed women were not chosen for study; or when women were employed, the aftermath of their job loss was not examined.[35] Only recently, as we have begun to recognize women's need for jobs, have researchers begun to explore the effects of job displacement on women and compare them to the effects on men.

To date, these researchers[36] have begun to compare the impacts of job displacement on men and women, looking at things like the duration of unemployment, reemployment outcomes, income losses, and economic distress. Their work also examines the effects of displacement and unemployment on men's and women's family relations, psychological distress, and physical health.

The findings of this research clearly refute the idea that women are impervious to the economic and personal impacts of job displacement and unemployment. On many of the measures of economic and psychological distress, women suffer just as severely, sometimes even more severely, than men. Indeed, those who are heads of households are likely to be hit harder than male breadwinners in intact families.

But before we can understand the way job displacement affects men and women, we need to go beyond simply comparing the sexes on indices of suffering. In order to flesh out the experiences of men and women as they go through the harrowing process of job loss and unemployment, we must first look at the differential effects of displacement on each sex separately. It is important to realize that married women's behavior is not likely to "fit" the patterns which are typical for married men. We need to understand the larger context of men's and women's labor market options and family roles before we can understand the ways in which men and women experience the distress of losing their jobs. The alternative is to wind up comparing the proverbial apples and oranges.

In the following chapter we will take a look at the impact of job loss and unemployment on the economic well-being of the women's families and the women's personal and psychological responses to the alternatives they confront. But first we will look at the differences in men's and women's labor market situations and the impact this has on their job displacement experience.

First of all, and perhaps most importantly, men and women tend to have different jobs. Like most blue-collar women, the women in this study were not employed in traditionally male industries. They work in a secondary labor market, a "woman's labor market." When they were displaced, they went from one "woman's job" to another, a phenomenon which, *given the availability of women's production jobs in New England,* accounted for their "success" in finding work. Sex segregation in production work then is an important factor in explaining the options and limits women confront, not only when they are working, but also when they are displaced.

Different opportunities in male and female labor markets determine the options that are available to men and women when they are displaced. For example, studies of displaced men show that older workers, who have less education and more years of tenure on the job, fare worst in finding new jobs.[37] Such men, especially those displaced from unskilled and semiskilled jobs, have the most difficult time transferring their specialized production skills to other jobs. Skilled men have the most favorable reemployment options.

The options are considerably different for blue-collar women. First of all, the vast majority of women production workers are employed in "unskilled" and "semiskilled" occupations. Most blue-collar women then, are therefore likely to be excluded from getting whatever skilled production jobs become available. Secondly, as we have seen in New England, older women in traditional female jobs have a fairly easy time of finding new jobs. In more depressed regions like the Rust Belt, older men in traditional male jobs do not. This is because low-wage production jobs continue to be available to women in New England, jobs which these women are willing to take.

For New England's displaced blue-collar women, then, reemployment does not seem to be linked to "human capital" as it is for men. As we have seen, the Portuguese women and the older, American-born women, women with the fewest years of education, were more likely to find new jobs when they were not recalled. Apparently, at low wages, the skills of these displaced women factory workers were "transferrable" to other factory settings. Jobs were available to them, when they were willing to lose wages.

Certainly displaced men are caught in the same bind—that of having to accept lower wages if they want to work at all.[38] Indeed, men in "high-wage" jobs are more likely to suffer from what Bendick[39] has called the "handicap of affluence"; namely, those who earned the highest wages have the most to lose when they take new jobs. Some studies report that displaced men lose up to 40 percent of their hourly wages when they find new jobs. In 1961 displaced workers at Mack Truck lost 40 percent of their wages.[40] In a more recent study,[41] steelworkers laid off in the Buffalo area between 1982 and 1983 went from earning about $10.00 to $6.62 per hour, a 34 percent drop.

One might argue that these high-wage men suffer most because they have the most to lose. Yet studies which compare displaced men and women *in the same industry* find that women lose more income than men. Gordon, Schervish, and Bluestone[42] report that displaced women auto workers in Michigan lost more income than displaced men when they were finally reemployed, though the women had less seniority and made less money than their male counterparts to begin with. Perrucci et al.[43] found that among RCA workers laid off, reemployed men earned 67 percent of their former weekly salaries; reemployed women received only 59 percent of their former weekly paychecks. Nowak and Snyder[44] found the same pattern in their research. When women work in higher-paying, "men's" industries and are displaced, they have *further to fall* because their alternative is usually a low-paying women's job. The availability of jobs for men and women, at men's and women's wages, are, of course, an essential element in their reemployment. The regional mix of production jobs for both sexes inevitably has a lot to do with how displaced men and women fare.

Yet in manufacturing production jobs, men and women are not likely to be found in the same industries or occupations. The women in our study, in traditional female production jobs, did not earn anywhere near the $10.00 average hourly wage that blue-collar men earned in Buffalo. The women in our study also did not lose anywhere near 40 percent of their wages when they took new jobs. Those with high wages lost only about half of that, or 19 percent of their previous hourly wages, while those with average wages only took about a 12 percent wage cut. These displaced women lost a smaller proportion of what they had formerly earned than the men did—but only because they took wages that no man would be likely to accept. Women with high wages in this study started with an hourly wage of about $5.65 and wound up with an average of $4.60. Women with average wages started at an hourly wage of $4.51 per hour and wound up with $3.96. They *did* find new jobs, it is true. But, the new jobs these women had to take if they wanted to continue doing production work paid no where near the $6.25 an hour the men's new jobs paid in the recent Buffalo study, only 63 percent of that, or $3.96 an hour.

Conclusion

In this chapter I have tried to chronicle the events in the lives of New England's contemporary women factory workers as they lose their jobs—to begin to share their untold stories with a world which seems to have forgotten them. Bringing to light the choices these blue-collar women face reaffirms what others are now beginning to discover—that there are many women who are affected by the changes which are reshaping America's industrial contours, women who are becoming displaced workers. These women are vulnerable to the loss of valued jobs. As married women with husbands to "support" them, as "secondary" earners rather than breadwinners in the traditional sense, as workers in traditionally female occupations and industries, their experiences are different from those of displaced men. Nevertheless, as we have seen, their marital situation hardly insulates them from the effects of displacement.

Married women who lose their jobs may gain some economic security from their husbands' paychecks. But to emphasize this point is to ignore the different life circumstances of women and men. When men are displaced it is their obligation to find a job to "support" the family in a labor market which affirms a man's obligation to provide this support. But displaced women face a different context of choice and obligation. As we have seen, women must consider their need for earnings in the context of a variety of different family commitments, commitments which vary with the women's culture and their stage in the life cycle.

As we have also seen, women make these choices in a women's labor market, one characterized by women's jobs and women's low wages. Therefore, if there are those who argue that displaced men have the most to lose because they hold high-wage jobs, it is also arguable that women suffer doubly when they lose their jobs. They suffer first as displaced workers facing unemployment and second from the lower wages that are the fate of women.

Displaced women look for jobs in a sex-segregated labor market and face reemployment in new female ghettoes. Ultimately then, the effects of job displacement on both men and women seem to reproduce the wage gap. More research needs to be done to substantiate this trend. But if it is occurring, the changing employment structure may be working directly at cross-purposes with the goals of equalizing wages between men and women.

In a situation of fewer jobs, lower wages, and declining unionization it is enormously difficult for these women to develop effective strategies to fight back. In an era when women workers are trying to develop strategies for improving their wages and working conditions, the women we studied were finding themselves increasingly defenseless. This increased vulnerability is reflected in their personal and family lives, an issue to be addressed in the following chapter.

8

Layoffs and Women's Lives

IN THE PRECEDING CHAPTER I tried to explore the ways in which the workings of a declining job market have created a series of difficult choices for New England's blue-collar women. In this chapter I will try to assess the impact of these choices on the women and their families. How are their lives affected by the continuing experience of job insecurity in a context of real financial need? What indeed is the financial effect on these women's families in terms of earnings losses and retrenchments in the families' standard of living? And perhaps more importantly, how does the consequence of financial deprivation, the potential need to increasingly do without, affect the women's sense of efficacy and control? How does it affect their relationships with their families?

As we have seen, a majority of the displaced blue-collar women we studied did find new jobs. Others chose to be without work—at least for a time. Yet, as I have tried to emphasize, neither of these "choices" necessarily represents a wholly positive or a negative outcome. Displaced women make choices about when it makes sense to return to work based on the circumstances of their lives. If continued unemployment is not always the outcome of last resort, neither does taking a new job always resolve the problems created by displacement. As I will try to show, working hard at a miserable job can intensify the anguish of losing a good job as it whittles away a woman's sense of optimism and hope for a better future.

What I have to report here are not cataclysmic events. During the six-month period between the women's layoff and the time we interviewed them, none of the married women reported losing a home or becoming destitute. No one told us that they or their families had gone hungry. Instead we heard about "little tragedies"—fears for a child's education, the abandonment of a long-deferred vacation, concerns about savings for retirement. We heard about the pain of lost friendships and the trauma of readjustment to a less desirable workplace. In short, we heard about the demise of the women's hopes and dreams for a richer, simpler, easier life.

Because this book has been one of the first in-depth looks at the personal and family consequences of job displacement among women workers, because it is a pioneering effort, its scope is inevitably limited. One of its most serious limitations is the absence of a follow-up study. As a result of our inability to follow the women beyond the six-month point after which they lost their jobs, we do not know about the long-term effects of displacement for these women. Further, we have only interviewed women and therefore cannot make any definitive comparisons between men and women. However, where appropriate, we will compare our findings about the personal and family impacts of displacement with studies that have already been done on men.[1] It is crucial to begin sorting out some of the ways in which the differences of men's and women's lives inform their responses to job instability and displacement.

There have, of course, been an increasing number of new efforts in this direction. Recognizing the importance of women's labor force participation today, researchers have begun to do studies which compare the impact of job loss on men and women. Most of this work is based on case studies of individual plants or workers in specific labor market areas.[2] Though this work begins to answer some important questions, the findings are still fragmentary, even somewhat contradictory. For example, in their study Snyder and Nowak[3] found that displaced women had worse reemployment alternatives than do men. Snyder and Nowak studied men and women laid off from production jobs where they made thermostat controls in the depressed steelmaking region of western Pennsylvania in the early 1980s. One year after job loss, 59 percent of the women compared to 42 percent of the men were still unemployed. These researchers noted that worse labor market options were available to the displaced women as compared with those available to displaced men. This contributed to the women's (but not the men's) increased levels of demoralization even after they were reemployed. The experience of economic distress seemed to have effects even after the women had found new jobs. Warren[4] also reports that unemployed women experienced more stress than unemployed men. At the same time, Perrucci et al.[5] have found that displaced men are more likely than women to increase their alcohol consumption. These researchers also found that job loss was more likely to increase depression in men than in women.

However, the underlying question raised in doing this research ought not to be simply "who suffers more?" Do men suffer more than married women because they are breadwinners? Do married women suffer just as much because their earnings are essential to their family's well-being? Before we can more fully understand how job displacement affects the personal lives of married men and women, we need to do more than just examine a series of outcome measures. We need to locate the distress of men and women who lose their jobs in the context of their needs and desires to find both meaning in their lives as well as to fulfill their roles as spouses and parents.

This chapter in particular is an attempt to begin such a task. First I will look at some of the financial impacts of women's job loss on their families. How much money do the women and their families lose when they lose jobs? What is the actual loss to their families, in terms of dollars and cents? Even more importantly, what does the loss of dollars and cents represent in experiential terms? What does it mean to women and their families to know that there are things they can no longer have, things these families were previously able to buy and now cannot? Finally, and perhaps most importantly, how do retrenchments in living standards affect the women's personal lives? How does it affect their emotional well-being and the conflict they experience between work and family life?

These are, of course, complex questions to ask. Moreover, the answers to them are not always likely to be direct and straightforward. The loss of a job may not only bring losses in earnings, but also a need to restructure one's life to adapt to being out of work—or perhaps to adjust to a new work situation. Does it matter to the women whether they are recalled, whether they get new jobs, or remain, willingly or unwillingly, out of work? How does each of these situations affect the women's sense of well-being? How do they spill over into family life, increasing the conflict women already feel between working and caring for their families? In what follows we will see how these effects vary among the three groups of women whose lives we are studying. We will see how blue-collar women cope with job loss in the context of different cultures and stages in their life cycles.

Economic Impacts

What are the earnings losses for women and their families when New England's blue-collar women get laid off? One would expect that since the blue-collar women in our sample returned to work, on average, only thirteen weeks after they were terminated and most collected unemployment insurance, the financial effects on their families would not be too staggering. On the other hand, as we have seen, women tended to earn between 40 and 50 percent of their families' annual income, so that their income losses could have a sizable effect on their families' budgets—even in the short term.

We calculated the job loser's family income losses for each group of women—the American-born, younger women, the American-born, older women, and the Portuguese women.[6] Younger, American-born women lost about 15 percent of their families' yearly income. Older women lost 14 percent and the Portuguese women lost 13 percent. This is consistent with

our earlier finding that unemployment compensation allows secondary earners to replace about 85 percent of their family incomes.

Losing 15 percent of one's family income is hardly negligible. However, such a loss does not seem likely to generate extensive impoverishment
either. Indeed the loss of 15 percent compares favorably to the 42 percent
household income losses reported of displaced married women auto workers
in the 1984 study by Gordon, Schervish, and Bluestone. One reason the
women auto workers lost substantially more earnings is because they suffered from much longer periods of unemployment than the women in this
study.

But when we look at the women's own earnings we find that this 15
percent figure underestimates how much the women have really lost. First
of all, even if the women had not been laid off, they still would have earned
substantially less than their employed counterparts, as evidenced by their
lower potential yearly income and their lower hourly wages. Indeed, it is
both the women's current earnings losses and their initially lower hourly
wages which account for their families' lower overall incomes. Job losers did
not have lower family incomes because their husbands earned less than the
husbands of employed women. *Their family incomes were lower because they
themselves earned less than fully employed women. This was true for each of the three
groups of women we studied* (see table 8.1).

How can we account for this earnings differential between employed
blue-collar women and job losers, when the two groups of women were
working at the same kinds of jobs? Do the employed women have more
"human capital"? Or, is there some other disadvantage that the job losers
suffer which has reduced their capacity to earn as well as women who have
remained employed?

One possibility is that repeated layoffs rather than continuity of employment have generated a "skidding" effect that other researchers have
documented, a pattern of layoff followed by less and less desirable employment options as one's work career proceeds. Jacobson[7] has shown that
male workers who get laid off are frequently unable to find jobs which pay as
well as their previous ones, leading to an earnings loss which persists over a
lifetime. As we have already seen in chapter 7, blue-collar women who lose
jobs and take new jobs also tend to lose wages.

To test these alternative hypotheses we first compared the number of
layoffs experienced by our employed control group and our job losers. Before
doing this we subtracted one from the number of layoffs reported by job
losers to adjust for their most recent job loss. Even after this adjustment was
made, job losers reported having been laid off an average of 2.8 times in the
past ten years while employed women reported only 1.7 layoffs. Job losers,
then, have been laid off significantly more often than employed women.[8]
Then a discriminant function analysis was done using the employment

Table 8.1   *Average (mean) Family Income for Employed Women and Job Losers*

Means	Employed Women's Means	Potential Income of Job Losers[a] Estimated	Actual Income of Job Losers[c] Means
Younger, American-born			
Total family income	$27,192	$25,370	$21,512
Women's earnings	11,545	9,445	5,578
Husband's earnings	14,692		13,419 $p > .01$
Other income[b]	855		2,506
Women's hourly wage	$6.16		$4.80 $p < .01$
Older, American-born			
Total family income	25,413	23,231	20,073
Women's earnings	12,386	8,496	5,311
Husband's earnings	8,884		10,743 $p > .01$
Other income	4,143		4,019[d]
Women's hourly wage	$5.92		$4.27 $p < .01$
Portuguese Women			
Total family income	25,341	22,549	19,719
Women's earnings	9,897	8,241	5,411
Husband's earnings	12,701		11,733 $p > .01$
Other income	2,743		2,575
Women's hourly wage	$4.89		$4.33 $p < .01$

[a]Had job losers not lost their jobs.

[b]Includes spouse's pension, disability, or unemployment compensation, rental income, and earnings of other family members.

[c]Based on hourly wages on jobs from which the women were laid off.

[d]Some older women have employed children living at home who contribute to the family's income.

group (job losers versus employed) as the dependent variable in order to find out whether being a job loser (and earning lower wages) was an effect of women's having less human capital and/or experiencing more layoffs (see table 8.2).

The results show quite clearly that neither age nor education (measures of human capital), nor industry discriminates between being a job loser or a member of the employed sample. Moreover, even when we hold constant these factors and the women's length of tenure, we find that having been laid off more frequently in the past ten years is still an effective discriminator between being a current job loser and remaining employed. Therefore, the difference between being employed (and earning higher wages) and being a job loser (and earning lower wages) is not due to the women's human capital. It has nothing to do with their skill or experience but is a function of having been laid off more frequently in the past ten years. This clearly suggests a skidding effect produced by the recurrent job displacement.

Snyder and Nowak[9] argue that the economic consequences of job dis-

Table 8.2   *Results of Discriminant Function Analysis: Relative Ability of Factors to Discriminate between Job Losers and Continuously Employed Women* (N = 201)

Variable	Coefficient[a]	F	Significance
Number of times laid off in past ten years	−.6248	7.808	.006
Length of tenure	.8570	11.110	.001
Years of education	−.0522	0.0026	.960
Age	−.2696	0.4630	.497
Apparel workers[c]	.6073	0.3596	.550
Electrical worker[d]	.6447	0.8577	.356

Canonical correlation[b] = .3561; Wilks' Lambda = .8731

[a]Standardized canonical discriminant function.
[b]The canonical correlation is similar to the use of the multiple R in regression analysis.
[c]Apparel workers = 1, nonapparel workers = 0. (Outgroup is composed of workers in other industries.)
[d]Electrical workers = 1, nonelectrical workers = 0. (Outgroup is composed of workers in other industries.)
Percent of "grouped" cases correctly classified 65.17%.

placement for women must be understood in terms of regional differences in labor market opportunities. Using aggregate data from the five year Bureau of Labor Statistics survey, they show that 54 percent of semiskilled white women in manufacturing were reemployed in New England (a figure close to the 62 percent found in this study) while only 37 percent were reemployed in the mid-Atlantic states. They conclude that New England offers a more "optimistic" outcome for displaced women than does the Rust Belt where women's production jobs are considerably less prevalent than are mens' and new job opportunities for displaced women are worse.

New England certainly does have a tradition of employing more women in female production jobs than western Pennsylvania. The patterns of displacement, however, have been different than the ones found in the midwest. What we are seeing here is what might be called a "trickle-out effect." In other words, small firms which employ these women have been leaving the region slowly and continuously over the past twenty years. At the same time, few new recruits to these low-paying jobs are available. Therefore, when a small firm closes, displaced women probably find new production jobs in the firms which remain. Only a small percentage of women *at any one time* are left jobless for long periods of time.

Yet the potential for displacement does not disappear, as firms which reemploy these women continue to close. Inevitably this has meant a loss of union membership which contributes to the unions' increasing powerlessness to prevent a decline in real wages. The repeated job losses of women in our study suggest how each year the process of displacement and reemployment at lower pay continues. As a result, the gap between production jobs (which used to pay better than women's sales and service work) has been narrowed. The ability to find a new production job or work in the same industry may make the women's job loss experience easier to bear in the short run, but over a longer time period it has lead to a continuous reduction of earnings.

This reduced earning capacity has a substantial effect on the overall income of the women's families. Table 8.3 shows the percentage of women whose families had annual incomes of less than $20,517, the income level that was calculated by the Bureau of Labor Statistics as the intermediate level of living for an urban family of four in 1979.[10] It also compares job losers and employed women whose husbands were employed full time and less than full time during the twelve months prior to our interview.[11]

Not surprisingly, for each of the three groups of women, job losers were more likely to report family incomes below the intermediate level of living than women who were continuously employed. What is most striking, however, is that job losers, *even those who had fully employed husbands,* were more likely to fall below the intermediate level of living than employed women whose husbands did not work full time during the preceding year. Their low family income was *not* due to the fact that the job losers' husbands earned less. Although the numbers are small and hardly conclusive, they suggest the importance of the economic contribution blue-

Table 8.3   *Percentage of Women Reporting Annual Family Income below the Intermediate Level of Living For an Urban Family of Four*

	Younger, American-born	
	Employed ($n = 29$)	Job Losers ($n = 44$)
Husband employed full time	8%	38%
Husband not employed full time	25%	71%
	Older, American-born	
	Employed ($n = 34$)	Job Losers ($n = 58$)
Husband employed full time	6%	15%
Husband not employed full time	7%	17%
	Portuguese	
	Employed ($n = 28$)	Job Losers ($n = 40$)
Husband employed full time	22%	37%
Husband not employed full time	20%	0%*

Note: Intermediate level of living = $20,517 per year. Figure based on Bureau of Labor Statistics for 1979.

*There were no women among the Portuguese who reported husbands who were employed less than full time during the previous year.

collar women make to their families. Indeed, such blue-collar families are as seriously affected financially when a working wife loses her job as when her husband is out of work or not fully employed for some time during the year.

The data also highlight some important differences between the three groups of women. The older, American-born women appear to be least financially vulnerable to the loss of their jobs and their lower wages. The younger women, both the Portuguese and their American-born counterparts, are most vulnerable and have the largest proportion of families that fall below the intermediate level of living because of a woman's loss of her job.

This effect is, in part, attributable to the fact that older women, many of whom have grown children, have fewer family members. Younger women, with their children still at home and economically dependent, need to have larger family incomes to live at the same standard of living as older women whose families have grown. Some of the older women also have employed children living at home who are likely to make financial contributions to the family. As we will remember, among the women born in America, older women were more likely to take the available, lower-paying jobs than younger women. With fewer dependent children to support, they can do this and still feel that they will be able to make ends meet. On the other hand, younger women who have lost their jobs have the most to lose when they take such lower-wage jobs.

The Consequences of Earnings Loss

Calculating the lost dollars and cents, however, doesn't give us much insight into the qualitative changes that are wrought in families where blue-collar women lose their jobs. How do the more limited resources, the newly felt absence of so many dollars and cents a week, affect the families' standard of living? And finally, how does the change in the families' standard of living affect the quality of the women's lives?

First of all, even in the short run, the women and their families inevitably pull in their belts. We asked our respondents whether or not they had "either made cutbacks, postponed purchases, or been unable to pay [their] bills for each of the following items." Not surprisingly, out of a list of twenty-two items we mentioned, job losers reported making more curtailments in family spending than employed women on five out of the twenty-two items we mentioned (see table 8.4).

What were the things they cut back on? They were the things one might expect over the short haul, the "little pleasures" which make life more enjoyable—groceries, clothes, and recreation. Families ate more hamburger and spaghetti rather than sirloin. They made do with last year's wardrobe instead of buying new Easter outfits. No one told us that she had

Table 8.4   *Cutbacks in Family Spending on Specified Items*

Groceries*	Vacations
Childcare	Club dues
Children's needs	Charitable/Religious contributions
Household maintenance*	Telephone
Household repairs	Fuel
Clothing*	Utilities
Cars	Financial care for relatives
Car repairs/maintenance*	Gifts
Appliances	Insurance
Mortgage/rent	Medical care
Recreation*	Furniture

*Job losers (n = 142) reported making significantly more cutbacks than employed women (n = 91) on specified items. (One tailed t-test, p = < .05.)

lost her home or had her car repossessed. But job losers did tell us they made more cutbacks on car repairs and more cutbacks on home maintenance than employed women. Sonia May is a woman who lost her job in an electrical assembly plant. When we spoke with her she was unemployed; this is how she experienced the impact of lost earnings and cutbacks. As she puts it, "Fred and I don't owe a tremendous amount, but we live like everybody else—a little above our means, knowing Sonia's getting paid on Friday. . . . Food has gone up. How much can you cut back on food? You have to eat. The electric company doesn't want to hear it [that she lost her job]. The phone company doesn't want to hear it. . . ."

For all women, losing a job meant losing money. But which families in particular were most vulnerable to the need to reduce their standard of living? How did the women's employment options, in conjunction with their family situations, contribute to their reduced purchasing power? Which women had to make the largest number of cutbacks? To explore this question we developed a scale of cutbacks based on the number of items each woman reported cutting back on. To do this we simply added together the total number of items which women said they had cut back on, had been unable to pay a bill for, or had postponed a purchase.[12] We then used this scale of cutbacks as a dependent variable in a multiple regression equation in order to see how various aspects of the women's work and family situation contributed to their need to do with less.

The primary purpose was to see if the job losers' reemployment choices had anything to do with their present financial well-being. Were the women who were reemployed, in recall jobs or new jobs, less likely to make cutbacks than the women who were still out of work? How did these three groups of women compare to those who had not lost their jobs at all?[13]

We made a point of controlling for age because we believed that older women would be likely to make fewer cutbacks. Some of the items we asked about were not likely to apply to older women—for example, children's needs and childcare. Older women were also more likely to have lower mortgage bills. We also controlled for total family income and country of origin.

We can see from table 8.5 that even when we controlled for age (a factor that was highly significant—older women made fewer cutbacks), total family income, and country of origin, though job losers made more cutbacks than women who remained employed, job losers' reemployment outcomes apparently had very little to do with whether they had to pull in their belts. Going back to work or not in the short term (either taking a new job or being recalled) or remaining unemployed had virtually nothing to do with the number of cutbacks the women reported. Evidently, going back to work after a layoff is not always the best strategy for all blue-collar women to optimize their resources.

It is, of course, quite possible that women who had to make the most cutbacks could have pushed hardest to find a new job. Taking new low-wage jobs may have been a way, then, of avoiding the need to pull in one's belt beyond limits acceptable to one's family. Unlike displaced blue-collar women in more highly depressed manufacturing regions, this was an option available to women production workers in New England where at least some jobs were available even if they were at considerably lower wages.

Table 8.5   *Number of Reported Cutbacks*[a]—*Results of Multiple Regression Equation*

	B	Beta	F	Significance
Job losers recalled[b]	.6706	.0639	0.794	—
Job losers with new jobs[c]	1.2829	.1046	2.106	—
Job losers out of work[d]	.6814	.0644	0.700	—
Total family income[e]	−.0001	−.1909	7.306	**
Country of origin[f]	.5431	.0565	0.658	—
Age[g]	−.1065	−.2614	14.330	***

Constant = 12.9775; N = 224; R^2 = .1160; F = 4.7456

[a]Numbers of items respondents reported making cutbacks on.
[b]Workers recalled to former jobs = 1, all others = 0.
[c]Workers laid off who have found new jobs = 1, all others = 0.
[d]Workers laid off remaining out of work = 1, all others = 0. (Outgroup = workers continuously employed.)
[e]Measured in dollars.
[f]American-born = 0, Portuguese = 1.
[g]Measured in years.
**$p < .01$
***$p < .001$

But curtailments in family spending were not spread evenly through-out our sample. As we can see, they varied with the women's family re-sources, resources which, as we have seen, are *linked directly to the women's experience with layoffs,* both past and present. Even when we controlled for age, country of origin, and reemployment outcomes, women with lower family incomes made more cutbacks. Evidently, the experience of repeated layoffs in declining industries has important consequences for the standard of living of blue-collar women's families.

Finally, younger women, regardless of whether they were American-born or Portuguese, reported making the largest number of cutbacks. Older women, as we have seen, are more willing to take new jobs where they lose wages. However, younger women, because of their greater economic needs for growing families, feel more reluctant to do this. Presumably, these younger women, who earn more to begin with but need the higher earnings for growing families, have more expenditures to reduce than their older counterparts whose financial needs are declining. Older women make fewer cutbacks most likely because they are able to manage with lower absolute incomes (see table 8.5).

Conflict between Work and Family

What happens to the quality of women's lives when they have to make cutbacks, when they have to deny themselves and their children the small luxuries that make life more enjoyable? What are the tensions in-volved in needing to worry about things like maintaining a home and keep-ing cars in running order? How does the strain of economic deprivation affect the way the women feel about the "double burden"? To explore this question we looked at the effect of cutbacks on the tensions women experi-enced between work and family life. To do this we used the work-family conflict scale developed in chapter 7 [14] as a dependent variable in a multiple regression equation. In this analysis, the number of reported cutbacks was used as an independent variable. We controlled for family income, age, number of children, country of origin, and reemployment outcome (see table 8.6). Not surprisingly, we found that women who reported making more cutbacks felt a greater conflict about working and taking care of their families.

As we have seen, when women lose their jobs, they report that their husbands and children do with less. But pulling in their belts takes its toll on the women indirectly as well by increasing the conflict they experience between work and family life. What seems to be happening is that the lack of resources embodied in the need to reduce expenditures makes the double day seem harder to bear.

Regardless of their age, country of origin, or family income, those who make more cutbacks experience more work-family conflicts than those who do not have to reduce their family's standard of living as much. It appears, then, that it is not only the objective realities of the daily grind that intensify women's sense of having a "double burden" but the experience of fewer rewards for their efforts.

Remaining unemployed, instead of getting back to work, might be expected to be a cause for experiencing stress. Yet, the data show, perhaps not surprisingly, that job losers who are still unemployed, report not more, but fewer, work-family tensions. As we have already argued, these findings confirm that blue-collar women feel there are advantages to being able to stay home for a while after losing a job (see table 8.6). When we control for the number of cutbacks, those women who lost their jobs and remained without work experienced less conflict than any of the other three groups of women in the sample—less than either the continuously employed women or the job losers who were reemployed (at new jobs and at recall jobs). Blue-

Table 8.6   *Conflict between Work and Family Life*[a]*—Results of Multiple Regression Equation*

	B	Beta	F	Significance
Job losers recalled[b]	.5861	.1164	2.827	—
Job losers with new jobs[c]	.1228	.0209	0.089	—
Job losers out of work[d]	1.0126	.1996	7.209	**
Number of cutbacks in family spending[e]	−.0704	−.1462	5.026	*
Total family income[f]	.0000	.0849	1.506	—
Number of dependent children 18 or under[g]	−.2310	−.1427	3.717	—
Age[h]	.0058	.0294	0.150	—
Country of origin[i]	−1.1634	−.2521	13.369	***

Constant = 5.7021; N = 223; R^2 = .1915; F = 6.3373

[a]Measured by sum of responses to two questions: (1) I have sometimes felt it was unfair to work and also spend so much time taking care of my home and family; and (2) I sometimes feel that I cannot do enough for my family when I work. Responses (1) very true, (2) somewhat true, (3) a little true, (4) not at all true. (Range = 2–8, Mean = 4.7, S.D. = 2.1.)
[b]Workers recalled to former jobs = 1, all others = 0.
[c]Workers laid off who have found new jobs = 1, all others = 0.
[d]Workers laid off remaining out of work = 1, all others = 0. (Outgroup = workers continuously employed.)
[e]Measured in reported number of cutbacks.
[f]Measured in dollars.
[g]Number of children eighteen years old or under living in household.
[h]Measured in years.
[i]American-born = 0, Portuguese = 1.
   *$p < .05$
  **$p < .01$
 ***$p < .001$

collar women who were unemployed when we interviewed them were clearly benefiting from their "brief vacations"—like Sonia May who told us, "I've really enjoyed being laid off for the summer. For the first time in years I've been able not to worry about going to work at 3:30. I take the girls to the beach. I can go someplace with them. My girls have been very involved in softball this summer and to see them enjoy it . . . I think more than in a long time, I have enjoyed my children this summer."

Valerie Delos, a 59-year-old woman whose children are grown, reported the same kind of experience about being without work. Though she didn't like foregoing her paycheck and feels she can't live on unemployment insurance, she saw some definite advantages in being out of work. She enjoyed "not getting up in the morning! Staying in bed late! Being home!" Then she added, "And my grandchildren are here too!"

But Sarah Candinski saw her situation somewhat differently. She calculated her options as follows, saying, "My last day of employment was . . . I had some vacation days coming. . . . My severance pay is still sitting there waiting for me and I still have two vacation days. . . . And next year I'm not going to be collecting [unemployment insurance]—it doesn't last forever. Sooner or later I'll have to go back to work. I hope I'm doing something I like. I know I will never make the money I did at . . . Electric."

Life becomes a balancing act for blue-collar women job losers. They must constantly calculate and recalculate the losses and benefits involved in staying out of work versus finding a new job. Each woman must figure out just how long she can afford to stay home before seriously exploring the low-wage employment options open to her.

Since blue-collar women work primarily for the money they earn, we expected that women who lost their jobs and later returned to their former jobs—those who were recalled—might experience less conflict between work and family life. Since women who were laid off and got new jobs tended to lose wages, we thought the need to work just as hard for less pay or the adjustment to a new work situation might increase their experience of work-family conflict as compared with the women who were recalled.

For example, Doris Viera, a garment worker, took a new, lower-paying job in another garment shop when the firm she had worked in for seven years closed its doors. She describes the adjustment she has had to make to her new work situation. She said that at her old firm, "We did just collars. Here the girls who have been here a long time, they know all the styles because they have been here, but seeing that I'm new at the job, I don't know. And we are forever learning. It's difficult to make a dollar here. Compared to my other job I am not making out. I don't mind the learning part, but I can't work this way and not make my money." Her adjustment is taking its toll on her family. She said, "You've got to neglect something.

Because if you come home and you are tired you are not going to do what you are supposed to do that night. Or you have to save housework for the weekend."

Dottie Nardello described the deprivation she felt in having to take a new job as somewhat like being on a treadmill. As she put it,

> When they said they were going to close, there were people who had worked there twenty years and they had *lost everything*. They can't collect their pensions until they are sixty-two. When they got laid off they took other jobs and had to stay there when the factory reopened. At the new place they had to *start all over again*.
>
> The twenty years were just lost. It seems like since I've been working its worse and worse. They want more and more out of you.

For these women, the wearying round of continuing to work just as hard or harder for less and less is experienced as "losing everything," as having to "start all over again."

Yet the data show (see table 8.6) only marginal differences between the women who were recalled and those who got new jobs with respect to their experience of work-family conflicts. Recalled women do report less work-family tension than those who got new jobs. However, the differences between the groups were not statistically significant. More research needs to be done to explore this issue further. We know that needing to reduce the family's standard of living by making more cutbacks generates more stress as blue-collar women confront the demands of work and family life. But we also need to know more about the relationship between the need for women who lose their jobs to adjust to a less satisfactory job (one that pays less or where the pressures are more intense) and the impact this adjustment has on the way they experience the conflicts between work and family life.

Finally, the Portuguese, not surprisingly, seem to experience the greatest conflict between work and family life, even when we control for reemployment outcome, the number of cutbacks they report, family income, and number of children. Presumably this sense of conflict is related less to their job situation than to their more patriarchal family situations.

Job Loss and Emotional Well-being

When women lose their jobs, reduced earnings contribute to reduced living standards. These appear to have important consequences for the way they experience their double burden. But what are the psychological effects on the women of having to make cutbacks? What role does the subsequent increase in work-family tensions play in the overall emotional well-being of blue-collar women who lose their jobs?

There is an extensive body of research, dating back to the Great Depression, which documents the relationship between job loss and the impairment of mental health. [15] These studies provide rich qualitative descriptions of the emotional experiences of male, blue-collar breadwinners who suffered from long-term unemployment. The unemployed experienced despair, resignation, and loss of self-esteem as the duration of their unemployment increased and their resources were depleted.

More recent case studies of plant closings have also shown that unemployment, particularly long-term unemployment accompanied by severe economic deprivation, not only creates dissatisfaction with personal and family life, but also a wide range of physical ailments and mental health problems. [16] In addition to the numerous case studies, the work of M. Harvey Brenner documents this phenomenon on an aggregate level. Brenner shows that as unemployment in manufacturing increases, there are changes in standard institutional indicators of "well-being." For example, infant mortality goes up and first admissions to psychiatric institutions increase as unemployment rates rise. [17]

We have known for a long time then, that job loss and unemployment do not bode well for a person's happiness or sense of well-being. But most of the research that has been done deals with the impact of job loss on men. Further, some of the most serious effects of job loss are associated with long-term unemployment. Is it likely to expect the same consequences for our married women factory workers, women who see their roles as "secondary" earners? Moreover, when the women actually wanted or needed to go back to work, most were able to find jobs within a six-month period. Even those who were still out of work and wanted jobs could not be defined as suffering from "long-term unemployment." [18] Is short-term unemployment, then, likely to have any measurable effects on the women's emotional state? How do the repercussions of different reemployment outcomes affect the nature of emotional distress for each of the four groups of women?

In order to answer these questions we administered the Psychiatric Epidemiology Research Interview (PERI) to our respondents as part of our structured interviews. The PERI is a series of twenty-seven questions designed to measure levels of "demoralization." What exactly is "demoralization"? According to the formulation by Jerome Frank, [19] "A person becomes demoralized when he finds that he cannot meet the demands placed on him by the environment and cannot extricate himself from his predicament." [20]

It is important to note that demoralization is not necessarily associated with psychiatric impairment, though it may be. At the same time it is often associated with emotional help-seeking from friends, relatives, clergymen, or mental health professionals. It is what one might want to call "the blues" and is related to environmental stress or simply "existential despair." The measure is explicitly designed to be highly correlated with physical symptoms.

We chose this measure over other measures of psychiatric symptomatology that are available because we did not expect to find the same type or extent of despair among the women in our sample that is often found among unemployed male breadwinners who are out of work for long periods of time. We wanted to see how a variety of different experiences associated with the job loss, in conjunction with stresses produced at home, might alter the women's overall sense of well-being—for each of the three groups we were studying as well as for all the women.

Much to our surprise we found no relationship between the women's reemployment outcomes and their reported levels of demoralization. The women were no more or less demoralized than the employed whether they were recalled, found new jobs, or remained unemployed. Job losers were no more demoralized than the women who remained employed (see table 8.7).[21]

Table 8.7   *Demoralization*[a] *and Job Loss—Results of Multiple Regression Equation*

	B	Beta	F	Significance
Job losers recalled[b]	.1889	.0156	0.057	—
Job losers with new jobs[c]	.9396	.0665	1.011	—
Job losers out of work[d]	.0287	.0022	0.001	—
Physical symptoms[e]	11.9335	.4907	62.783	•••
Number of reported cutbacks[f]	.0946	.0811	1.739	—
Work satisfaction[g]	.6942	.1047	3.037	—
Work-family conflicts[h]	−.2632	−.1063	2.761	—
Total family income[i]	−.0000	−.0494	0.608	—

Constant $= 5.7335$; $N = 206$; $R^2 = .3531$; $F = 11.8878$

[a]Measured by the Psychiatric Epidemiology Research Instrument (see Bruce P. Dohrenwend, Patrick E. Shrout, Gladys Egri, Frederick S. Mendelsohn, "What Psychiatric Scales Measure in the General Population: Part II: The Components of Demoralization by Contrast with Other Dimensions of Psychopathology," unpublished paper (Columbia University School of Public Health and Administrative Medicine, 1979). Mean $= 10.007$, S.D. $= 5.194$.
[b]Workers recalled to former jobs $= 1$, all others $= 0$.
[c]Workers laid off who have found new jobs $= 1$, all others $= 0$.
[d]Workers laid off remaining out of work $= 1$, all others $= 0$. (Outgroup $=$ workers continuously employed.)
[e]Checklist of fifty reported physical symptoms, scored 0-2. (The scale was constructed by Drs. Ramsey and Joan Liem for the 1979 Work and Unemployment Project, Department of Psychology, Boston College.) Mean $= 1.297$, S.D. $= .2136$.
[f]Measured in reported number of cutbacks.
[g]Response to question, "All in all, how satisfied would you say you are with your job": $1 =$ very satisfied, $2 =$ somewhat satisfied, $3 =$ not too satisfied, $4 =$ not at all satisfied. (Taken from 1977 Quality of Employment Survey, Institute for Survey Research, University of Michigan.) Mean $= 1.777$, S.D. $= .783$.
[h]See Table 8.6 [a].
[i]Measured in dollars.
••• $p < .001$

Further, other factors we thought might be associated with variations in stress levels, such as family income, numbers of dependent children, and women's work satisfaction were not associated with demoralization either. Nor were our measures of cutbacks or work-family tensions. Only the measure of physical symptoms we included in this analysis was highly related to demoralization. Women who said they were more demoralized tended to report many more symptoms of physical illness than those who were less demoralized—for each of the three groups of women and even more strongly for the group as a whole. Such findings seem to substantiate the claim of Dohrenwend, Shrout, Egri, and Mendelsohn[22] that demoralization is highly sensitive to physical illness.

These results seem to suggest that married women are not as emotionally vulnerable to job loss and displacement as men seem to be. Moreover, they are consistent with other findings comparing displaced men and women. For example, when Perrucci et al.[23] compared men and women who lost jobs due to plant closings, they found that only men and not women were more depressed. In two recent studies that focused on displaced men[24] the researchers found that men remaining unemployed because of a plant shutdown were more stressed than those who found new jobs. This was clearly not true for the blue-collar women we studied.

According to Snyder and Nowak,[25] displaced women who do not live with spouses (single women, women living with children alone, women living with parents or roommates) tend to be more demoralized than men— even when they are reemployed. Snyder and Nowak attribute this to the women's experience of greater economic insecurity in the period between job loss and reemployment. As women in an area which is economically depressed, they have more difficulty finding jobs that will enable them to support themselves than men do. Snyder and Nowak argue that this sense of insecurity remains with them even when they do get new jobs. At the same time, married women reported the least degree of demoralization in Snyder and Nowak's work. In our work, which focuses exclusively on married women, most of whom have husbands who are fully employed, the reemployment outcome of women who have lost jobs appears to have no bearing on the extent of the women's demoralization.

These findings seem at odds with the pain and anguish we heard from so many of the women who lost their jobs. Are we to believe then, that when married blue-collar women lose jobs there are no impacts on their emotional well-being? Are these women's jobs relatively unimportant to them because they do not see themselves as breadwinners? Or, do married women have more financial and emotional resources than men do, resources which allow them to accommodate better than men can to losing a job?

Though more research is needed to understand how displaced women respond to their situation, there are a variety of interrelated explanations for these negative findings. Perhaps most importantly, the women we studied suffered from short-term unemployment. They lost their jobs, on average, only six months before we interviewed them. According to Kasl and Cobb,[26] the length of an individual's unemployment has to exceed some lengthy threshold and lead to fairly severe economic consequences before an impact on mental health is likely to occur. Though the displaced women we studied reported making cutbacks, few could be seen as suffering from severe economic deprivation. Many of the women we studied were still eligible for and, if they had not returned to work, were still receiving unemployment insurance.

The blue-collar women we studied believed they would find jobs when they were ready. What they feared was having to take lower wages. About 60 percent of the women had, within a period of six months from the time of their layoff, gone back to work. Some had been called back. Others, particularly older women and Portuguese women, had accepted the limitations of their age, ethnicity, limited skills, and education in the declining labor market and had chosen to take whatever jobs were available to them— albeit at lower wages. For those who were still out of work, most typically the younger, American-born women, remaining without work was also a choice, a choice made in the context of available family resources as well as in the hope of finding better alternatives fairly soon.

In the short term, displaced men tend to behave similarly. Where resources from supplementary unemployment benefits, unemployment insurance, and family resources have been available, unemployed men tend to hold out for new jobs which pay as much or almost as much as their former wages. The problem for men has been the lack of such jobs. Long-term unemployment has too often been the inevitable result.

New England's female, traditional, blue-collar industries, however, have not died a cataclysmic death as have many steel and auto plants in the Rust Belt where largely men are employed. Instead, the number of jobs in New England's female, traditional, labor-intensive industries has steadily declined in these communities over a period of more than twenty years, as the overall wages of the remaining jobs have continued to decrease. Women employed in and displaced from these industries have therefore had a different set of options than most displaced men. Without the education or skills to make a change, older and new groups of ethnic women have chosen to remain in these industries and accept the slowly but steadily declining wages.

In New England then, women's family roles as well as the employment options available to them in this labor market give them different choices than most displaced men have when they lose their jobs. Moreover, as we have already pointed out, married blue-collar women do not want to define themselves as primary breadwinners. Indeed, as we have seen, it is this very posture which gives them some of the emotional freedom they need to be able to come to terms with the bitter choices they face both as workers with family responsibilities and as women with low-paid work available to them.

Conclusions

How can we assess the impact of job displacement on the personal lives of the women we have studied? The married women who work in factories have somehow managed to adjust to the periodic loss of their jobs. They worry about lost earnings but hope for the best, accepting the fact that they will find other work, even if it is not as valued or lucrative as the work they have lost. The periodic setbacks many experience are not simply taken in stride as part of the accepted cost of working in declining industries. Instead the women find ways to maintain their emotional balance by optimizing the choice they feel they have as women—to be only "supplementary" earners. They both welcome and justify the time off as time for themselves and their families. Married blue-collar women cannot choose whether to go back to work. But to some extent, they try to choose the right job at the right moment.

Though the women in our study were not more demoralized than their employed counterparts, each time a woman loses her job there are measurable costs to her and her family. As we have seen, the problem is not simply one of being out of work. Indeed, as I have argued, unemployment creates a short respite for many of the women from the double burden they face on a daily basis. But the rest from the wearying round of paid work and family work is purchased at the expense of the family's financial well-being.

Each time a woman gets laid off—on average about every three to four years—she can expect to lose earnings, even with unemployment insurance. If she is not called back to her former job (where she can at least expect to stay even), she is likely to return to a job that pays less than the one she held before. Ultimately, then, the problem of unstable employment in these declining industries means a career of declining wages and decreasing family income. Blue-collar women increasingly face underemployment.

There is for some women, of course, the possibility of giving up on these declining industries. One might argue that blue-collar women can become white- or pink-collar women as the growing sales and service sector expands. Some of the women could, of course, seek retraining for alternative work. Such women would most likely be younger, born in America, have high school educations and/or some office experience, and have supportive husbands. Yet for women like these, higher-paying factory work frequently seemed more attractive. Sarah Ponetti was an electrical assembler who worked in an office before her growing children induced her to take a higher-paying factory job. She said, "What I would like to do is take a course in typing and some type of office work. They have a course at a junior college for medical reception types of things, and I want to look into that. Probably the beginning of the year. I know myself, I am not qualified to walk into a place and say I can type and do this, because it has been so long. I have to improve my skills before I present myself to somebody as competent. The most I could do now is probably be a receptionist . . ." Yet even if she went back to school to learn office skills, it is not clear that she could earn as much money as she made before she lost her factory job.

Moreover, as many women see it, going back to school is an option they cannot afford. Like Carrie Malten, a former electrical assembler whose husband's job is shaky. She said, "You know what it costs to go to school? That's a drawback right there. My husband can't afford to send me to college."

Of course for older and Portuguese women, such options hold much less promise than trying to hold on to their "trade." Indeed, the limited options for subsidized retraining for displaced women will be discussed in the following chapter.

Our story is about those who feel they cannot leave these industries for greener pastures, those who must deal with the bitter choices, choices which take their toll on the women's lives in subtle ways. As we have seen, women's reduced family incomes mean a reduced standard of living. Though we found no cataclysmic losses in the short term, the evidence suggests that each layoff means the women are able to contribute less and less to the family purse in a context where, as we have seen, their contributions are of major importance.

It is because they work *for the money* that the effects of displacement weigh so heavily on blue-collar women. They must continue to work just as hard but earn less and less, making it feel as if working is getting them "nowhere." It is hardly surprising, then, that so many of the women told us that they seek the major gratification in their lives from their families. At times like these it may make emotional sense to try to deny the centrality of paid work in their lives.

Yet despite many of the women's stated wishes that they shouldn't have to work, or shouldn't have to work so hard, in the long term, their family lives do not benefit from the loss of their jobs. Family life does not become more gratifying if the women hold poorly paying jobs. Instead, their continued need to reduce what their wages can buy for their families means that the conflicts they feel between work and family life intensify. Earning less makes it feel harder and harder for them to continue to work and take care of their families. Ultimately, this dynamic has serious implications, not only for women who work in factories, but for all working women who work *because they have to.*

9 Conclusions: A New Social Agenda

THE WORK THAT INITIALLY LED to this volume began with what seemed a simple, straightforward question. How did working women—married blue-collar women—react to and cope with the loss of their jobs? After virtually decades of research exploring the effects of job displacement and unemployment on working men, we needed to know how wives and mothers rather than male breadwinners dealt with this growing problem. However, the more I began to explore the issue, the more it became apparent that the difficulties women faced were embedded in a much larger economic, historical, and social context, raising questions that went beyond the immediacy of women's reactions to the loss of their jobs. It went beyond the lost earnings and personal anxieties which emerge in response to a crisis situation.

I came to understand the connection between personal problems and public issues, discovering the effects of a new global economy which, during the past twenty years or so, has been vitally transforming the nature of work for hundreds of thousands of women who work in America's production jobs. The growth of this new international division of labor has begun to undermine the wages and working conditions of women who continue to work in our older mills and factories.

To conclude, let me say that in documenting the effects of these events on New England's blue-collar women I have tried to bring to light a new and important problem faced by some of today's women workers. But I have also tried to contribute to a better understanding of how class and gender are experienced by working-class women—both at work and at home. In some ways then, the issues raised in this book go beyond the problems of women who work in factories. Other working-class women, like their blue-collar counterparts, are also members of dual-earner families who must deal with some of the same problems—low wages, stressful working conditions, and the need to balance paid work with domestic obligations. As technological and administrative changes occur in other indus-

165

tries and occupations where women are heavily employed, many working-class women are also beginning to experience layoffs.

To understand what it means for a married working-class woman to lose her unionized production job, it is essential to realize what she feels is being lost, how she views what Simone de Beauvoir has called her "situation"—how she sees the quality of her job and her family responsibilities. These vary with her age and stage in the life cycle. They vary with the views of her family and culture about the meaning and importance of her employment. I have tried to show that New England's blue-collar women have specific understandings of the limits of their lives and the possibilities which shape their interests as women. In concluding, I will try to show how their vision defines their views of the contemporary women's movement, and in doing so to suggest some possibilities for defining a working-class feminism in America.

Finally, in looking at the meaning of work for blue-collar wives and mothers I have made both implicit and explicit comparisons with blue-collar husbands and fathers, attempting to explore the way each gender experiences the impact of job displacement. I have tried to point out how men's and women's different work and family roles and different labor market opportunities create different options and goals for workers when they are displaced from their jobs. Hopefully, this pioneering effort will inspire others to compare this question in a new light. Perhaps we need to do more than just compare the scores of male and female job losers on a traditional series of outcome measures. Different indices of distress may be needed to compare the sufferings of men and women.

Documenting the plight of New England's blue-collar women is not the same thing as offering solutions. Ultimately, little has been done to deal with the problems created by the demise of women's production work because the displacement of women workers has been virtually ignored as a public policy issue. In this final chapter I will try to show why we can no longer close our eyes to the damage which is being done to so many women who work for a living in our declining mills and factories. What strategies might be effective in protecting the livelihoods of our nation's women factory workers?

Social Policy and the Family Wage

Some have argued that the emergence of the two-paycheck, working-class family exacts a heavy price from women in added toil, a price working-class women could choose not to pay if their men could earn a family wage. But the lessons of the past implicitly deny the value of such hopes, as do the lessons of the present—great tides of women have entered the labor force. No doubt blue-collar women "have to work." But it is not only their need to contribute financially to their families which keeps them at work. Making that contribution also adds to their personal sense of efficacy, autonomy, and control.

The findings of this book reaffirm the value of well-paid work for women. They lead us to reject the idea that a family wage is the way to alleviate the trials of working-class women's double day. Equal wages rather than a family wage must be the goal of social policy. In emphasizing how women's jobs affect their families, it has become clear that "good jobs," jobs that pay well, seem to motivate women's commitment to work; poor jobs have the opposite effect. At the same time, the quality of women's work lives tends to ease or intensify the way they experience the double burden—in much the same way this works among middle-class women with "careers."

When we compare the lives of working-class women of a generation or even a decade ago to New England's contemporary blue-collar women, we see a different sensibility. Studies of working-class families of the 1950s, 1960s, and 1970s described women who were primarily homemakers. Though some worked part time, by and large their salaries were described as making only marginal financial contributions to the family income. In view of the inadequacy of the "family wage" and the supposed authoritarianism of working-class husbands, these women led lives of "quiet desperation," single-handedly managing their families with virtually no control over the resources to do this.

These observations are not meant to deny that many of the blue-collar women we studied felt burdened by the demands of having to work in factories. Some saw their paid work in contrast to domestic work as the primary source of these burdens. Many saw the ideal solution in having husbands whose earnings could "support" them. Yet few of the American-born women, even those whose husbands earned relatively well, actually wanted to relinquish their jobs. It is their earnings which bind them tightly to the labor force.

Blue-Collar Women at Work

This book is more than just a set of hypotheses supported by a technically competent analysis of "hard" data. As I said at the outset, in letting the women speak for themselves, I have tried to offer a written portrait of their lives, to present, frequently in their own words, the stories of how they grew up as daughters of the working class and how as adult women they came to work in New England's mills and factories.

Despite the perceptions of intellectuals and other observers that factory jobs are "alienating," the women who work in factories hardly ever described their jobs in this way. We never heard that factory work was "boring." Instead the women told us how hard their work was, most often describing their jobs as involving too much "pressure." The pressure, as most saw it, was embodied in the demands of the piece-rate system.

In many ways then, the women's description of factory life records an experience of what could be described as "class conflict." But the women do not play out the conflict on the shop floor with clenched fists. Instead they use whatever resource their jobs provide to develop strategies to cope with the pressures. Their goal is to carve out a sense of personal control which makes the workplace livable for them. They also do this by seeking to establish rules, often through their unions. The unions which represent them are losing power and influence in these declining industries and often cannot enforce the rules they have negotiated. Nevertheless, the contract sets a benchmark defining the forms of exploitation that are legitimate and those that are not. In that sense it offers some modicum of protection and with it a basis for self-respect that is not available to nonunion women.

Just as importantly, blue-collar women try to develop relationships with co-workers and supervisors which moderate the tensions and pressures of their jobs. Friendships in the workplace are important then, not merely because as women these factory workers are naturally unambitious and gregarious. Close relationships with workmates are gratifying, of course. They contribute to a sense of solidarity among the women and function to make the workplace livable.

Women's strategies to make the workplace livable vary with the jobs they hold—how good the wage is, how easy it is to "make good money." The strategies used also vary with the women doing the job—their age, ethnicity, or stage in the life cycle. These are factors which account for how the women see their role as family members and their own economic needs at the moment. Despite a generalized dissatisfaction with the piece-rate system, despite the women's realization that it is exploitative, some women, often younger women, feel it gives them some control over their work and allows them to earn well and to manage the amount of earnings they take home at the end of the week.

Indeed, blue-collar women frequently see their factory jobs as providing an opportunity to earn "good money." For this many are willing to work hard and sometimes to forego the higher status of other types of work. Yet to point out that women work in factories only for the money is to miss the fact that material possessions provide important psychic benefits to those whose lives are financially insecure. Women's paychecks sometimes contribute to fully applianced kitchens and to summer vacations for their families. Sometimes their wages simply pay the bills. But whatever additions their incomes make to family purchases, their earnings give them increased control over the vagaries of an uncertain economic future and add to their self-esteem.

Factory Jobs and Women's Family Roles

The resources women derive from their jobs often carry over into family life. The younger, American-born women in particular often describe a degree of sharing at home which seems to emanate from the essential nature of their financial contributions. Bringing in almost half the family income can serve as a basis for women to make legitimate requests from husbands for help with children and housework and for input into financial decision making, requests which are often complied with. The ability to contribute so extensively to the family purse, then, both legitimates the right of blue-collar women to work and justifies their absence from home and children. It permits women some control over the family's finances and motivates husbands to commit time and effort to housework and childcare.

However, blue-collar women don't work to enhance their "power" in the family or to ensure that husbands carry an equal share of family work. Particularly in Portuguese families, holding down a full-time factory job and coming home to a full load of housework is the norm for wives and mothers. Even in American families, where it is seen as desirable for husbands to "help" their wives, shopping, cleaning, cooking, doing the laundry, and taking care of children are still seen as essentially women's obligations. Blue-collar women support the notion of separate spheres in spite of the persistent experience of "overload." Housework and childcare are women's responsibilities; husbands are seen as being responsible for supporting the family.

The attempt to protect men and women's separate spheres is a way that blue-collar women have developed to bind their working-class families together. The women's wish to preserve the fiction (despite their sometimes hefty paychecks) that they are only "supplementary" earners is a way of protecting their husbands' manhood. In doing this they ensure the continuation of their employment. Yet support for the notion of separate spheres is also a way of reinforcing a husband's obligation and willingness to continue providing support for his family. Blue-collar women cannot earn enough to support themselves and their children alone, seeing that "every woman is only a husband away from welfare."

Blue-Collar Women and Feminism

Ultimately, it is these felt needs, rooted in the structural conditions of their working-class lives, which activate the vision New England's blue-collar women have of feminism. They are acutely aware of the opportunities available to women of higher classes. Indeed, their lack of opportunity shapes the way they see the goals and ideals of "women's liberation."

Blue-collar women have a different set of interests than those of middle-class women. Their experience, then, generates a different set of moral principles.

As Ferree, Rapp and particularly Benenson, have argued,[1] middle-class feminism often challenges the traditional family and the traditional division of family labor. Middle-class wives ask that their husbands participate in domestic labor. They seek to dismantle the boundaries between male and female roles. They do not ask for reciprocity but for greater equality. If wives are to seek career goals similar to their husbands, husbands need to provide wives with parallel supports at home.

This hardly means that middle-class, dual-career marriages are more egalitarian. Nor does it mean that women with "careers" rather than "jobs" actually receive more help with domestic work. However, because they do have better labor market opportunities (both for earning more money and for enjoying the work they do) they can be more confident than their working-class peers about making demands which enhance their own satisfaction even if these demands have the potential to challenge the stability of their marriages. Divorce is less likely to lead to poverty for educated women with professional skills.[2] Women with job skills are also better able to financially, and therefore emotionally, surmount the trauma of marital separation, even emerging from it with an increased sense of mastery over their lives.[3]

For these reasons middle-class feminism is not acceptable to many of the working-class women we spoke with, because it poses a real challenge to the stability of the nuclear family. As Sen argues,[4] the working-class family is an institution of crucial resource pooling and an important source of emotional security for working-class women, despite their real subordination within it. Sen writes, "The family is almost the only institution in capitalist society that bears both an ideology and a reality of love, of sharing, and of generosity. The fact that it also sustains an ideology and a reality of inequality and subordination places women in a very contradictory position."

As we have seen, and as Ferree argues,[5] women try to deal with this Faustian bargain by trying to live in and balance both worlds. They work to escape patriarchal domination and seek the support of their families to avoid capitalist exploitation.

The underlying class differences between middle-class and working-class women became apparent from the women's own comments about the feminist movement. Though we have no hard data to support this view, it seemed that it was not just indifference which characterized the stance women factory workers had toward the women's movement. Instead, they conveyed a strong sense of anger and hostility about "women's liberation" which seemed to mask an envy of working women who have "interesting careers." What surfaced was an acute and painful recognition of middle-class women's class privilege. For example, Millie Barnes described the women's movement as, ". . . a bunch of middle-class women who don't have anything else to do, going to meetings and rallies and stuff." She added thoughtfully, "It hasn't really done anything for us at the bottom of the social and labor scale."

As these married, women factory workers see it, very few of the employment policies which the feminist movement has struggled for, like antidiscrimination laws, equal employment opportunity, affirmative action, or comparable worth can help them as individuals to deal with the immediate problems they currently face—maintaining or improving their wage levels—and most importantly, holding onto their jobs.

Certainly upgrading the wages and status of women in other industries would have some important effects on blue-collar women who become displaced from their factory jobs. If women's wages were higher in the fast-growing sales and service industries, making a transition to a new job might not be so painful. Women displaced from factory jobs who wanted to make a work transition would have a much more hopeful future than they do now. But such, unfortunately, is not the case and displaced women confront the reality of that situation.

As we have seen, blue-collar women most definitely do chafe and bridle at the injustices they experience at work and the overload they feel at home. They would love to claim a sexual equality that would permit them the freedom enjoyed by middle-class women who have careers. As we have seen, all the women would like to earn more money. Over and over we heard that women should get paid well; that if they want to or need to they should be hired at men's jobs—particularly if they are heads of households.

Nevertheless, as many see it, a woman who holds a man's job takes it away from a man who has a family to support. In that sense, she is depriving another wife of her rightful due. Working-class women therefore hurt themselves as women by claiming equality with men. Terry Sullivan, a garment worker, expressed this dilemma quite forcefully when she said, "When I see the women go and drive the bus or deliver the mail, when there are so many young men who need jobs, I think men should have these jobs, not women. I think women hurt themselves by being equal to men."

Or, as Carla Thomas told us, "I don't believe in women's lib because it's a man's world. It's easier for a woman with a man."

As things are, then, making a claim for equality can be a very dangerous thing. In doing so women see themselves as forfeiting the right to be taken care of in a work world which offers them few opportunities to take care of themselves. As Millie Barnes put it, "I think liberation can really ruin a relationship. I mean there are certain things I would not do to my husband only because it would take away from his manhood, his pride. Maybe that's why I don't worry about a job as much, because I figure he's supporting this family; its his obligation somehow."

Perhaps then we need to rethink what we mean by feminism, recognizing how much our image of what it means to be "liberated" is based on access to opportunities which are only available to middle-class women. These opportunities involve the chance to pursue the discovery of self, to seek emotional independence through well-paid, creative work. Only the possibility of financial independence allows for the pursuit of sexual relationships based on equality between men and women. Married blue-collar women have few opportunities for financial independence.

It is certainly true that blue-collar women seek and get a sense of efficacy, autonomy, and control over their lives through their paid work. But there can never be the same motivation to work in a factory as there is to work as a professional or managerial woman. Nor can factory work provide the same opportunities for economic independence. Therefore we need to interpret what blue-collar women say they want in the context of their situation. As we have seen, they want more and better jobs. But the absence of opportunities for better work defines their vision and their goals, shaping the possibilities they see for equality at home.

Job Loss

The lives of women factory workers then are circumscribed by the need to work and the nature of their jobs. For those who lose their jobs, however, problems are even worse. The instability of their work histories and the tenuousness of the jobs they hold further diminishes their sense of security. Therefore we must interpret what they say in the context of this situation, a situation which creates the deeply held belief that it is desirable for husbands to earn enough to support the family, that at home husbands and wives should not be "equal."

This sensibility is in part a reflection of the women's experiences with job instability. As I have shown, in New England, women's layoffs do not come as a sudden blow after years of stable employment. The continuing round of layoff, unemployment, and reemployment is something the job losers we studied have lived with—at least for the past ten years—whether they are eventually recalled or face the more dismal prospect of having to find new jobs at lower wages.

Of course, layoffs are not always perceived as an unmitigated evil. Husbands do provide a cushion against the prospect of impoverishment. Where women have hopes for recall, particularly where layoffs are expected to be temporary or fairly brief, the women are likely to be pleased with the prospect of collecting what they see as well-deserved unemployment compensation and are hardly averse to a brief respite from the tiring round of factory work and family obligations.

Nevertheless, this research enables us to rethink the way we understand the financial role of "primary breadwinners" in today's two-paycheck, working-class families. No matter how much the husbands of these women earn, their salaries are not enough to fully support the family—whatever the style to which these families have grown accustomed. A husband's salary may keep the wolf from the door, but it is hardly a guarantee of full financial support.

When a blue-collar wife is unemployed, she is not taking a vacation at the government's expense. Most women, despite the fact that they receive unemployment compensation, still look for work. Few refuse jobs and few stay out of work long enough to exhaust their benefits. In a declining labor market there are few wage benefits to be gained by postponing the return to work. Marriage does give blue-collar women more flexibility in responding to the demands of a declining labor market. But their pleasure in having "free time" is constantly marred by the anxiety so many feel at the loss of their earnings.

In 1964 displaced married women often remained out of work because they wanted to. But today's married blue-collar women are no less likely than single women to return to work in a six-month period—despite the differences in their family resources and despite the number and the ages of their children. The labor market behavior of these women is becoming more and more similar to that of married men. Both work because they have families to support. Yet at the same time married men and women don't have the same experiences when they lose their jobs. The relationships between age, skill, education, and options for reemployment are different for men and women. This is because women and men have different family responsibilities and different labor market opportunities.

In the long run, the influx of married women with children into the labor force may create more congruity between men's and women's roles. The trend may be for working-class husbands and wives to increasingly share financial and domestic responsibilities. The 40 to 50 percent of family income New England's blue-collar women bring home is evidence of their financial contribution. But the instability of the work available to them impairs their ability to provide.

I have tried to show that it is not the need for these women to work which threatens the stability of their families. Nor does working undermine the satisfactions of the women themselves. What hurts most is losing one's job and the ensuing need to confront some difficult choices—work at lower and lower wages or no work at all. New England's blue-collar women do not suffer from long-term unemployment but from long-term underemployment.

As we have seen, women who lose their jobs learn to accept and to cope emotionally with the dilemmas posed by repeated bouts of layoffs and unemployment, assimilating the losses they incur into their expectations about the vicissitudes of life for women like themselves—women with little education and few valued job skills. Yet the instability of employment, the financial insecurity, and the repeated threat of having to do without does take its toll. These trials make the double burden, the conflict between working and caring for their families, increasingly difficult to bear.

Displaced Blue-Collar Women—Salvaging the Future

The last word on the women factory workers in America today who are being displaced from their jobs has yet to be written. Ultimately then, this book is only a first step in bringing to light the choices they face, an initial effort to make their private problems a public issue. Since this research was done, more and more women have lost jobs in production work. Exactly how many women have been affected is difficult to know for certain, just as it is difficult to assess the long-term effects on the women and their families. How do they fare, how do they cope a year, two years, three years, or more after being displaced from their frequently well-paying factory jobs? At this writing more and more researchers are beginning to investigate this issue further.[6]

When both laymen and specialists in industrial policy[7] engage in discussions about saving American manufacturing jobs, the focus is most often on jobs in the highly paid "heavy" industries where male workers are heavily employed as machinists, steel workers, and auto workers. It is often assumed that most of the industries where women are employed as production workers may have to be written off since they are typically labor intensive. American women can't compete with the wages women earn in Taiwan, Sri Lanka, or beyond the Mexican border.

But despite this frame of reference, women production workers in manufacturing have not disappeared from America's labor market. As I pointed out in chapter 2, there are still about 5.5 million women who were employed in such work in 1985.[8] There has, of course, been a veritable hemorrhaging of jobs in the fiber industries (apparel, textiles) in the past five years or so. In 1979, 2.2 million workers were employed in these industries. By 1985, it was estimated that only 1.9 million remained.[9] But even with these egregious losses in employment and union membership, as I mentioned earlier, there are still more workers in the domestic fiber industries than are employed in basic steel, auto, and chemical refining industries combined. They are employed in forty out of fifty states. In view of these numbers, it is difficult to justify simply writing them off as a lost cause. While some suggest that it is more important to save production jobs in more highly paid industries, it is important to remember that for many women production workers the jobs they do are relatively well-paid compared to available alternatives.

Despite the fact that younger women are staying in school and preparing for the growing numbers of jobs in the "white-collar" sectors, there remain large numbers of older women who have devoted their lives to production work. Just as we have seen in New England, many of these women currently face impoverishment at the loss of their life's work and can only look forward to a retirement of penury due to the loss of hard-earned pension benefits. Large numbers of workers in these industries in urban areas, like the women in our sample, are immigrant women. [10] Or, they are women in rural areas where the closing of a textile mill, garment shop, or other industrial plant means there is virtually no other work that will allow them to support themselves and their families. [11]

It would take another whole study, done on a national scale, to explore the problems America's displaced women production workers now confront in order to develop viable alternatives to the choices they now face. In addition to looking at the ways in which women respond to layoffs based on their cultures, stage in the life cycle, and marital status, such a study would require an in-depth look at the economics of a variety of industries where women are heavily employed—region by region and community by community.

At this point, however, two strategies suggest themselves as ways of dealing with the loss of women's production jobs. The first strategy involves a focus on a managed trade policy which would specifically be aimed at protecting the industries where women workers are employed, most importantly the fiber, textile, and apparel industries. In the context of protection, technological advances could lead to the restructuring of "women's" industries so they might better compete with the growing offshore production. These policies could protect the remaining jobs for women who need them most—immigrant and older women. The second strategy involves a commitment to the retraining of displaced women for alternative jobs. Younger women with more education might be good candidates for retraining programs.

Such strategies are hardly new or original. Indeed they have already been extensively discussed. However, my main goal in addressing these issues is to compare the different experiences in industries which employ men and women and to compare the sources of the problems in "men's" and "women's" industries. Secondly, and perhaps most importantly, I want to highlight the fact that job displacement is, in large part, an issue which concerns women workers. In writing this I hope to encourage more public debate about the problems America's blue-collar women face. There is a need to commit energy and resources to solving these problems. Ultimately, such a commitment must be seen as part of the larger struggle (along with efforts like affirmative action and comparable worth) to to improve the employment conditions of America's wage-earning women.

Managed Trade and Technological Innovation

The problems of foreign competition have plagued virtually all of American manufacturing. American industry itself has been faulted for its inability to compete. For example, the American steel industry, with its declining profit rates, has been criticized for making a choice to diversify its holdings and milk its outdated plant capacity rather than recommit itself to the new technologies which would make the production of American steel competitive on the world market. The auto industry has been blamed for failing to anticipate the demand for higher-quality, smaller cars, as well as for its failure to bring state of the art technology to its aging plants. The American steel and auto industries have typically dealt with foreign competition by developing intermittent and voluntary agreements to restrict imports. Such agreements have been on again, off again throughout the past fifteen to twenty years. More recently, U.S. automakers have also engaged in collaborative efforts with foreign automakers to produce more cars in the United States in order to utilize American labor.

Efforts to save jobs have been different in the textile, fiber, apparel complex where most blue-collar women are employed. These efforts have revolved around regulating imports. In the 1950s the first Multi-Fiber Arrangement was negotiated. This agreement limits the growth of imports on a yearly basis. Robert Kuttner, in a recent article,[12] sees this Multi-Fiber Arrangement as a successful model of managed trade, "which combines a dose of protectionism with a dose of modernization." How does it work? As Kuttner describes it,

> Essentially, textiles have been removed from the free-trade regime by an international market sharing agreement. In the late 1950s, the American textile industry began suffering insurmountable competition from cheap imports. The United States first imposed quotas on imports of cotton fibers, then on synthetics, and eventually on most textiles and apparel as well. A so-called Multi-Fiber Arrangement eventually was negotiated with other nations which shelters the textile industries of Europe and the United States from wholesale import penetration. Under M.F.A., import growth in textiles was limited to 6% per year.

The rationale was that if domestic industries were given some protection, it would make sense for them to invest in state of the art technology which would enable them to increase productivity and compete with imported goods.

The textile industry, in some part comprised of large manufacturers,[13] has done just that. Since 1974 investments in new plant and equipment have averaged 1.3 billion dollars per year, including 1.7 billion dollars in 1984.[14] The men's clothing industry where large manufacturers make up a sizable portion of the industry, has also followed such a policy. The women's clothing industry, however, is composed of thousands of "mom and pop" shops which employ an average of only fifty workers or so. Many employers in this very marginal and fragmented industry are contractors who get work from jobbers and manufacturers. Such firms find it virtually impossible to finance new technologies to improve productivity.

The women's apparel industry has perhaps suffered most in recent years. Not only have there been extensive layoffs, but there is also more and more underemployment and increasingly degraded working conditions for many women who still nominally have jobs in these industries. For example, 25 percent of domestic stitchers in the garment industry are working two to three days a week and only twenty-eight weeks a year. As the industry declines so has the bargaining power of the unions representing its workers. This year (1985) a new contract was signed with a zero percent wage increase for the coming year. There has also been a decline in union membership in these industries along with a growth in the number of nonunion jobs. We are also seeing more sweatshops. It is estimated that about 9 percent of all domestic garment workers are employed in such sweatshop conditions, reminding us that the global assembly line in the Third World is coming home to roost. For example,

> Conditions common in Asian or Latin economies for decades—complete freedom from union demands, welfare state programs, health and safety protections, minimum wage, child labor or homework laws, and even taxes—are now found in thousands of small workplaces in major U.S. cities. Piece work wages in these shops run between $1.50 and $2.00 an hour—barely more than in relatively prosperous Third World countries and far below the U.S. minimum wage of $3.35. A typical day runs from 8:00 A.M. to 8:00 P.M.—longer if the shop is busy. The work week is sixty to seventy hours. There are no time clocks or other records of these long hours. Wages are paid in cash, with time-and-a-half for overtime unheard of . . . By not issuing checks shopowners can avoid deducting taxes or paying Social Security, workers' compensation, and unemployment insurance. Some weeks there is no pay either.[15]

There is certainly a great deal of unemployment in the auto and steel industries today. There have been an increasing number of virulent union-managment struggles in heavy industry over concessions and givebacks. Wages in these high-paying industries have declined, and the earnings of workers taking jobs outside these once high-paying industries have plummeted. But for most men who still hold manufacturing jobs in heavy industries like auto and steel, there are, as far as I know, no sweatshops.

But what of the industries in the fiber complex where extensive technological modernization has been implemented? Here, despite official quotas, imports have soared far beyond the expectations of the hopeful architects of this plan. As a result, even large, productive textile firms have been forced to close because they cannot sell their wares to domestic clothing and garment manufacturers. [16] In 1984 there were at least sixty-one textile plant closings in North and South Carolina alone. [17]

Why has the Multi-Fiber Arrangement failed? Quotas developed country by country, fabric by fabric, and product by product have been easily circumvented by manufacturers who, taking advantage of an abundant supply of cheap female labor, have been able to shift production from less underdeveloped to more underdeveloped countries. For example, if Sri Lanka had no quotas for sweaters, manufacturers could establish sweater production there and export these products without being subject to quotas. As a result, instead of imports rising by 6 percent on a yearly basis, as planned in the 1981 MFA negotiations, in some years they went up as much as 20 percent. Imports shot up dramatically by 25 to 30 percent in 1983–84 in the apparel industry, where they now represent a full 52 percent of all purchased garments and 45 percent of the textile and garment market combined. At no time during recent years did the penetration of auto imports exceed 27 percent. Imports were no higher than 22 percent in basic steel. Indeed, if imports in these women's industries continue to grow at the same rate they did in 1983, it is estimated that foreign textiles and apparel will capture the entire U.S. market by 1990.

If American consumers have benefitted from cheaper, smaller, better-made Japanese cars and electronics products and from the lower prices of foreign steel, they have not benefitted from cheaply made textiles and apparel. Prices of foreign-made garments are frequently the same as American-made products. Retailers simply mark up their cheaply made clothing and vastly increase their profits. A study by Market Research Corporation of America showed identical retail prices on identical garments, whether they were imported or made in the United States.

In capital-intensive industries like the automobile industry, it may be feasible to overcome the wage gap between Japan and the United States through technological innovations. The Chrysler bailout in 1981 has shown that with government subsidies and the commitment to technological retooling, the auto industry may be able to produce competitive products and stabilize its declining labor force.

Recently GM and the UAW announced plans to build a new auto assembly complex in Tennessee. Hailed as a landmark agreement, the new complex is expected to create jobs for 6,000 new workers and create 20,000 new jobs. Auto workers at this site will be recruited from GM's employees, including those who are currently on layoff. The agreement between the UAW and GM stipulates that no less than 80 percent of all workers initially employed by this new plant, constructed to produce the GM Saturn, will be protected with permanent job security. According to the *Boston Globe*,[18] starting base rates will be $13.45 per hour for hourly production workers and $15.49 for skilled trades. There will also be a high percentage of domestically produced material in the car. How many of these new production jobs will be taken by women remains to be seen.

Yet despite technological innovation in the still labor-intensive women's industries, new technology alone cannot work if protection fails. Even with the best technology in the world, the fiber, fabric, and apparel industries have simply been unable to compete with the new reserve army of cheap female labor which has been created by the new global economy. Even if extensive unionization were to occur among Third World women employed in these industries, the improvement in wages and working conditions which would be likely to result would probably still not even the difference between Third World and American women factory workers. Offshore production would still be an attractive alternative to domestic production.

In 1985 new legislation was proposed to stem the tide of imports. Called the Textile and Apparel Trade Enforcement Act of 1985, the bill was an attempt to "achieve the objectives" of the MFA on a national level. It was supported by a coalition of textile and garment manufacturers associations and the trade unions which typically organize these industries, the ILGWU and the ACTWU. The bill was passed by both the House and the Senate but was later vetoed by President Reagan. Congress attempted to override the veto but failed by eight votes.[19]

One of the major provisions of the bill would have been to plug the loopholes in the import quotas originally set in 1981. Therefore, the "major exporting countries," like South Korea, Hong Kong, Taiwan, and the People's Republic of China, would have to roll back their exports of textiles and apparel to the levels where they would have been if they had only increased exports to 6 percent a year since 1980. Thereafter, their imports could grow by only 1 percent a year. Spokesmen for the bill believed that, if passed and enforced, it would roll back imports from about the current 50 percent of the American market to about 38 percent.

Though no one, unions or manufacturers, expected this bill to be a panacea, the feeling was that without it the American fiber industries would be doomed. With it, these industries might be able to be stabilized to some extent. With more goods made in America there would be more work for American workers. But those industries and firms which are most productive, particularly the large textile manufacturers, would stand most to gain from protection. Much of the women's apparel industry, particularly the small contractors and mom and pop shops, needs to be reorganized into larger units of production before it could benefit from a variety of economies of scale.

Reemployment and Retraining

Responding to the needs of all displaced workers is a problem of major proportion in today's economy. As I have already pointed out in chapter 1, between 1979 and 1983, 11.5 million workers lost jobs due to plant closings or relocation, abolition of a position or a shift, or slack work. Of these, workers who had held their jobs for at least three years (5.1 million workers) were considered "displaced." Not surprisingly, manufacturing industries were some of the hardest hit. Nearly half of all the 5.1 million workers counted as "displaced" during this period worked in steel, auto, industrial equipment, textiles and apparel, or other similar industries.[20]

Three types of help are needed by workers when they are displaced from their jobs: (1) financial subsidies to help families maintain a decent standard of living while unemployed workers consider career transitions and/or look for new jobs, (2) help in finding new jobs and/or exploring the possibilities of starting new careers, and (3) retraining in fields where employment growth promises a real opportunity for lucrative and stable work.

As researchers have begun to make us aware of the personal, family, and community effects of large-scale job displacement, government and industry have begun to see the need to provide resources for those who industrial transformations are leaving behind. Compared to other countries, however, the U.S. has a poor record in providing such resources.[21]

There have been two basic federal programs designed to meet the reemployment and training needs of dislocated workers in the recent past. These programs are Title III of the Job Training and Partnership Act and a program called Trade Adjustment Assistance. There are also a variety of dislocated worker programs sponsored jointly by state governments, departing industries, and the unions with which these companies have collective bargaining agreements. Yet it appears that much of the money spent and efforts made through these programs have reached only a tiny proportion of all displaced workers. Moreover, though there is little data comparing the benefits received by men and women through these programs, what little evidence we do have suggests that reemployment and training programs are even less likely to benefit dislocated women workers than they are to benefit dislocated men.

Trade Adjustment Assistance was established in 1962 "to compensate and retrain workers who lost their jobs to foreign competition due to lowered tariffs." The program reached few workers until 1974 when Congress liberalized TAA. The liberalization made it easier to establish eligibility and extended benefits. In the late 1970s and early 1980s this program provided the most generous benefit levels of any federal program of its kind. Eligible workers were entitled to benefits of up to 90 percent of their former weekly earnings for up to fifty-two weeks. Workers could also become eligible for relocation and allowances for approved retraining. According to the recent study done by the Office of Technology Assessment, "In its first 4 years [fiscal years 1976–79] the revised TAA program cost about $844 million, providing assistance to about 500,000 displaced workers, on average 125,000 people per year. But in 1980 and 1981, with large layoffs in the auto industry, spending shot up to $3.1 billion. Over 800,000 workers received TAA assistance in those two years."[22]

As we have already seen, many of the women in this study were recipients of TAA benefits during this peak funding period. However, under the Reagan administration, TAA was severely cut back. By fiscal year 1984–85 the program was funded at only $70 million per year, serving only 30,000 dislocated workers, or less than 8 percent of the workers who were funded during the peak years of 1980–81. At the time of this writing, the program continues to be funded at about these same levels, but the resources are focused on retraining and job placement efforts rather than on income maintenance.

The year 1982 saw the passage of the Job Training and Partnership Act as a replacement for the Comprehensive Employment and Training Act. Title III of this act was targeted specifically at dislocated workers. This funding approach was seen as a way to aid all displaced workers rather than only those whose jobs were lost as a direct result of import competition. Title III was funded at $223 million in 1984 when it served 132,200 displaced workers.

It is virtually impossible to assess the effectiveness of Title III compared to TAA by simply looking at funding levels or numbers served. What seems to be the case is that the program emphasis of this administration, as exemplified by the changed focus of TAA and the mandate of Title III, is now heavily concentrated on job placement and retraining rather than income maintenance.

What is clear, however, is that current funding for displaced workers is grossly inadequate. It is estimated that only 5 percent of all displaced workers were served by Title III in fiscal year 1984–85. Furthermore, Reagan proposed to cut federal spending for this program by $120 million in fiscal year 1985–86. Such limited federal efforts on behalf of dislocated workers has meant that state governments and the private sector have been left to voluntarily provide the remainder of reemployment and retraining services for dislocated workers. While we have very little data which would clearly show that women are discriminated against in federal programs, evidence about local, state, and private efforts on behalf of displaced workers suggests that women are not treated equitably.

Many such programs to reemploy and retrain displaced workers have been provided by large manufacturers in heavy industry *where few women are employed.* They tend to be implemented in companies which are solvent but which may shut down a branch plant. They are also implemented where a firm is a large employer in a community and fears the potential notoriety involved in a large shutdown. In these cases substantial efforts are sometimes made to ease the pain of job loss for workers, as state governments and private companies make contributions to such programs over and above the funding provided by Title III.

For example, on 24 July 1985, the Quincy Shipyard, a branch of General Dynamics and the South Shore of Massachusetts' largest employer, announced that it would close down permanently by the spring of 1986, gradually laying off about 4,200 of its remaining workers. During the past months, 2,000 workers had already been laid off. According to the *Boston Globe*,[23] in addition to the usual unemployment compensation benefits, these workers will also get "bonuses of up to $3,600 or three months of salary and retain free medical coverage for up to three months after being laid off."

In addition to these benefits the *Globe* article reports that,

> General Dynamics this Spring established a job placement center in Braintree and funded it with $10 million. Already 600 workers of 1400 laid off have come to the center and 200 of these have found work. The center, which uses a computer to match employees' skills with jobs all over the country, also provides free typing of resumes and letters and free telephone calls. As workers get their layoff notices, they are given an appointment at the center. . . . The state has given $800,000 to the center and has requested additional federal funding of up to $2.5 million for the Braintree Center.

While there is no evidence that women who have been employed in this plant will experience sex discrimination in access to these programs, the vast majority of workers at this facility are, of course, men.

The Downriver Community Conference in Wyandotte, Michigan, ran a similar type of program when a Ford assembly plant closed there. A second example of such a large-scale effort occurred at the closing of another Ford plant in Milpitas, California. According to the 1986 Report by the Office of Technology Assessment, "The Ford Milpitas project was an outstanding example of a prompt, positive response to a plant closing. Important factors in its success were the six-month advance notice required by the Ford-UAW bargaining agreement; early provision of an array of effective services; the excellent leadership provided by the Ford Staff and UAW members, who together ran the program; and the help provided by the State of California."[24]

Buss and Redburn[25] have documented similar types of programs in other large plant closings. They argue that helping displaced workers find jobs is a less costly strategy than merely offering severance pay. If workers fail to become reemployed, they tend to use up large sums of severance pay, a tactic which ultimately costs employers more than helping workers find new jobs.

It is difficult to determine how many companies that close their doors make significant efforts to help their former workers become reemployed. The evidence suggests they are few and far between. Moreover, programs like this, funded at such high levels and offering a comprehensive set of services, tend to be provided by large national and multinational corporations who may sponsor them independently or engage private firms to initiate and manage them. Kevin Balfe is a private consultant, formerly employed by the National Alliance of Business. He has worked with between thirty and forty companies to initiate plant closing support programs typically run by union-managment teams which provide services like counseling, job search instruction, job clubs, testing and assessment, educational counseling, occupational training, on-the-job training, remedial education (including G.E.D. certification), job development, personal financial counseling, stress counseling, and social service referrals.

Most of the companies who use his services, he says,[25] are Fortune 500 firms like General Electric, United States Steel, and International Harvester. They may be responding to collective bargaining agreements in these industries which require such help for displaced workers. They tend to be large, still solvent companies who must continue to maintain effective labor management relationships in their existing plants. Some managers, he says, are becoming increasingly aware of the deep personal tragedies that accompany mass layoffs and feel a commitment to averting some of this.

Such services are, of course, expensive. The Ford Milpitas program in California cost approximately $3,000 per worker while the typical JTPA Title III programs cost an average of $895 per worker in fiscal year 1984–85. The higher cost represents funding for the provision of income supports, retraining services, and basic-skills education rather than the job placement services which constitute the bulk of Title III programs. Further, only 6 percent of Title III funds may be spent on support services. This limit may be especially prejudicial to women who need special services, particularly for childcare.

Despite the fact that few displaced male workers have been able to avail themselves of such help after a layoff, retraining and support services are available to still fewer displaced women. Though there are women job losers who participate in programs like these—women laid off from large firms like General Electric or Ford—these opportunities have not been available to workers in the labor intensive industries where most of the women job losers tend to work. Most garment manufacturers, textile plant owners, even those who run high-tech industries, either are not unionized or do not have contracts which require severance pay to displaced workers. They do not generally initiate efforts to help their displaced women workers. Moreover, such employers do not tend to give much advance notice of closings. As I have already pointed out, advance notice of a closing has been shown to help workers make job transitions by allowing them to prepare for the future. Advance notice also permits lead time to set up worker assistance programs.

In December of 1985, a few weeks before Christmas, P & L Sportswear, one of the largest garment shops in Boston's Chinatown, shut down without notice, suddenly laying off 350 women garment workers, mostly Chinese and Italians. Several months later, Beverly Rose, another sportswear manufacturer, shut its doors, leaving another 150 women production workers without jobs. In total, about five hundred garment workers were left jobless with virtually no assistance aside from unemployment insurance. At the time of the shutdowns, the Colonial Provisions Products Company had also recently closed, laying off about three hundred fifty people. Workers from this firm, with a larger proportion of higher-paid male workers, were interviewed daily on the six o'clock news by all the major Boston networks. Reports of large-scale worker assistance programs for the Colonial workers, funded by state, federal, and private money, were broadcast. The plight of the garment workers was totally ignored by major print and broadcast media.

It was only when the children of the Chinese and Italian garment workers (most of whom could not speak English) told their parents about TV news stories reporting large-scale efforts to establish assistance programs for Colonial workers that the garment workers began to organize. They wrote letters and held rallies, demanding comparable programs from state and federal agencies.

Their efforts have not been in vain. The Massachusetts Industrial Services Program finally came up with $350,000 for ESL and job retraining programs. This may be the first time that displaced women production workers have fought for such rights—and won them. Their struggle sets an example for other women production workers who have been overlooked. Their success is a tribute to the effectiveness of their organizing efforts. Yet it took eleven months, almost a year after the initial plant closing at P & L, for the money to finally be made available. Colonial workers, however, found a full-scale, well-funded worker assistance program only days after the final shutdown.

It might be argued that men are more needy of such help because they tend to suffer more wage slippage after displacement. But it could also be argued that counseling, job search help, and retraining could help displaced women even more than men. Women displaced from low-wage manufacturing industries might be able to earn as much or even more than they were initially making if they got training for skilled craft jobs or other work which has traditionally been the preserve of male workers. As we have already seen, the majority of women in our job loss sample said they would like retraining for other jobs. Most of these were the younger American-born women, women who were more likely than the Portuguese or the older women to already have had some experience working in offices and other nonmanufacturing jobs. With a little help retooling, many of these women might begin to develop lucrative alternative careers.

Ultimately, however, it seems that today's married, displaced women are caught between the cracks of public policy programs designed to improve women's employment opportunities. Women are encouraged to get job training if they are heads of households, "displaced homemakers," "welfare mothers," or even "battered women." Today, however, if a woman is married, and she loses her job, all she can do is collect unemployment insurance for a while, pull in her belt, and hope for the best.

Public funding should play a larger rather than a smaller role in the effort to help displaced women factory workers. While married women usually can expect to benefit from the resources provided by spouses, as I have tried to show in this book, they need to work and they need jobs which will allow them and their families to participate in the economic mainstream of American life. As yet, we know very little about the potential for sex discrimination in federal programs to help dislocated workers. In particular, more research is needed to compare the benefits offered to men and women by Title III.

Finally, every effort needs to be made to stabilize employment in declining industries, to save as many jobs as possible. Massachusetts is taking some initiatives in doing this by committing a substantial proportion of its Title III funds to administer Cooperative Regional Industrial Laboratories. It has funded a variety of programs around the state to foster discussions between labor and management about developing new ways to use the skills and human resources of workers in dying industries. Such projects are already in place in the machine tool industry of western Massachusetts.

As part of this effort, the Office of Economic Affairs has awarded a small planning grant to a coalition of union and management groups in the garment industry. This Needle Trades Action Project is an attempt to develop worker-management cooperation in developing a plan to stabilize the apparel industry in the Fall River–New Bedford area, which is the third largest center of apparel production in the country. Janet Boguslaw, a sociologist at Boston College who has studied the industry in this region and serves as a consultant to the project, suggests that what is needed is a strategy to consolidate the large number of small independent contractors into a larger manufacturing unit so that they may benefit from a variety of economies of scale—in both production and marketing strategies.[27] At this point, cooperation between manufacturers and contractors has not been forthcoming and definitive proposals have not yet emerged.

I do not know what ever happened to Sylvia DeNiso, the married 43-year-old woman with three teenage children, who we met at the beginning of this book, the woman who was laid off from her job at Cerulean Electric where she had worked for eighteen years. I wish it were possible to find her and hear what has happened to her and her family since 1980. But it has not been possible.

Sylvia had not gone back to work when we spoke to her after almost six months of unemployment. Most likely, like the other women we interviewed, she found a job. Perhaps she is still working at her new job, perhaps not. It is unlikely, however, that she is still making the equivalent of the $8.25 an hour that she earned at Cerulean. I wonder if she has kept up with the friends she worked with. I wonder how her children are. Have they been able to go to college as she and her husband had hoped? As Sylvia approaches fifty she is probably looking towards retirement. Will she want to, or have to, continue working—at a new job she loves or hates? How many more layoffs will Sylvia, and so many women like her, have to face in the years of working ahead of them? Thousands of women are losing their jobs in these industries every year. Thousands are becoming unemployed and underemployed. How will our labor force cope with the displacement of so many workers? How will we fit, or refit, most of these women into our changing employment structure? The future does not look bright.

Appendix:
_____ Methodological Procedures

This appendix will describe the methodological procedures that were used to gather the extensive body of qualitative and quantitative data that became the source material for this work. The research was initially based on lengthy, structured interviews with 414 "blue-collar" women who were currently or had recently been employed in traditional female production jobs in declining manufacturing industries in eastern New England. A subsample of forty of these women were reinterviewed a second time in depth. These in-depth interviews were done to explore some of the personal aspects of the women's lives and daily experiences. This work was made possible by a generous grant from the Employment and Training Administration of the Department of Labor. The interviews took place in 1980.

Sampling Procedures

Since the purpose of the research was to explore the impact of job displacement on women production workers in New England, we needed to identify both employed and displaced women in declining traditional female industries and occupations. According to a recent survey done by the Bureau of Labor Statistics,[1] a displaced worker is one who has lost a job "because of the closing down or moving of a plant or company, slack work, or the abolishment of a position or shift." The Bureau of Labor Statistics included workers in this category only if they had been employed for at least three years. In our study, a worker was defined as displaced if she had been employed in the same firm for at least one year. A woman worker defined as continuously employed is one who had worked in the same firm for at least one year.

We needed to locate a large and representative sample of these women in order to meet our sampling goals—originally planned to include up to six hundred interviews. To do this our approach was twofold: (1) to work with trade union leaders in the appropriate industries—union officials, we believed, would have access to information about women who had been laid off in recent months; and (2) to institute screening procedures at appropriate claims offices of the Massachusetts Department of Employment Security (DES)—we planned to institute screening procedures at appropriate offices which would allow us to identify working women

187

who met our sampling criteria, namely, women laid off from traditional female production jobs.

The decision to combine these two sampling methods was made on the following grounds. Consultation with contemporary researchers of job displacement in metropolitan areas[2] had made us aware of the difficulties of recruiting a sufficient number of participants in this kind of study. We believed, quite correctly, that union leaders would be able to identify and help us locate an interview sample of sufficient size.

Organized Labor

During the initial phase of our research, contacts were made with a number of trade union officials in the eastern New England area. Participating unions were The International Ladies' Garment Workers' Union (ILGWU), The International Union of Electrical Workers (IUE), The Amalgamated Clothing and Textile Workers' Union (ACTWU), The Brotherhood of Electrical Workers (IBEW), The Union of Electrical Workers (UE), and the Bakery, Confectionery, and Tobacco Workers Union.

Officials from each of these unions were initially contacted by the principal investigator. Subsequently meetings were arranged between union leaders and the research staff in order to explain the purposes of the study, to provide information and materials about the project, and to request the cooperation of the union staff in locating women who had experienced a layoff in recent months and comparable women workers who remained employed.

Each of the above-mentioned unions cooperated with us, providing lists of women workers who had been laid off and women in the same jobs and industries who continued to work. Such lists provided our sampling frame; however, in many cases they were inaccurate and incomplete. In selecting and communicating with the listed women (by mail and then by phone) we discovered the following problems: (1) women were reported as laid off when they had actually left their jobs voluntarily; (2) layoff dates were incorrect; and (3) individuals were named with incorrect addresses and/or wrong phone numbers.

Where problems were obvious before sampling (i.e., no available phone number provided and no directory phone listing), we excluded the women from our initial sampling frame. Frequently, however, some of the above-mentioned problems were not discernible until after contact had been made with potential respondents, in which case potential respondents were also deleted from our sampling frame.

We followed two sampling procedures. Where the sampling frame was small (approximately 75 names or less) we attempted to contact all the individuals. Where the sampling frame was high (76 to 350 names) we contacted every nth individual. The same procedures were followed for the job loss and continuously employed samples.

As a result of our meetings and discussions with union officials, a total of 1,531 names were provided to our research staff. These included the names, addresses, and sometimes telephone numbers of 923 women who had experienced a job loss. Of these we contacted 727 by mail. They also included the names of 608 women who had been fully and continuously employed in comparable industries and occupations. We sent 407 of these women letters requesting their participation in the study.

The Massachusetts Department of Employment Security

Arrangements were made with the director of research at the Massachusetts Department of Employment Security to screen unemployed female workers at several claims offices in the eastern Massachusetts area. A screening interview was designed in cooperation with the director of research and local managers of DES claims offices in Lawrence, Lowell, Salem, Brockton, Taunton, Fall River, and New Bedford. Although it was not possible for us to screen in Boston area offices or in Rhode Island offices, we chose these Massachusetts offices because of their proximity to industrial communities in eastern Massachusetts.

The screening procedure involved a member of our research staff being stationed in each office several mornings a month from September to November 1979. Women claimants were typically approached after receiving their checks and asked to voluntarily participate in a brief interview which would allow our staff to ascertain the type of their previous employment, reason for job separation, age, and marital status. We also asked for names, addresses, and telephone numbers from those women who met our sampling criteria. A total of 805 claimants were screened. Out of these, 212 met our sampling criteria. We had enough information to send letters requesting participation in our study to 134 of these women.

As can be seen from table A.1, the DES screening procedure proved to be a relatively inefficient way of finding large numbers of working women appropriate to our sampling criteria. We located only 68 women out of our total job loss sample of 273 in this way, or about 25 percent of our job loss sample. Obviously, this method did not yield respondents who were employed. Moreover, despite our attempt to choose claims offices where large numbers of women factory workers were likely to be found, a full 43 percent of the 805 women we screened were inappropriate because they had been employed in other industries and occupations, typically sales, service, and clerical work. Another 23 percent were production workers who were only "partially" unemployed, that is, they were working part of each week and were therefore underemployed rather than unemployed. Eight percent were unwilling to cooperate and another ten percent failed to provide us with enough information to contact them after the initial screening. We contacted only 17 percent of the women we screened and ultimately interviewed only 8 percent of these women. Our union sampling procedure generated results which were considerably better. Of the 1,531 employed and unemployed women whose names we received, 23 percent were eventually interviewed.

There were, however, trade-offs between the two sampling procedures. The union method yielded higher numbers of potential and actual respondents than the DES method, but refusal rates among the union sample were substantially higher than those of the DES sample (see table A.1). The higher response rate among the DES sample may be due to the fact that the women at claims offices had personal

Table A.1   *Composition of Samples: Screening Procedures*

Number of People	Total Job Loss Group Sampled			Total Employed Group Sampled Union Sample
	DES Sample	Union Sample	Total	
Interviewed	68	205	273	141
Refused	34	174	208	108
Inappropriate	14	78	92	49
Unreachable	10	156	166	83
With language barrier	5	48	53	4
Too late to interview	3	66	69	22
Total letters sent	134	727	861	*Total* 407
Refusal Rate	25.4%	45.9%	—	43.4%

contact with the researchers. Discussions with our research staff suggest that initial personal contact may increase respondents' trust of the researchers. Interviewers later reported that where peer networks within firms facilitated the transmission of positive information about the research, respondents were more likely to grant an interview. Such positive information could also be transmitted to workers by union personnel where such individuals gave overt support for the research. Such word of mouth information, however, may also bias our sample in favor of individuals who tend to participate in social networks within a plant.

Development of a Structured Interview Guide

During the initial phase of this research, a lengthy questionnaire was developed. Questions were designed to provide both qualitative and quantitative indices of each of the labor market, work, and family variables necessary for a comprehensive analysis of the research questions. Two versions of the questionnaires were developed—one for displaced women and another for women who remained employed. The questionnaires were improved and modified by our research team several times and reworked again in the context of our pilot interviews.

Pilot Interviews

As we began collecting our sample of both job losers and employed women, we began our pilot interviews. After each one was completed, a meeting was held between the interviewers and the research staff to discuss the problems of reliability and validity in the interview quide. Ambiguities in the structuring of questions, issues of motivating respondents' cooperation with the research, and difficulties in developing interviewer-respondent rapport were discussed. Analysis of our pilot interviews enabled us to make changes in the interview guide as the questionnaire was refined and finalized.

Interview Design

The proposed research design for these structured interviews required that respondents in our job loss sample be interviewed approximately six months after their layoff date. This interval was chosen to permit respondents enough time for adjustment to job loss, job search activity, recall and/or reemployment in a different job. A six-month time period seemed to be a short enough interval to permit workers to be recalled. Exactly six months between layoff and interview was not always feasible, since the exigencies of interviewers' and respondents' lives generated scheduling difficulties. The actual intervals between layoff and interview varied between four and ten months.

Structured Interviews

As our sampling proceeded and our pilot interviews helped perfect the questionnaire, we began the primary part of the data collection—the structured interviews with 273 displaced women and a comparison group of 141 employed women. Among the job losers, individuals were sorted according to the dates on which they had been laid off from their jobs. As the sixth month after the layoff approached, initial contact with the women to be interviewed was made by a letter from the principal investigator. The letter informed the respondent of the way she had been identified (through her union or her participation in the DES screening interview), described the goals of the research, asked her cooperation in granting us an interview, and insured her of the confidentiality and anonymity of all her responses. Where possible, an additional letter, asking the respondent to cooperate with the research, was also enclosed from an appropriate union official. Several days after sending this letter, a data sheet with name, address, telephone number, industry, source of contact, and layoff date was provided to an interviewer. Telephone contact with the respondent was then made by interviewers who arranged appointments for interviews to be done at the women's homes or other locations where the interview could be conducted in privacy. Interviews typically took one and one-half to two hours to complete.

Portuguese Interviews

As our research proceeded, informal discussions with workers and union leaders and information garnered from our interviewers made it clear that a large number of women who fit our sampling criteria were recent immigrant and ethnic women whose lives were embedded in cohesive ethnic communities in New England's industrial towns. Many of these women were Greek, Italian, and Hispanic and could not speak English well enough to participate in our interview. The largest number of foreign-born and non-English speaking women workers in the industries we were studying were Portuguese women, typically recent immigrants from the Azores.

We realized then, that a significant proportion of the women eligible to be studied in this research would have to be excluded because of a language barrier.

This raised not only procedural but substantive questions with respect to our sampling and interviewing strategies. Because such women were likely to have different family and cultural patterns from American-born women and represented an important component of New England's blue-collar work force, we felt it was necessary to include them in our study. At the same time we realized it was impossible to translate the interview guide into so many different languages and to find interviewers who could be trained to administer them.

We resolved this problem with a compromise solution. Since the majority of foreign-born, non-English-speaking women workers were from the Portuguese Azores, we made a decision to translate our questionnaire into Portuguese and to interview the Portuguese-speaking women in their native language. The Cambridge Organization of Portuguese Americans (COPA), a community-based social service agency in Cambridge, was engaged to translate the final version of our questionnaire—both the employed and the job loss version. Interviewers fluent in Portuguese administered the questionnaire to our immigrant respondents in their native language. The women's responses were then translated back into English in conference with the principal investigator before they were coded.

Interviewer Selection and Training

The recruitment process for our interviewing staff began with a search among women graduate students at the Boston College School of Social Work. We believed that women with clinical and research skills required by social work students would be especially qualified to develop the rapport with respondents that was needed to make the data collection successful. Seven women were hired initially. They were selected based on their previous interviewing experience, recommendations from their department and a personal interview with the principal investigator. Two college students, fluent in Portuguese, were also hired in the New Bedford–Fall River area to do the interviews with the Portuguese-speaking women.

Once the field work began, two problems became evident. First we discovered that it would be difficult for nine interviewers to complete enough interviews to complete our fieldwork on schedule. Second, many of our respondents lived in areas that required a drive of an hour to an hour and one-half—to places like New Bedford, Fall River, Lawrence and Lowell, Massachusetts, and Providence, Rhode Island.

Seven additional interviewers were subsequently hired. Four of these were from southeastern Massachusetts and three were from the Providence area. These interviewers were hired with the help of faculty at Bristol Community College in Fall River and the staff of the Sarah Doyle Women's Center at Brown University.

All of the interviewers were carefully trained. They participated in a series of three training seminars. The first was designed to familiarize them with the research and its goals. The second seminar focused on the interpersonal skills required for achieving validity and reliability in data collection. The third seminar was geared to familiarizing interviewers with the research instruments. Role playing was also used; we used videotaping sessions in which interviewers practiced interviewing each other. This technique provided the opportunity for each interviewer to resolve problems and engage in mutual criticism before going into the field. Finally, each interviewer was required to do a pilot interview before being qualified to go into the field and collect data to be used in the actual data base.

Intensive (In-Depth) Interviews

The structured interviews were designed to provide a data base to statistically analyze the financial, personal, and social costs of job displacement for women production workers. However, a series of forty intensive interviews were also done to collect in-depth information about the work and family lives, problems, worries, and motivations of these blue-collar women, information which could not be obtained by the structured interviews. Given the small number of such interviews, the intent was to use the data from them, where necessary and appropriate, to yield greater insights into the meaning of the statistical relationahips derived from our larger data base.

The sample for these intensive interviews was drawn from the larger data base of both employed and unemployed women. Those who were selected, however, worked exclusively in the apparel and electrical industries. Excluded from the sampling frame were those whose first interview was conducted in Portuguese. This sample was stratified in the following way. Half (twenty) of the women worked in the apparel industries; the other twenty worked in general assembly jobs. Half of each subset ($N = 10$) was drawn from the overall employed sample, while the other half was drawn from the sample of job losers. The final sample consisted of thirty-two married women, four who were currently separated or divorced and four who were single.

Sampling Results

Our sample was heavily represented by women employed in the electrical goods industry (SIC 364) and the apparel industry (SIC 23). As we can see from table A.2, these two industries employed 81 percent of the 273 women in our sample who had been displaced from their jobs. These two industries also employed 92 percent of the 141 women in our control group of continuously employed women. A total of sixty-four women (fifty-three job losers and eleven employed women) worked in a variety of other light manufacturing industries—food processing, leather production (mostly shoes), and textiles. The women were all employed in occupations which were classified as "operatives, except transport," according to the *Alphabetical Index of Industries and Occupations*.[3] They were employed in traditional, female jobs—unskilled and semiskilled production work.

Their job titles were coded in accordance with the job categories developed by the *Classified Index of Industries and Occupations*.[4] The vast majority of apparel workers (76 percent) were sewers and stitchers. Seventy-four percent of job losers and 79 percent of the employed women worked in this occupation. Sewers and stitchers operate a wide variety of sewing machines. The remainder of apparel workers do tasks which include trimming threads from sewn garments, sorting and moving

Table A.2   *Composition of Samples: Industry Representation and Employment Status*

Industry	Job Loss Sample (%)		Employed Sample (%)	
Apparel	119 (43.6)	} 81%	57 (40.4)	} 92%
Electrical	101 (37.0)		73 (51.8)	
Food	20 (7.0)		9 (6.4)	
Other	33 (12.1)		2 (1.4)	
Total	273 (100)		141 (100)	

bundles of cut fabric from one sewing operation to another, or pressing and/or packing the finished products for shipment.

Our respondents in the electrical industry were most likely to be assemblers, checkers and examiners, and machine operatives. These three job titles accounted for 82 percent of the women job losers and 67 percent of the employed women. The electrical workers assembled lighting fixtures or were employed in a variety of stages in the manufacture of electrical cords. Some cut and wound copper wires, others operated molding machines which set the plugs in place, and still others did labeling and packaging.

A small group of women worked in production jobs in other industries. Those in food processing were employed packing and wrapping candy or bread. One woman was an assembler in a small firm which manufactured hospital supplies. Another woman made calendars, and a third, novelties. Several women worked as solderers or machine operatives in a firm which made missiles.

The women we interviewed (80 percent) lived and worked in the small and medium-sized cities of eastern Massachusetts, from Lowell and Lawrence in the north to New Bedford and Fall River in the south. The remaining 20 percent were drawn from communities which surround Providence, Rhode Island. We chose to focus on Massachusetts because it employs the largest concentration of women production workers in New England. In 1970, about 50 percent of the region's female production workers were employed in this state.[5] These women comprised 23 percent of all the blue-collar workers in the state.[6]

Massachusetts also has a considerable concentration of women production workers in the apparel and the electrical goods industries. In 1975, almost 71 percent of women apparel workers in New England were employed in this state, as well as almost half (48.3 percent) of women workers in the electrical goods industry (SIC 36).[7]

Sampling Biases

Clearly the sampling methods chosen could not provide us with a truly representative sample. First and foremost, our sample overrepresents unionized women. In 1970, 44 percent of women workers in blue-collar jobs in New England were union members.[8] In our sample 92 percent of the women were unionized. As a result of this difference we did not make any statistical comparisons between union and nonunion workers. The conclusions reached here also are likely to apply to women who are in unions. Secondly, our sample overrepresents women in the apparel and electrical goods industries. This may be the result of the specific unions we contacted in trying to locate displaced women, or it may be a consequence of the fact that women are being displaced from these industries in relatively large numbers. However, we do know that the women's ages are roughly comparable to those of women employed in similar industries in New England. Their educational attainment and marital status are roughly comparable to that of blue-collar women in the nation as a whole.[9]

Notes

Chapter 1

1. All the names of people, places, and companies have been changed to protect the anonymity of respondents.

2. This was in 1980 when we interviewed her.

3. U.S. Department of Labor, Bureau of Labor Statistics, *Employment and Earnings* 28, no. 10 (October 1981): table A-21.

4. Nancy S. Barrett, "Women in the Job Market: Occupations, Earnings and Career Opportunities," in *The Subtle Revolution: Women at Work,* edited by Ralph Smith (Washington, D.C.: The Urban Institute 1979); Joan Smith, "The Paradox of Women's Poverty: Wage-Earning Women and Economic Transformation," *Signs* 10, no. 2 (1984): 291–310.

5. Alice Kessler-Harris, *Out to Work: A History of Wage Earning Women in the United States* (New York: Oxford University Press, 1982); Tamara Hareven and Ralph Langenbach, *Amoskeag: Life and Work in An American Industrial City* (New York: Pantheon, 1980); Thomas Dublin, *Women at Work: The Transformation of Work and Community in Lowell, Massachusetts, 1826–1860* (New York: Columbia University Press, 1981).

6. See Mary Frank Fox and Sharlene Hesse-Biber, *Women at Work* (Palo Alto, CA: Mayfield Publishing Company, 1984). They define "ordinary" working women as those who are "neither at the top nor at the bottom, but somewhere in the middle—in the ordinary white- and blue-collar jobs" (p. 97).

7. Stephen Dubnoff, "Beyond Sex Typing: Capitalism, Patriarchy and the Growth of Female Employment, 1940–1970" (Paper presented at the annual meetings of the Eastern Sociological Society, New York, March 1970); Stephen Dubnoff and Philip Kraft, "Gender Stratification in Computer Programming" (Center for Survey Research, University of Massachusetts, 1984); Sarah Kuhn, "Computer Programming and Women's Roles: A Look at a Changing Occupation" (Department of Urban Studies and Planning, MIT, 1980); Rosalyn Feldberg and Evelyn Glenn, "Effects of Technological Change on Clerical Work: Review and Reassessment" (Paper presented at the American Sociological Association Meetings, New York, 1979); Sally Hacker, "Sex Stratification, Technology and Organizational Change: A Longitudinal Case Study of AT & T, *Social Problems* 26 (June 1979): 539–57; Joan Greenbaum, *In the Name of Efficiency: Management Theory and Shopfloor Practices in Data Processing Work* (Philadelphia: Temple University Press, 1979).

8. See Francine Blau and Marianne Ferber, "Women in the Labor Market: The Last Twenty Years," in *Women and Work: An Annual Review*, vol. 1, edited by Laurie Larwood, Ann Stromberg and Barbara Gutek (Beverly Hills, CA: Sage Publications, 1985).

9. The most recent and best stated expression of this position is to be found in "The New Immiseration: Stagflation, Inequality and the Working Class" by Elliott Currie, Robert Dunn, and David Fogarty, *Socialist Review*, no. 54 (November-December 1980): 7–31.

10. Patricia Sexton, *Women and Work*, R & D Monograph 46 (U.S. Department of Labor: Employment and Training Administration, 1977).

11. See Jane Hood, *Becoming a Two Job Family* (New York: Praeger, 1983); Laura Lein, *Families Without Victims* (Lexington, MA: Lexington Books, 1984).

12. Myra Marx Ferree, "Between Two Worlds: German Feminist Approaches to Working-Class Women and Work," *Signs* 10, no. 35 (1985): 517–36; Harold Benenson, "Women's Occupational and Family Achievement in the U.S. Class System," *British Journal of Sociology* 35, no. 1 (1984): 19–41; Rayna Rapp, "Family and Class in Contemporary America: Notes Towards an Understanding of Ideology," in *Rethinking the Family: Some Feminist Questions*, edited by Barrie Thorne (New York: Longmans, 1982).

13. Barry Bluestone and Bennett Harrison in their book *The Deindustrialization of America* (New York: Basic Books, 1983) are perhaps the best spokesmen for the view that disinvestment and plant closings are serious problems for America's workers that ought to be addressed through fundamental social policy changes.

14. Address by Sol Chaikin, President of the International Ladies Garment Workers Union, Conference on Industrial Policy, sponsored by the ILGWU and the Industrial Union Department of the AFL-CIO, Boston, 4 May 1984.

15. Paul O. Flaim and Ellen Sehgal, "Displaced Workers of 1979–1983: How Well Have They Fared?," *Monthly Labor Review*, U.S. Department of Labor, Bureau of Labor Statistics, vol. 108, no. 6 (June 1985): 8; calculated from table 4.

16. Kay A. Snyder and Thomas C. Nowak, "Job Loss and Demoralization: Do Women Fare Better than Men?," *Journal of Mental Health* 13, no. 1–2 (1984): 92–106; Thomas C. Nowak and Kay A. Snyder, "Women's Struggle to Survive a Plant Shutdown," *The Journal of Intergroup Relations* 11, no. 4 (Winter 1983): 25–44; Carolyn C. Perrucci, Robert Perrucci, Dena B. Targ, and Harry Targ, "Impact of a Plant Closing on Workers and the Community," in *Research in the Sociology of Work: A Research Annual*, vol. 3, edited by I. H. Simpson and R. L. Simpson (Greenwich, CT: JAI Press, 1985); Avery F. Gordon, Paul Schervish, and Barry Bluestone, "The Unemployment and Reemployment Experiences of Michigan Auto Workers," Report on the Michigan Auto Industry Worker Study, submitted to Office of Automotive Industry Affairs, United States Department of Commerce and to the Transportation Systems Center, U.S. Department of Transportation, 1984; Ellen I. Rosen, *Hobson's Choice: Employment and Unemployment among Blue-Collar Women Workers in New England*, Final Report to the U.S. Department of Labor, Employment and Training Administration, December 1982.

17. For a more detailed discussion of the methodological procedures through which the study was done, see the Appendix.

18. The Department of Labor classifies production workers into three skill categories. They are craft workers (or "skilled" workers), operatives, transport operatives and laborers (defined as "semiskilled" and "unskilled"). Such classifications exist despite the complexity of the work these women do, the speed at which they work, or the experience they sometimes need to do their jobs well.

19. U.S. Department of Labor, Bureau of Labor Statistics, *Employment and Earnings* 27, no. 3 (March 1980): 41.

20. Diana Pearce, "The Feminization of Poverty: Women, Work and Welfare," *Urban and Social Change Review* 11, nos. 1 and 2 (February 1978): 28–36; Isabel Sawhill, "Discrimination and Poverty Among Women Who Head Families," in *Women and the Workplace,* edited by Martha Blaxall and Barbara Reagan (Chicago: University of Chicago Press, 1976).

21. See Barbara Garson, *All the Livelong Day: The Meaning and Demeaning of Routine Work* (New York: Pantheon, 1975).

Chapter 2

1. See Heidi Hartmann, "Capitalism, Patriarchy and Job Segregation by Sex," in *Women and the Workplace,* edited by Martha Blaxall and Barbara Reagan (Chicago: University of Chicago Press, 1976).

2. See Tamara Hareven and Randolph Langenbach, *Amoskeag: Life and Work in an American Factory City* (New York: Pantheon, 1978); and Alice Kessler-Harris, *Women Have Always Worked* (Old Westbury, New York: Feminist Press, 1981).

3. For an excellent discussion of protective labor legislation for women in the early twentieth century, see Ronnie Steinberg, *Wages and Hours: Labor and Reform in Twentieth Century America* (New Brunswick, NJ: Rutgers University Press, 1982).

4. Ralph Smith, *The Subtle Revolution* (Washington, D.C.: The Urban Institute, 1979).

5. There are of course, notable exceptions to this general rule. One of the earliest and best treatments of women employed in factory jobs is Robert Blauner's *Alienation and Freedom* (Chicago: University of Chicago Press, 1964). Also see Judith Buber Agassi, *Women on the Job* (Lexington, MA: Lexington Books, 1981) for a cross-cultural study of women factory workers. Also see Karen Sacks and Dorothy Remy, eds., *My Troubles Are Going to Have Trouble with Me* (New Brunswick, NJ: Rutgers University Press, 1984); and Barbara Epstein, "Women's Work and Family Change in the Silicon Valley: Report on Work in Progress," Working Paper no. 7 (Center for the Study, Education and Advancement of Women, University of California, Berkeley, 1983); Ruth Cavendish, *Women on the Line* (London: Routledge and Kegan Paul, 1982).

6. Nancy Gabin, "They Have Placed a Penalty on Womanhood: The Protest Actions of Women Auto Workers in the Detroit Area UAW Locals, 1945–47," *Feminist Studies* 8 (Summer 1982): 373–98.

7. Folker Fröbel, Jurgen Heinrichs, and Otto Kreye, *The New International Division of Labor,* translated by Peter Burgess (Cambridge: Cambridge University Press, 1980); Marlene Dixon, Susanne Jonas, and Ed McCaughan, "Immigration,

Low Wage Labor in the Core Capitalist Countries, and the Transnational Labor Force," (San Francisco: Institute for the Study of Labor and Economic Crisis, 1982); June Nash and Maria Patricia Fernandez-Kelly, *Women, Men and the International Division of Labor* (Albany, NY: State University of New York Press, 1983).

8. See Nash and Fernandez-Kelly, *The International Division of Labor.*

9. Rachel Grossman, "Women's Place in the Integrated Circuit," Pacific Studies Center, *Pacific Research* 9, no. 5 (1978): Barbara Ehrenreich and Annette Fuentes, "Life on the Global Assembly Line," *Ms. Magazine* 9, no. 7 (January 1981): 52–59.

10. See the work of contributors in Nash and Fernandez-Kelly, *The International Division of Labor.*

11. See chapter 1, note 14.

12. See articles by Frankel, Shapiro-Perl, Lamphere, Fernandez, and Remy in Karen Sacks and Dorothy Remy, eds., *My Troubles Are Going to Have Trouble with Me* (New Brunswick, NJ: Rutgers University Press, 1984).

13. Victor Becerra, "The Los Angeles Garment Industry: A Cloak of Shame," unpublished ms. (August 1981); Institute for the Study of Labor and Economic Crisis, "Sweatshop Renaissance: The Third World Comes Home, *Dollars and Sense,* no. 96 (April 1984): 6–8.

14. Naomi Katz and David Kemnitzer, "Women and Work in Silicon Valley: Options and Futures," in *My Troubles Are Going to Have Trouble with Me,* edited by Karen Sacks and Dorothy Remy (New Brunswick, NJ: Rutgers University Press, 1984).

15. In 1980, 95 percent of all women workers who were employed in unskilled and semiskilled production work were classified as "operatives."

16. Calculated from *Money Income of Families and Persons in the U.S.,* Current Population Reports, series P–60, no. 85 (December 1972): Table 55, 127–28; no. 123 (June 1980): Table 55, 246–47; (1983): Table 54, 194–95.

17. Ellen I. Rosen, "The Changing Jobs of American Women Factory Workers" (Paper presented at the Conference on the Changing Jobs of American Women Workers, sponsored by the Professional and Business Women's Foundation, George Washington University, and the Service Employees International Union, 5–6 January 1982).

18. Calculated from Linda Le Grande, "Women in Labor Organizations: Their Ranks are Increasing," *Monthly Labor Review* 101, no. 8 (August 1978): 8–14.

19. Jules Bernstein, "Union Busting: From Benign Neglect to Malignant Growth," *University of California Law Review* 13, no. 3 (Summer 1980): 3–78. There are also four volumes of government testimony which provide evidence of the wide variety of tactics and methods of "persuasion" used by employers to defeat union drives. See *Pressures in Today's Workplace,* Oversight Hearings before the Subcommittee on Labor-Management Relations, 16–18 October 1979, Washington D.C.

20. See Robert Howard, "Second Class in Silicon Valley," *Working Papers Magazine* 8, no. 5 (September-October 1981): 21–31.

21. See Le Grande, "Women in Labor Organizations."

22. See Rosen, "The Changing Jobs of American Women Factory Workers."

Chapter 3

1. Many of the immigrant women who work in New England's traditional female manufacturing jobs today are from European countries like Italy, Greece, or the Portuguese Azores, or from places like Puerto Rico, Haiti, and Southeast Asia.

2. Only 29 percent report having a high school diploma.

3. See Alice Kessler-Harris, *Women Have Always Worked* (Old Westbury, NY: Feminist Press, 1981).

4. Helen Safa, "Women, Production, and Reproduction in Industrial Capitalism: A Comparison of Brazilian and U.S. Factory Workers," in *Women, Men and the International Division of Labor,* edited by June Nash and Maria Patricia Fernandez-Kelly (Albany, NY: State University of New York Press, 1983).

5. Judith Buber Agassi, *Women on the Job* (Lexington, MA: Lexington Books, 1979).

6. There is very little research done on the Portuguese immigrant communities in America. There are, however, three important sources which have provided the background for this analysis. They are Rita Moniz, "The Portuguese of New Bedford, Massachusetts, and Providence, Rhode Island: A Comparative Micro-Analysis of Political Attitudes and Behavior" (Ph.D. diss., Department of Political Science, Brown University, 1979); James Adler, "Ethnic Minorities in Cambridge: The Portuguese" (Prepared for the Cambridge Planning and Development Department, 1972); Louise Lamphere, Ewa Hauser, Dee Rubin, Sonya Michel, and Christina Simmons, "The Economic Struggles of Female Factory Workers: A Comparison of French, Polish, and Portuguese Immigrants" (Prepared for the Conference on the Educational and Occupational Needs of White Ethnic Women, National Institute of Education, September 1980).

7. It will be remembered that 74 percent of native-born, older women told us their fathers had been industrial workers.

8. These family patterns are consistent with those found among other preindustrial peasant societies. See Louise Tilly and Joan Scott, *Women, Work and Family* (New York: Holt, Rinehart and Winston, 1978).

9. About 70 percent of the American born women in the same age groups were married.

10. These figures are consistent with the findings of other research. See Adler, "Ethnic Minorities in Cambridge."

11. See Alice Kessler-Harris, *Women Have Always Worked.*

12. Four years of school is all that is legally required there.

13. See Marlene Dixon, Susanne Jonas, and Ed McCaughan, "Immigration, Low Wage Labor in the Core Capitalist Countries, and the Transnational Labor Force" (San Francisco: Institute for the Study of Labor and Economic Crisis, 1982); also article by Naomi Katz and David Kemnitzer, in *My Troubles Are Going to Have Trouble with Me,* edited by Karen Sacks and Dorothy Remy (New Brunswick, NJ: Rutgers University Press, 1984).

14. The relative comfort we found among these women's families, which will be discussed further in coming chapters, may be related to the fact that immigration policies have been very favorable for the Portuguese, creating a situation in

New England where there are few illegals. Furthermore, our sample was largely comprised of unionized workers who at least received the minimum wage.

15. See Tilly and Scott, *Women, Work, and Family;* Stephen Thernstrom, *Poverty and Progress: Social Mobility in a 19th Century City* (Cambridge: Harvard University Press, 1964).

16. The average age of the women at marriage was twenty-one.

17. See Lillian Breslow Rubin, *Worlds of Pain: Life in the Working Class Family* (New York: Basic Books, 1977) for a good statement of this position.

18. See Eli Chinoy, *The Automobile Worker and the American Dream* (New York: Doubleday, 1955).

Chapter 4

1. Harry Braverman, *Labor and Monopoly Capital: The Degradation of Work in the Twentieth Century* (New York: Monthly Review Press, 1974).

2. See Heidi Hartmann's "Capitalism, Patriarchy, and Job Segregation," in *Women and the Workplace,* edited by Martha Blaxall and Barbara Reagan (Chicago: University of Chicago Press, 1976).

3. J. Rubery, "Structured Labour Markets, Worker Organization and Low Pay," *Cambridge Journal of Economics* 2, no. 1 (1978): 17–36.

4. Peter Armstrong, "If It's Only Women It Doesn't Matter So Much," in *Work, Women and the Labour Market,* edited by Jackie West (London: Routledge & Kegan Paul, 1982).

5. Angela Coyle, "Sex and Skill in the Organization of the Clothing Industry," in West, *Work, Women and the Labour Market.*

6. Elizabeth Allison, "Disadvantaged Workers in the Apparel Industry," Industrial Relations Research Seminar, Sloan School of Management, MIT, 6 November 1979.

7. In unionized firms piece rates, like wage rates, are usually a subject for contract negotiations.

8. Louise Lamphere, "Fighting the Piece Rate," in *My Troubles Are Going To Have Trouble with Me,* edited by Karen Sacks and Dorothy Remy (New Brunswick, NJ: Rutgers University Press, 1984).

9. Problems with broken or poorly repaired machinery are, of course, not limited to women who work on piece rates. When machinery is not functioning properly, there are fearful safety hazards which inevitably affect everyone in the plant. Repeatedly we heard stories of women who got cut or burned when fingers or entire hands were caught in presses or molds because safety equipment was not working properly. In one firm, workers repeatedly tripped on a hole in the floor which had gone unrepaired for months. Several women told us they hurt their backs after tripping or having equipment fall on them because of this hole.

10. Blue-collar women report some of the lowest levels of work satisfaction. See *Dual Careers: A Longitudinal Study of the Labor Market Experience of Women,* U.S. Department of Labor, Manpower Research Monograph no. 21, vol. 1, 1974; also see Ellen Rosen, *Hobson's Choice: Employment and Unemployment among Blue-Collar Women Workers in New England,* Final Report to the U.S. Department of Labor, Employment and Training Administration, December 1982.

11. Ann Bookman, "The Process of Political Socialization among Women and Immigrant Workers: A Case Study of Unionization in the Electronics Industry" (Ph.D. diss., Department of Anthropology, Harvard University, 1977); also see Barbara Garson, *All the Livelong Day: The Meaning and Demeaning of Routine Work* (New York: Pantheon, 1975).

12. See Karen Sacks and Dorothy Remy, eds., *My Troubles Are Going to Have Trouble with Me* (New Brunswick, NJ: Rutgers University Press, 1984).

13. About 65 percent of the women we studied worked on a piece rate. The average wage for piece workers was $4.66 and the average for those on a standard rate was $4.87. These differences were not statistically significant. $F = .354$; Level of confidence $= .552$.

14. See Robert Blauner, *Alienation and Freedom* (Chicago: University of Chicago Press, 1964).

15. There is no way of knowing whether these numbers are representative of women employed in the industries we studied because we did not have a representative sample. There may be some reason to believe that their calculated median wage is somewhat low because women employed in the apparel industry, who earn less than women in other industries, are overrepresented in our sample. At the same time, the women in our sample were mostly unionized workers who tend to earn more than nonunionized workers.

16. Eli Chinoy, in *The Automobile Worker and the American Dream* (New York: Doubleday, 1955) describes a scenario in which blue-collar men feel trapped in factory jobs because they feel responsible for supporting their families. As we will see in the following chapter, blue-collar women experience some of the same dilemmas.

17. See the articles by Lamphere, Remy, Shapiro-Perl, in Sacks and Remy, *My Troubles*.

18. Myra Marx Ferree, "Between Two Worlds: German Feminist Approaches to Working-Class Women and Work," *Signs* 10, no. 35 (1985): 517–36.

19. Blauner, *Alienation;* Garson, *All the Livelong Day;* and Elinor Langer, "Inside the New York Telephone Company," in *Women at Work,* edited by William L. O'Neill (Chicago: Quadrangle Books, 1972).

Chapter 5

1. See "Dual Careers: A Longitudinal Study of the Labor Market Experience of Women," U.S. Department of Labor, Manpower Research Monograph no. 21, vol. 1., 1974; Ellen Rosen, *Hobson's Choice: Employment and Unemployment among Blue-Collar Women Workers in New England,* Final Report to the U.S. Department of Labor, Employment and Training Administration, December 1982.

2. See James Adler, "Ethnic Minorities in Cambridge: The Portuguese" (Prepared for the Cambridge Planning and Development Department, 1972); Louise Lamphere, "Fighting the Piece Rate," in *My Troubles Are Going to Have Trouble with Me,* edited by Karen Sacks and Dorothy Remy (New Brunswick, NJ: Rutgers University Press, 1984); and Rita Moniz, "The Portuguese of New Bedford, Massachusetts, and Providence, Rhode Island: A Comparative Micro-Analysis of Political Attitudes and Behavior" (Ph.D. diss., Department of Political Science, Brown University, 1979).

3. See Lamphere, "Fighting the Piece Rate," in Sacks and Remy, *My Troubles*.

4. The data on hourly wages represents the reported hourly wages of the employed women and the hourly wages of the job losers on the jobs they had before they were laid off. The wage difference between Portuguese women and American women was statistically significant: $F = 10.074$; Level of confidence $= .002$.

5. This was statistically significant: $F = 8.864$; significance $= .004$.

6. Older, American-born women earned on average $4.87 per hour and younger women earned $5.32 per hour.

7. The independent variables were the womens' reports of their opportunities to chat with co-workers, having a physically comfortable job, having a sense of accomplishment from their jobs, and the women's satisfaction with their wages. Overall work satisfaction was measured by the response to the question, "All in all, how satisfied would you say you are with the job you have?" The responses were coded (1) very satisfied, (2) somewhat satisfied, (3) not too satisfied, and (4) not at all satisfied. The independent variables were measured by the women's responses to four statements. These were (1) I have a chance to chat with other workers, (2) doing my work was physically comfortable, (3) doing my job gives me a sense of accomplishment, and (4) the pay is good. These were coded (1) very true, (2) somewhat true, (3) a little true, and (4) not at all true.

8. Kendall's tau, sig. $= .029$.

9. On average, Portuguese women earned $4.56 an hour compared to $4.87 for older, American-born women. These differences were not statistically significant: $F = .761$; significance $= .386$.

10. The difference between piece-rate and standard-rate wages for this group was statistically significant: $F = 12.768$; significance $= .001$.

11. See Judith Buber-Agassi, *Women on the Job* (Lexington, MA: Lexington Books, 1978).

12. $F = .867$; Significance $= .356$.

13. Why this is so is not something that can be explained with the available data.

14. See Barry Bluestone and Bennett Harrison, *The Deindustrialization of America* (New York: Basic Books, 1983).

Chapter 6

1. Grace Baruch, Rosalind Barnett, and Caryl Rivers, *Lifeprints: New Patterns of Love And Work for Today's Women* (New York: McGraw Hill, 1983).

2. For a good statement of this position by contemporary socialists who defend the family wage, see Elliott Currie, Robert Dunn, and David Fogarty, "The New Immiseration: Stagflation, Inequality and the Working Class," *Socialist Review* 54 (November-December 1980): 7–31; Jane Humphries, "Class Struggle and the Persistence of the Working Class Family," *Cambridge Journal of Economics* 1, no. 3 (September 1977): 241–58; and "The Working Class Family, Women's Liberation and Class Struggle: The Case of 19th Century British History," *Review of Radical Political Economics* 9, no. 1 (Fall 1977): 25–41, has also argued that the family wage has traditionally offered benefits to working-class women.

3. Zillah Eisenstein, *Capitalist Patriarchy* (New York: Monthly Review Press, 1977).

4. Myra Marx Ferree, "Between Two Worlds: German Feminist Approaches to Working-Class Women and Work," *Signs* 10, no. 35 (1985): 517–36.

5. Critics of the family wage argue that it is the poor quality of work available to women that underlies their stress at work and their continued economic dependence on the family. See Washington Area Marxist-Feminist Study Group, "None Dare Call It Patriarchy: A Critique of 'The New Immiseration,'" *Socialist Review* 12, no. 1 (January-February 1982): 105–11. According to Hartmann, this is a vestige of women's subordination in the family and exclusion from well-paid, male-defined jobs, a phenomenon which took place in the process of capitalist development. See Heidi Hartmann, "Capitalism, Patriarchy and Job Segregation by Sex," *Signs* 1, no. 3, part 2, (Spring 1976): 137–69.

6. See Ann Oakley, *The Sociology of Housework* (New York: Pantheon, 1974); and Laura Lein, *Families without Villains* (Lexington, MA: Lexington Books, 1984).

7. See the literature on women's employment and role bargaining: John Scanzoni, *Sexual Bargaining: Power Politics in the American Marriage* (Englewood Cliffs, NJ: Prentice-Hall, 1972); Jane Hood, *Becoming a Two-Job Family* (New York: Praeger, 1983).

8. By "provider" I mean women who make, if not half, at least a substantial contribution to their families' earnings, so that both spouses recognize that the family's economic stability and/or well-being depends on a wife's earnings.

9. For a good elaboration of this view, see Lillian Breslow Rubin, *Worlds of Pain: Life in the Working Class Family* (New York: Basic Books, 1977).

10. See Constantina Safilios-Rothschild, "Family Sociology or Wives' Family Sociology? A Cross-cultural Examination of Decision Making," *Journal of Marriage and the Family* 31 (1969): 290–301.

11. Lee Rainwater, Richard Coleman, and Gerald Handel, *Workingman's Wife* (New York: Oceana Publications, 1959); Arthur B. Shostak and William Gomberg, eds., *Blue Collar World: Studies of the American Worker* (Englewood Cliffs, NJ: Prentice-Hall, 1964).

12. Pat Sexton, "The Wife of the Happy Worker," in Shostak and Gomberg, *Blue Collar World,* 81.

13. See Lillian Breslow Rubin, *Worlds of Pain* (New York: Basic Books, 1976), 96.

14. Ibid., 168.

15. Linda Haas, "Domestic Role Sharing in Sweden," *Journal of Marriage and the Family* 43 (November 1981): 957–67; R. A. Berk and S. F. Berk, *Labor and Leisure at Home: Content and Organization of the Household Day* (Beverly Hills, CA: Sage Publications, (1979); C. Perucci, H. Potter, and D. Rhoads, "Determinants of Male Family-Role Performance," *Psychology of Women Quarterly 3,* no. 1 (Fall 1978): 53–66; John Scanzoni, *Opportunity and the Family* (New York: The Free Press, 1970); Lois W. Hoffman, "Parental Power Relations and the Division of Household Tasks," in *The Employed Mother in America,* edited by L. Hoffman and F. I. Nye (Chicago: Rand-McNally, 1963); R. Blood and D. Wolfe, *Husbands and Wives* (New York: The Free Press, 1960); Jane Hood, *Becoming a Two-Job Family* (New York: Praeger, 1983).

206 Notes to Pages 97—108

16. Rubin did her fieldwork for *Worlds of Pain* in California almost a decade earlier than the fieldwork for this book was done.

17. Rubin, *Worlds of Pain,* 106.

18. Based on the Bureau of Labor Statistics figures for 1979 for an urban family of four at a yearly income of $20,517. U.S. Department of Labor, Bureau of Labor Statistics, *Urban Family Budgets and Comparative Indexes for Selected Urban Areas, 1979,* U.S.D.L.: 80–278, 30 April 1980.

19. See Rainwater, Coleman, and Handel, *Workingman's Wife:* Mirra Komarovsky, *Blue-collar Marriage* (New York: Vintage Books, 1962).

20. Stephen Bahr, "Effects on Family Power and Division of Labor in the Family," in *Working Mothers,* edited by Lois Hoffman and F. Ivan Nye (San Francisco: Jossey-Bass, 1974).

21. See Rubin, *Worlds of Pain,* 107–12.

22. Twenty-two percent said their husbands liked having the money the wives earned. Only 14 percent said their husbands liked them to work because the women gained satisfaction from working.

23. For a comprehensive review of this research, see Joseph Pleck, "Husbands' Paid Work and Family Roles: Current Research Issues," in *Research in the Interweave of Social Roles,* edited by Helena Lopata and Joseph Pleck (Greenwich, CT: JAI Press, 1983).

24. See Hood, *Becoming a Two-Job Family;* and Lein, *Families without Villains.*

25. These inside tasks include (1) preparing meals, (2) grocery shopping, (3) washing dishes, (4) doing laundry, and (5) cleaning the house. Husbands were counted as helping if their wives reported husbands who either took full responsibility for the task or shared the task equally with their wives.

26. See Lein, *Families without Villains.*

27. Wives with high earnings are those who earn $5.26 an hour or more; medium earnings are between $4.26 and $5.25 an hour; low earnings are $4.25 an hour or less.

28. Unfortunately we did not collect data on the shifts of husbands and wives. Therefore we cannot know how much men's participation in housework is directly related to husbands and wives working different shifts.

29. $F = 1.077$, Significance $= .305$.

30. Marital satisfaction was measured by asking the women, "Taking everything together, how happy would you say your marriage is? Answers were coded in the following way: (1) extremely happy, (2) very happy, (3) happy, (4) somewhat happy, (5) not too happy, and (6) not happy at all. We divided these responses into two categories, combining 1 and 2 and 3 to 6.

31. $F = 4.788$, sig. $= .029$.

32. We developed a scale which attempted to measure the conflict women feel between work and family life. The scale was composed of the women's responses to two statements. They were: (1) I have sometimes felt it was unfair that I have to work and also spend so much time taking care of my home and family, and (2) I sometimes feel that I cannot do enough for my family when I work. The answers to these questions were coded as follows: (1) very true, (2) somewhat true, (3) a little true, and (4) not at all true. The responses to these questions were positively correlated ($r = .546$).

33. Kendall's tau, sig. = .373.

34. Kendall's tau, sig. = .007. Women's satisfaction with wages was measured by their response to the statement, "The pay is good." Very true = 1, somewhat true = 2, not very true = 3, not at all true = 4.

35. See Baruch, Barnet, and Rivers, *Lifeprints.*

36. Kendall's tau, sig. = .001.

37. When children leave home, older women report that their husbands do the same amount of "inside" work as that reported by women under forty-five years of age who had younger children. The average number of tasks reported by younger wives is 1.66. The average number of tasks reported by older women without children at home is 1.62.

38. Kendall's tau, sig. = .004.

39. $F = 3.009$, sig. = .019.

40. Since Portuguese wives earned less than American wives, the gap between Portuguese and American family incomes was narrowed by the contributions of employed children in Portuguese families and the income from rental property.

41. Rita Moniz, "The Portuguese of New Bedford, Massachusetts, and Providence, Rhode Island: A Comparative Micro-Analysis of Political Attitudes and Behavior" (Ph.D. diss., Department of Political Science, Brown University, 1979).

42. See Moniz, "The Portuguese of New Bedford, Massachusetts, and Providence, Rhode Island," 79–80.

43. Some of the families own more than one house, some of which have multiple dwellings. The additional apartments, those not lived in by the nuclear family, are rented, sometimes below market value, to relatives—parents, siblings, or cousins—who are saving to buy homes of their own. The owner can thereby take care of his extended family. Meanwhile, a rental unit is also a stable source of income in an often unstable job market.

44. See in particular, E. P. Thompson, *The Making of the English Working Class* (New York: Pantheon, 1964).

45. Kendall's tau, sig. = .001.

46. Kendall's tau, sig. = .004.

47. Kendall's tau, sig. = .001.

48. Kendall's tau, sig. = .003.

49. Kendall's tau, sig. = .041.

Chapter 7

1. Bureau of Labor Statistics Press Release, 30 November 1984.

2. We asked our respondents, "About how many times in the past ten years have you been laid off from your job?"

3. This figure is comparable to other studies of workers who have been laid off. See Kim Clarke and Lawrence Summers, "Labor Market Dynamics and Unemployment: A Reconsideration," *Brookings Papers on Economic Activity,* vol. 1 (1979): 13–72.

4. See The Governor's Commission on Mature Industries, Final Report, Boston, Massachusetts, June 1984. Employers claim that notifying workers well before the plant is closed will cause them to be negligent or to look for other jobs.

This, they believe, tends to disrupt production. Studies, however, show that early notification is beneficial for workers, allowing them to adjust to the situation and plan for the future. See Barry Bluestone and Bennett Harrison, *The Deindustrialization of America* (New York: Basic Books, 1983); Terry F. Buss and F. Stevens Redburn, *Shutdown at Youngstown: Public Policy for Mass Unemployment* (Albany: State University of New York Press, 1983).

5. Scenarios like this are typical of the way in which large conglomerates and multinational corporations "milk" the profits from high-wage plants and then close them. See Bluestone and Harrison, *The Deindustrialization of America.*

6. The remainder of the women in each group (25 percent younger American, 29 percent older American, and 19 percent Portuguese) saw the layoff as embodying both good and bad aspects.

7. Younger, American-born women, 89 percent; older, American-born women, 86 percent; and Portuguese women, 78 percent.

8. Younger, American-born women, 84 percent; older, American-born women, 78 percent; and Portuguese women, 80 percent.

9. Kay Lehman Schlozman, "Women and Unemployment: Assessing the Biggest Myth," in *Women: A Feminist Perspective,* edited by Jo Freeman (Palo Alto, CA: Mayfield Publishing Co., 1979): Kay A. Snyder and Thomas C. Nowak, "Job Loss and Demoralization: Do Women Fare Better than Men?" *Journal of Mental Health* 13, no. 1–2 (1984): 92–106; and "Women's Struggle to Survive a Plant Shutdown," *The Journal of Intergroup Relations* 11, no. 4 (Winter 1983): 25–44.

10. This range is one standard deviation above and below the mean.

11. These single women were evenly divided between older women who were widows or divorcees living alone with no dependent children at home ($n = 26$) and women who were widowed or divorced and supporting children ($n = 22$).

12. Kendall's tau, sig. = .001.

13. Kendall's tau, sig. = .008.

14. Chi square = .2924, sig. = .589.

15. To explore the differences among these four groups of women, we compared each of the three groups of women with single women. "Single" women were defined as those who were unmarried. They either lived alone, most often as widows or divorcees, or they were female heads of households living alone with dependent children. We compared each of the three groups of married women with single women with respect to their responses to the following statements: (1) After I was laid off I was pleased to have more time to take care of my home and family, (2) After I was laid off I was worried about how I (and my family) would continue to pay my (our) bills. (These variables were measured on a scale of 1 to 4. Agree strongly, 1, agree somewhat, 2, disagree somewhat, 3, and disagree strongly, 4.) The third dependent variable was a response of yes or no to the question, "Did you look for work after you were laid off?"

16. For a good discussion of the pros and cons of these arguments see Schlozman, "Women and Unemployment," in Freeman, *Women: A Feminist Perspective.*

17. Martin Feldstein, "Unemployment Insurance: Time for Reform," *Harvard Business Review* 53, no. 2 (March–April 1975): 51–61.

18. Ronald Ehrenberg and Ronald Oaxaca, "Unemployment Insurance, Du-

ration of Unemployment, and Subsequent Wage Gain," *American Economic Review* 66, no. 5 (December 1976): 754–66: Kim Clark and Lawrence Summers, "Labor Market Dynamics and Unemployment: A Reconsideration," *Brookings Papers on Economic Activity,* vol. 1 (1979): 113–72.

19. Stephen Marston, "The Impact of Unemployment Insurance on Job Search," *Brookings Papers on Economic Activity* 1 (1975): 13–60.

20. The average duration of unemployment for those who were reemployed was about thirteen weeks. A full 62 percent of the women in our sample were reemployed and working when we interviewed them. Another 16 percent had worked but were currently unemployed again.

21. Harold Sheppard and A. Harvey Belitsky, *The Job Hunt* (Baltimore, MD: W. E. Upjohn Institute for Employment Research, Johns Hopkins University Press, 1966).

22. Ibid., 34. Percentages used for comparing the two studies were calculated, in part, from p. 34.

23. Ibid., 33.

24. Chi square = .0994, sig. = .753.

25. Chi square = .2917, sig. = .589.

26. Chi square = .2767, sig. = .599.

27. Paul O. Flaim and Ellen Sehgal, "Displaced Workers of 1979–1983: How Well Have They Fared?" *Monthly Labor Review,* U.S. Department of Labor, Bureau of Labor Statistics, vol. 108, no. 6 (June 1985): 3–16.

28. Snyder and Nowak, "Job Loss and Demoralization."

29. Carolyn C. Perrucci, Robert Perrucci, Dena B. Targ, and Harry Targ, "Impact of a Plant Closing on Workers and the Community," in *Research in the Sociology of Work: A Research Annual,* vol. 3, edited by I. H. Simpson and R. L. Simpson (Greenwich, CT: JAI Press, 1985).

30. The other twenty-three women had been laid off again or had left their new jobs.

31. Chi square = 1.213, 2 df, sig. = .545.

32. Chi square = 14.794, 2 df, sig. = .000.

33. To calculate the average wage loss or gain from changing jobs, we subtracted the women's reported hourly wages on their pre-layoff jobs from the wages they reported on their new jobs. We used this wage gain or loss as a dependent variable in a multiple regression equation. The independent variables were their hourly wages on their pre-layoff jobs and whether or not they were recalled.

34. The willingness of immigrant women to take low-wage jobs is clearly what is transforming the ethnic mix of the female, blue-collar work force.

35. For good summaries of the innumerable studies which have explored the effects of job displacement on men see Bluestone and Harrison, *The Deindustrialization of America;* Steven Mick, "The Social and Personal Costs of Plant Shutdowns," *Industrial Relations* 14 (May 1975): 203–8; *Community Costs of Plant Closings: Bibliography and Survey of the Literature,* Prepared by C & R Associates for the Federal Trade Commission, July 1978.

36. See Schlozman, "Women and Unemployment"; Snyder and Nowak, "Job Loss and Demoralization"; Nowak and Snyder, "Women's Struggle to Survive a Plant Shutdown"; Avery F. Gordon, Paul Schervish, and Barry Bluestone, "The

Unemployment and Reemployment Experience of Michigan Auto Workers," Report on the Michigan Auto Industry Worker Study, submitted to the Office of Automotive Industry Affairs, United States Department of Commerce and to the the Transportation Systems Center, U.S. Department of Transportation 1984; Perrucci et al., "Impact of a Plant Closing on Workers and the Community."

37. C & R Associates, *Community Costs.*

38. L. M. Wright, "Case Study: Buffalo Worker Reemployment Center," Report prepared for the U.S. Department of Labor, Employment and Training Administration (Princeton, NJ: Mathematica Policy Research, Inc., 1985); John W. Dorsey, "The Mack Truck Case: A Study in Unemployment," in *Studies in the Economics of Income Maintenance,* edited by Otto Eckstein (Washington: The Brookings Institution, 1967); Herbert Parnes and Randy King, "Middle Aged Job Losers," in *Industrial Gerontology* 4, no. 2. (Spring 1977): 77–95; Louis S. Jacobson, "Earnings Losses of Workers Displaced from Manufacturing Industries," in *The Impact of International Trade and Investment on Employment,* edited by W. G. Dewald, a conference on the Department of Labor Research Results (Washington, D.C.: U.S. Government Printing Office, 1978).

39. Marc Bendick, *The Role of Public Programs and Private Markets in Reemploying Workers Dislocated by Economic Change* (Washington, D.C.: The Urban Institute, 1982).

40. John W. Dorsey, "The Mack Truck Case: A Study in Unemployment," in *Studies in the Economics of Income Maintenance,* edited by Otto Eckstein (Washington D.C.: The Brookings Institution, 1967).

41. L. M. Wright, Jr., "Case Study: Buffalo Worker Reemployment Center," Report prepared for the U.S. Department of Labor, Employment and Training Administration (Princeton, NJ: Mathematica Policy Research, Inc., 1985).

42. Gordon, Schervish, and Bluestone, "The Unemployment and Reemployment Experience of Michigan Auto Workers."

43. Perrucci et al., "Impact of a Plant Closing on Workers and the Community."

44. Nowak and Snyder, "Women's Struggle to Survive a Plant Shutdown."

Chapter 8

1. Barry Bluestone and Bennett Harrison, *The Deindustrialization of America* (New York: Basic Books, 1983); *Community Costs of Plant Closings: Bibliography and Survey of the Literature,* prepared by C & R Associates for the Federal Trade Commission, July 1978; J. P. Gordus, P. Jarley and L. Ferman, *Plant Closings and Economic Dislocation* (Kalamazoo, MI: W. E. Upjohn Institute for Employment Research, 1981); John Hayes and Peter Nutman, *Understanding the Unemployed: The Psychological Effects of Unemployment* (New York: Methuen, 1981); Stephen Mick, "Social and Personal Costs of Plant Shutdowns," *Industrial Relations* 14, no. 2 (May 1975): 203–7; M. Harvey Brenner, *Mental Illness and the Economy* (Cambridge: Harvard University Press, 1973); Ramsay Liem and Paula Rayman, "Health and Social Costs of Unemployment," in *American Psychologist* 37, no. 10 (October 1982): 1116–23.

2. See Kay Snyder and Thomas Nowak, "Job Loss and Demoralization: Do

Women Fare Better than Men?" *International Journal of Mental Health* 13, no. 1–2 (1984): 92–106; Thomas Nowak and Kay Snyder, "Women's Struggle to Survive a Plant Shutdown," *Journal of Intergroup Relations* 11, no. 4 (1983): 25–44; Carolyn Perrucci et al., "Impact of a Plant Closing on Workers and the Community," in *Research in the Sociology of Work: A Research Annual,* edited by I. H. Simpson and R. L. Simpson (Greenwich, CT: JAI Press, 1985); R. Warren, "Stress, Primary Support Systems and the Blue Collar Woman" in *Response to Major Layoffs and Plant Closings,* edited by P. Jarley (Lansing, Michigan Department of Mental Health, 1980); Kay Schlozman, "Women and Unemployment: Assessing the Biggest Myths," in *Women: A Feminist Perspective,* edited by Jo Freeman (Palo Alto, CA: Mayfield Publishing Co., 1979); Avery Gordon, Paul Schervish, and Barry Bluestone, "The Unemployment and Reemployment Experiences of Michigan Auto Workers," submitted to the Office of Automotive Industry Affairs, U.S. Department of Commerce and the Transportation Systems Center, U.S. Department of Transportation, 1984.

3. See Nowak and Snyder, "Women's Struggle to Survive A Plant Shutdown."

4. See Warren, "Stress and the Blue-Collar Woman."

5. Perruci et al., "Impact of a Plant Closing on Workers and the Community."

6. This was done by multiplying the reported hourly wages by the number of hours each woman worked per week. We then multiplied this figure by fifty-two weeks. Then we added the weekly earnings for each week respondents reported being out of work for the year prior to the interview. We subtracted this figure from the women's potential earnings had they worked a full year. Unemployment insurance and receipts from Trade Adjustment Assistance were added into this calculation as well. Finally, we calculated this as a proportion of what the women's total family income would have been had they not lost their jobs.

7. Louis Jacobson, "Earnings Losses of Workers Displaced from Manufacturing Industries," in *The Impact of International Trade and Investment on Employment,* edited by W. G. Dewald (Washington, D.C.: U.S. Government Printing Office, 1978).

8. $F = 6.958$, significance $= .009$.

9. See Snyder and Nowak, "Sex Differences in the Long-Term Consequences of Job Loss," paper presented at the Annual Meetings of the American Sociological Association, New York, 1986.

10. To calculate this figure, total annual family income was divided by the number of members of each household.

11. Husbands who were employed less than full time had been unemployed, disabled, in school, or out of the labor force some time during this twelve-month period.

12. See table 8.4 for a list of the twenty-two items we asked about. The mean number of cutbacks was 5.5, S.D. $= 4.40$. The *number* of cutbacks does not measure the severity of economic distress as well as the dollar amounts of each cutback would. However, we did not believe respondents would be able to provide dollar amounts of each cutback with accuracy.

13. Four dummy variables were created to measure this effect—employed women, job losers who were recalled, job losers who found new jobs, and job losers who were still out of work. The employed women were used as the outgroup.

14. In chapter 7 we developed a scale to measure work-family conflict. It was developed from the women's responses to two questions: (1) "I have sometimes felt it was unfair that I have to work and also spend so much time taking care of my home and my family," and (2) "I sometimes feel that I cannot do enough for my family when I work." See chapter 6, note 32.

15. R. Angell, *The Family Encounters the Depression* (New York: Scribner and Sons, 1936); E. W. Bakke, *Citizens Without Work* (New Haven: Yale University Press, 1940); Philip Eisenberg and Paul Lazarsfeld, "The Psychological Effects of Unemployment," *Psychological Bulletin* 35 (1938): 358–90.

16. Stanislav V. Kasl, "Work and Mental Health," in *Work and the Quality of Life,* edited by James O'Toole (Cambridge, MA: MIT Press, 1974); Stanislav V. Kasl and Sidney Cobb, "Some Mental Health Consequences of Plant Closings and Job Loss," in *Mental Health and the Economy,* edited by L. A. Ferman and J. P. Gordus (Kalamazoo, MI: W. E. Upjohn Institute for Employment Research, 1979); Ramsay Liem and Paula Rayman, "Health and Social Costs of Unemployment"; Terry Buss and F. Stevens Redburn, *Shutdown at Youngstown: Public Policy for Mass Unemployment,* (Albany: State University of New York Press, 1983). For further reviews of the literature also see Gordus, Jarley, and Ferman, *Plant Closings and Economic Dislocation;* Hayes and Nutman, *Understanding the Unemployed.*

17. M. Harvey Brenner's work *Mental Illness and the Economy,* done in New York State, has been replicated in Massachusetts with similar results. See Ramsay Liem and Joan Liem, "Economic Change and Individual Psychological Functioning," Final Report, Center for Metropolitan Studies, National Institute of Mental Health, September 1977.

18. Long-term unemployment is typically defined as being out of work for a year or more.

19. Jerome Frank, *Persuasion and Healing* (Baltimore, MD: Johns Hopkins University Press, 1973).

20. The scale we used was developed by Dohrenwend, Shrout, Egri, and Mendelsohn and included twenty-seven questions which comprised eight highly intercorrelated scales measuring: (1) self-esteem, (2) hopelessness-helplessness, (3) dread, (4) confused thinking, (5) sadness, (6) anxiety, (7) psycho-physiological symptoms; and (8) perceived physical health. The response to each question was coded on a scale of zero to four. The composite scale had a potential score of thirty-two. The mean for our sample was 9.99, S.D. = 5.18. See Bruce P. Dohrenwend, Patrick E. Shrout, Gladys Egri, Frederick S. Mendelsohn, "What Psychiatric Scales Measure in the General Population: Part II: The Components of Demoralization by Contrast with Other Dimensions of Psychopathology," unpublished paper (Columbia University School of Public Health and Administrative Medicine, 1979).

21. In another regression equation we found that among the unemployed women (those who had lost jobs but were not currently working), those who were looking for work were no more demoralized than women who were not looking or were reemployed. Levels of demoralization were not affected by any of these reemployment outcomes among the younger, American-born women, the older,

American-born women, or the Portuguese, even when we explored these relationships in separate regression equations.

22. Dohrenwend, Shrout, Egri, and Mendelsohn, "What Psychiatric Scales Measure in the General Population."

23. Perrucci et al., "Impact of a Plant Closing."

24. See Buss and Redburn, *Public Policy for Mass Unemployment;* and Kasl and Cobb, "Some Mental Health Consequences of Plant Closings and Job Loss."

25. See Snyder and Nowak, "Women's Struggle to Survive a Plant Shutdown."

26. See Kasl and Cobb, "Some Mental Health Consequences of Plant Closings and Job Loss."

Chapter 9

1. Myra Marx Ferree, "Between Two Worlds: German Feminist Approaches to Working-class Women and Work," *Signs* 10, no. 35 (1985): 517–36; Rayna Rapp, "Family and Class in Contemporary America: Notes Towards an Understanding of Ideology," in *Rethinking the Family: Some Feminist Questions,* edited by Barrie Thorne (New York: Longmans, 1982); Harold Benenson, "Women's Occupational and Family Achievement in the U.S. Class System," *British Journal of Sociology* 35, no. 1 (1984): 19–41.

2. See Barbara Ehrenreich, "The Nouveau Poor," *Ms. Magazine* 10, no. 1 (July/August 1982): 215–24.

3. See Grace Baruch, Rosalind Barnett, and Caryl Rivers, *Lifeprints: New Patterns of Love and Work for Today's Women* (New York: McGraw Hill, 1983).

4. Gita Sen, "The Sexual Division of Labor and the Working Class Family: Towards a Conceptual Synthesis of Class Relations and the Subordination of Women," *Review of Radical Political Economics* 12, no. 2 (Summer 1980): 76–86.

5. See Ferree, "Between Two Worlds."

6. See chapter 8 for this discussion.

7. Robert Kuttner, *The Economic Illusion* (Boston: Houghton Mifflin, 1984); Barry Bluestone and Bennett Harrison, *The Deindustrialization of America* (New York: Basic Books, 1983); Terry F. Buss and F. Stevens Redburn, *Shutdown at Youngstown: Public Policy for Mass Unemployment* (Albany: State University of New York Press, 1983).

8. U.S. Department of Labor, Bureau of Labor Statistics, *Employment and Earnings* 32, no. 3 (March 1985): 34 (table A–22).

9. Conversation with Carl Proper, Educational Director of the Boston local of the ILGWU, July 1985.

10. According to figures generated by the Fiber, Fabric and Apparel Coalition for Trade, 29 percent of the workers in these industries are minorities and 67 percent of the workers are women.

11. See particularly the work of Kay A. Snyder and Thomas C. Nowak, "Job Loss and Demoralization: Do Women Fare Better than Men?" *International Journal of Mental Health* 13, no. 1–2 (1984): 92–106; Thomas Nowak and Kay Snyder, "Women's Struggle to Survive a Plant Shutdown," *Journal of Intergroup Relations* 11, no. 4 (1983): 25–44.

12. Robert Kuttner, "Thinking About the Unthinkable: The Free Trade Fallacy," *The New Republic,* 28 March 1983, pp. 16–21.

13. The top five manufacturers in 1983 controlled 20 percent of the market. See Kuttner, "The Free Trade Fallacy."

14. Figures from the Fiber, Fabric and Apparel Coalition for Trade, 1985, unpublished data.

15. "Sweatshop Renaissance: The Third World Comes Home," *Dollars and Sense,* no. 96 (April 1984): 6–8.

16. Personal communication with Robert Kuttner, April 1985.

17. See figures from the Fiber, Fabric and Apparel Coalition for Trade, 1985, unpublished data.

18. *Boston Globe,* 27 July 1985.

19. *The New York Times,* 5 August 1986, p. 1.

20. U.S. Congress, Office of Technology Assessment, *Technology and Structural Unemployment: Reemploying Displaced Adults* OTA-ITE-250 (Washington, D.C.: G.P.O., February 1986), 3.

21. See Bluestone and Harrison, *The Deindustrialization of America,* for a good description of industry-government efforts to aid displaced workers in European countries.

22. See Office of Technology Assessment, *Technology and Structural Unemployment.*

23. *Boston Globe,* 25 July 1985.

24. See Office of Technology Assessment, *Technology and Structural Unemployment.*

25. Buss and Redburn, *Shutdown at Youngstown.*

26. Kevin Balfe, personal communication, July 1985.

27. Janet Boguslaw, personal communication, June 1985.

Appendix

1. Bureau of Labor Statistics Press Release, 30 November 1984.

2. Dr. Ramsay Liem, Department of Psychology, Boston College; Drs. Susan Gore and Joan Liem, Department of Sociology, University of Massachusetts, Boston.

3. U.S. Department of Commerce, Bureau of the Census, *Alphabetical Index of Industries and Occupations* (Washington, D.C.: U.S. Department of Commerce, 1971).

4. Ibid.

5. Ann Seidman, ed., *Working Women: A Study of Women in Paid Jobs* (Boulder, CO: Westview Press, 1978), 22–23.

6. Ibid., 22.

7. These figures were assessed through an analysis of the Social Security Department's Longitudinal Employer-Employee Data File.

8. See Seidman, *Working Women,* 105.

9. See Ellen I. Rosen, "Hobson's Choice: Employment and Unemployment among Blue Collar Women Workers in New England," Final Report to the Department of Labor, Employment and Training Administration, 1982. See chapter 3.

Index

Bitter Choices

Blue-Collar Women in and out of Work

Ellen Israel Rosen

Foreword by Catharine R. Stimpson

Ellen Israel Rosen presents a compelling portrait of married women who work on New England's assembly lines while they maintain their homes and marriages. With skill and sympathy, she documents the reasons these women work; their experiences on the job, in the union, and at home; sources of job satisfaction; and their management of the "double day." The major issue for this segment of the labor force, Rosen suggests, is not whether to work, but the availability and quality of jobs. Rosen argues that deindustrialization—plant closings and job displacement—confronts blue-collar women factory workers with a "bitter choice" between work at lower and lower wages or no work at all.

Drawing on quantitative and qualitative data from interviews with more than two hundred such women factory workers, Rosen traces the ways in which women who do "unskilled" factory work have gained in self-esteem as well as financial stability from holding paid jobs. Throughout, Rosen explores the relationship between public work experiences and private family life. She analyzes the dynamics of two-paycheck, working class families, clarifies relationships between class and gender, and explores the impact of patriarchy and capitalism on working class women. At the same time Rosen places women's job